P. T. FORSYTH

The Man, The Preachers' Theologian, Prophet for the 20th Century

A Contemporary assessment

by

Donald G. Miller, Browne Barr, Robert S. Paul

Containing a reprint of

P. T. Forsyth

Positive Preaching and Modern Mind

The Pickwick Press

Pittsburgh, Pennsylvania

1981

Library of Congress Cataloging in Publication Data

Miller, Donald G.
    P.T. Forsyth--the man, the preachers' theologian,
prophet for the 20th century.

    (The Pittsburgh theological monograph series ; 36)
    "Containing a reprint of P.T. Forsyth, Positive
preaching and modern mind."
    Bibliography: p.
    Includes indexes.
    1. Forsyth, Peter Taylor, 1848-1921--Addresses,
essays, lectures. 2. Preaching--Addresses, essays,
lectures. I. Barr, Browne. II. Paul, Robert S.
III. Forsyth, Peter Taylor, 1848-1921. Positive
preaching and modern mind. 1981. IV. Title. V. Series.
BX7260.F583M54   230'.58'0924   81-10668
ISBN 0-915138-48-4   AACR2

THE PITTSBURGH THEOLOGICAL MONOGRAPH SERIES

Dikran Y. Hadidian

General Editor

36

P. T. FORSYTH

The Man, The Preachers' Theologian,
Prophet for the 20th Century

PETER DANIEL FORSYTH, D.D.

TO

CHARLES S. DUTHIE

1911-1981

Principal of New College
University of London

1964-1977

CONTENTS

A Reprint of

POSITIVE PREACHING AND MODERN MIND

Peter Taylor Forsyth

PREFACE

Seventy-four years ago, Peter Taylor Forsyth, a Congregationalist, born in Scotland, Principal of Hackney Theological
College, Hampstead, (later known as New College, London) delivered the 1907 Lyman Beecher Lectures on Preaching. POSITIVE
PREACHING AND MODERN MIND has undergone many printings on both
sides of the Atlantic. ". . .no summary of his theology can
serve as a substitute for his books. There is no better book
to begin with than his POSITIVE PREACHING AND MODERN MIND"
states Sydney Cave.[1]

Seventy-four years later, P. T. Forsyth is sought, understood and appreciated as much or more than in his own life
time. To have a much wider audience for his lectures on preaching, three Forsythians out of several were asked to introduce
P. T. Forsyth to the seminarians and preachers (and to the
laity who would like to know what preaching is all about) in
the last decades of the Twentieth century, who in the first
decade of the twentieth century believed that "with its preaching Christianity stands or falls."[2]

In my association with Donald G. Miller, during and after
his presidency of the Pittsburgh Theological Seminary, it became quite obvious that among a few who had influenced his
thoughts on preaching, P. T. Forsyth took the lead. In his
book on preaching, he states: "At this point, as in many, I
have gotten great help from P. T. Forsyth."[3] At a special
dinner held in Richmond, Virginia in October, 1979, honoring
Donald G. Miller's seventieth birthday, his after dinner remarks were concluded with these words: "Let me quote from my

favorite theologian, P. T. Forsyth. He said, 'I should count a life well spent, and the world well lost, if, after testing all its experiences, and facing all its problems, I had no more to show at its close, or carry with me to another life, than the acquisition of a real, pure, humble, and grateful faith in the Eternal and Incarnate Son of God. That would be a life worth living, would it not?'"

His essay on "P. T. Forsyth: The Man" reveals Dr. Miller's unquestionable perceptivity of the depth of Forsyth's mind. A reader of his essay will find himself compelled to read at first hand the works of P. T. Forsyth.

Dr. Miller served as coordinator of the essays found in this volume.

As minister of the Congregational Church in Berkeley, California, Browne Barr, in the midst of academic turmoil, with particular concern for what was (or was not) happening in theological seminaries (or divinity schools), wrote an article, which appeared in the January 21, 1971 issue of *Christian Century* entitled, "Lineaments of Seminary Renewal." Ever since that reading I have looked for other contributions by Browne Barr, who is now Dean of San Francisco Theological Seminary and in all instances he has brought a fresh and ever penetrating insight into his concerns about the church.

Here we have an autobiographical essay but on "P. T. Forsyth: The Preachers' Theologian--A Witness and Confession." It is so personal that it carries the reader beyond and above the current whims of the church, preoccupied with trivialities, be it the use of the English language as a means of describing the gender of the Word or the concern about the divinity of the Word, to the Word which transcends them all.

It was over a year ago, during my sabbatical as librarian of Pittsburgh Theological Seminary, that it was my privilege to meet Browne Barr in person. It was his nudge during our con-

versation that made me decide as general editor of Pickwick
Press to proceed with the planning of this volume.

Robert S. Paul, an English Congregationalist, joined the
faculty of the Hartford Seminary Foundation in 1958. Our
friendship ever since then has carried us through Hartford and
Pittsburgh, and when he was invited to join the faculty of
Austin Presbyterian Theological Seminary in Austin, Texas,
distance did not prevent us from continuing to find occasions
to be together. How much P. T. Forsyth underlies his thoughts
may be seen by reading the various works which have come from
his pen. One quote from his Preface to *Kingdom Come!* will tell
it all. "If you have not met him before, or if he is one of
those former friends whom you knew long ago but dropped for
more exotic company, let me introduce Peter Taylor Forsyth--but
beyond him the one Forsyth acknowledged to be at the center of
his thought."[4]

So we have an English Congregationalist introducing a Congregationalist of Scottish descent with his essay on "P. T.
Forsyth: Prophet for the Twentieth Century?" Robert S. Paul
brings to us the prophetic words of P. T. Forsyth spoken in
the first decade of the 20th century as if he were our contemporary in the eighth decade of the same.

The Twentieth Century is in its *fin de siècle* quandry and
the Christian Church is "in search of itself" with a disparate
sense of disarray due to secularization.

Louis Dupré of Yale University believes that:

> . . .the source of our present unsettlement
> is religious. I do so with a great deal of
> misgiving. For I hold no evidence to support
> the view, quite common in some 'religious'
> quarters, that unbelief and apostasy from
> ecclesiastical institutions are at the root
> of our troubles. . .As I use the term 're-
> ligious' here, it will refer exclusively to
> the need for, and the presence of, a tran-

scendent dimension in human existence, in whatever form or shape it may be expressed. Consequently, I do not regard a simple revival of ancient beliefs and traditional institutions, *in itself* a solution to any of today's problems. For if my view is correct, those institutions and beliefs in their present state suffer as much under secularization crisis as the secular society itself. In fact, all too often they form one of the main obstacles on the road to genuine transcendence.[5]

To bring to the readers' attention the works by and about P. T. Forsyth there was no better way than to find a young Forsythian, Robert Benedetto, who during his seminary days discovered P. T. Forsyth and this led him to prepare for his own reading a bibliography which makes this volume all the more valuable. He also provided us with an index of scriptural references and authors and proper names index to POSITIVE PREACHING AND MODERN MIND.

We are grateful also to Robert Benedetto for providing us with a copy of the last Governor's Annual Report of New College, London. The College was closed on September 30, 1977. The report incorporated the address by Dr. H. F. Lovell Cocks delivered at the final Commemorative Service held on June 16, 1977. It is a special privilege to include in this volume the words of a "living link" with P. T. Forsyth and in doing so some needed correctives are offered and most of all a tribute by a pupil to his teacher and Principal.

It is fitting also that this volume be dedicated to the late Dr. Charles S. Duthie, the last Principal of New College, London, 1964-1977.

It is our hope that the availability of POSITIVE PREACHING AND MODERN MIND introduced by three of our contemporaries will infuse new and renewed understanding of what positive preaching and positive theology are within the context of modern mind.

Whitsuntide, 1981   Dikran Y. Hadidian

NOTES

1. "Dr. P. T. Forsyth, the Man and his Writings," *The Congregational Quarterly* 26 (1948):119.

2. *Positive Preaching and Modern Mind* (London, 1909):3.

3. *The Way to Biblical Preaching* (Nashville, 1977):131.

4. *Kingdom Come!* (Grand Rapids, 1974):10.

5. "The Religious Crisis of our Culture," *The Yale Review* 65 (1975-76):203-204.

P. T. FORSYTH: THE MAN

*Donald G. Miller**

Strange are the quirks of Christian history. Often, the church is found "killing the prophets and stoning those who are sent" to them, then later building "the tombs of [those] prophets" and adorning "the monuments of the righteous." At other times, the church recognizes her "day of visitation," perhaps belatedly honoring her prophets during their lifetime, then straightway forgetting them.

The latter has been at least the temporary fate of Peter Taylor Forsyth. There is a certain Melchizedek quality about his role in the church. He appeared suddenly from nowhere. The great R. W. Dale, near the end of his life, upon reading one of Forsyth's deliverances, raised with a companion who walked with him in the garden the question: "Who is this P. T. Forsyth? He has recovered for us a word we had all but lost--the word grace." Others, too, suddenly discovered the power and depth of Forsyth's thought and his profound grasp of the essentials of the faith, and showered accolades upon him during his latter years. He was elected to the highest honor of his denomination, the Chairmanship of the Congregational Union of England and Wales. James Denney, Scotland's greatest New Testament scholar, said that Forsyth had "more true or important things to say than any other man writing theology." He was dubbed by some of his contemporaries "genius," "the greatest prophet of our times. . .an Amos with the vision of

*Donald G. Miller is past President of Pittsburgh Theolog-- ical Seminary, Pittsburgh, Pennsylvania.

the cross." J. D. Jones, describing the impression Forsyth made on his audience by his address at an International Congregational Council at Boston, wrote: "He spoke as a man inspired. He flamed, he burned. . . . I wonder whether it was that great afternoon which made us realize here in England what a great gift God had given our churches in P. T. Forsyth." Even the agnostic John Morley, at a Manchester University social function, having asked D. R. Davies, then a student, what book he had under his arm, upon being handed the book, said: "Ah! by Forsyth. One of the most brilliant minds in Europe." Forsyth was one of the very few Nonconformist theologians to gain the notice of the theologians of the Established Church in England. He numbered among his friends such as Bishop Charles Gore. Since his day, he has been seriously studied and appreciated by such Anglican theologians as J. K. Mozley, Alec Vidler and R. R. Williams. The Swiss theologian, Emil Brunner, called him "the greatest of modern British theologians." He has been labeled by Horton Davies "Dissent's greatest twentieth-century theologian," and hailed by Robert McAfee Brown as a "prophet for today." D. R. Davies, in 1948, could say: "He has, at last, been recognized as one of the great theologians, not only of our century and of Great Britain, but of all the centuries and of every land."

In spite of this, Forsyth's influence faded quickly from the scene following his death in 1921. The major theological trends against which he toiled during his latter years became paramount in Britain and America, and his protests were laid politely and silently to rest. He came into his own once more during and shortly after the Second World War, when the Hitler debacle shattered the easy-going optimism of Liberalism and the name of Karl Barth was on all theological lips. He had anticipated Barth to the extent that the Swiss theologian remarked that they did not need him in Great Britain because they had P. T. Forsyth, and added that "If Forsyth had not said what he said when he said it, I would have said he was quoting me." This is not to peg Forsyth as "a Barthian before Barth" as some have done (incidently, Barth did not like Barthians!), but merely to point out the circumstances under which Forsyth again came into his own. D. R. Davies, in a foreword to a reprinting of Forsyth's *Justification of God*, remarked that the best book written on the Second World War was written during the First World War! Several of Forsyth's major works were reprinted and his name came into vogue once more. Between 1952 and 1966 serious studies of Forsyth's theology appeared, and as recently as 1974 A. M. Hunter could say that "interest in Forsyth continues unabated."

If that were true then, it is not so now, at least in America. Bradley's prediction in 1952 that although "the present interest in Forsyth will decline. . .it is unlikely that he will be forgotten as he was before" has turned out to be untrue. I have frequently asked recent graduates of some of the better seminaries whether they had been introduced to Forsyth during their theological studies, only to find that they had never heard of him, much less been acquainted with his writings. One searches in vain, too, for references to Forsyth in most current theological writing. In a time when both theologians and the public seem to be more interested in things human than in things divine, when there is more concern that people should realize their "full humanity" than that God's name be hallowed, when we are more concerned about our pain than about our sin, when God's love has been sentimentalized into an indulgence of human desires rather than the holy judgment of the Cross, when the benefits of God's kindness to us are more central than their cost to God, when freedom is self-indulgence which allows us to do as we please rather than freedom to do what God pleases, when material wel-

fare is more valued than moral progress, Forsyth's piercing
insights have been laid aside and forgotten as they were during
his own early career and between the two World Wars. This is
a great loss to the church and to the world. The republication
of *Positive Preaching and Modern Mind*, first given as the Yale
Lyman Beecher Lectures on Preaching in 1907, is designed to re-
introduce Forsyth to our generation in the hope that his message may be recovered and the church may have a positive word
to say to the world when "the lid comes off hell" again, and
the ugly face of human sin is unmasked in all its ghastly
horror and seen for what it really is.

I

His Career

Who was this man Forsyth? No full scale biography
of him has appeared. His hope that "no one will ever write a
dreary official full-dress biography" of him has been fulfilled,
to our great loss. Those of us who never knew him personally
are left with a few brief memoirs, some sketchy biographical
allusions made in his own writings, some very brief encyclopedia articles, a few reminiscences written by those who were
moved by his public addresses or books, and some scattered
notices of his death. From these we may try to reconstruct
something of the man.[1]

His beginnings would have doomed a lesser man to obscurity. He was born in Aberdeen, May 12, 1848, of humble
parents. His mother was the daughter of a Highland tenant-
farmer who began her career at the age of twelve as housekeeper
for her widowed uncle. She later became housemaid in the home
of Peter Taylor, a prominent merchant in Aberdeen. Her devo-

tion to duty was such that she delayed her marriage nine years to fulfill a promise to Taylor's dying wife that she would faithfully take care of her husband. At his death, Taylor bequeathed his house to the Forsyth's, and for him their first-born son was named.

Forsyth's father, a weaver's son, intelligent, hard working and thrifty, was never able to rise above the poverty level. He began as a small trader, then became a bookseller, and finally a postman, an employment reluctantly accepted to insure an income for a family of five children. The stipend was assured, but pitifully small, never more than eighteen shillings per week. Forsyth's mother regularly took in boarders, mostly students, in a struggle to make ends meet. If the students were at times too poor to requite her for board and lodging, she carried them without charge. In later years, when elected Chairman of the Congregational Union of England and Wales, Forsyth overcame the reticence of personal reference ("it is not well that a man should expose his own soul to his people") sufficiently to speak of his poverty-stricken boyhood. "I want to say. . .how much I owe to two Scotch peasants, long passed away, but for whose scraping and toil and self-denial I should not have been here tonight." On another occasion, while addressing the Congregational Union, he indirectly revealed a bit of his early experience: "Do not take my arm and lead me away to the dwellings of the pound-a-weeks and the nothing-a-weeks and tell me, if I want realities, to consider there. I was there, and worked there, and con-sidered there, and have been considering ever since." His daughter speaks touchingly of an apology her father once wrote to her for forgetting her birthday: "Forgive a poor boy who never had any birthdays or any presents."

Although poverty and boyhood illness were his lot ("I can-not remember since boyhood passing a day without pain"), his

childhood was a happy one. His lack of robustness may have
kept him from indulging in organized sports (one of his boyhood chums remarked: "While we were at our bats, he was at
his books"), yet he entered into the spontaneous games and
snowball fights on the school grounds, and spent a good deal
of time mingling with the sailors along the wharves. His
daughter insisted that there "was no play or prank conceivable
by impish wits that he was not leader in, up and down the
streets, in and out of the wynds and along the quayside." She
attributed his later internationalism to his boyhood "intercourse with the ships and crews from all shores to be found in
the harbour at his door." He himself wistfully recalled his
youthful seaside days, when "at dead of night, when all was
quiet, I used to hear the sea singing a lullaby to the fisher
children on the shore beneath the moon and her family of stars."

His quick mind first came under discipline at the Grammar
School in Aberdeen. With this preparation he entered the annual Bursary Competition for the University, which consisted
of translating an English text into Latin. The winning of
such a competition was for him, as for many other poor Scottish lads, the only possible guarantee of a university education. He placed twenty-first among two hundred and four, and
won the Cargill Bursary for four years of study at Aberdeen
University. There, under the famous Professor Bain, professor
of Logic and Philosophy, from whom his own thought widely di-
gressed, the set of his mind and his habits of study were developed. A striking personality, he captivated his fellow
students and made his presence known on the campus. Vigorous
and disciplined study took a further toll on his health. Too
poor to buy essential books, he would, at times, take one from
the library and work right through it for twenty-four hours before it had to be returned. After taking several prizes in
his first and second year, with a lapse for illness during the

third year, he took a brilliant first in Classics during his senior year and tied for first prize in Moral Philosophy.

During his University career, he had earned money by tutoring. Following graduation, he spent a year as a private tutor, then worked another year as assistant to the Professor of Latin. After that, at the suggestion of his friend, W. Robertson Smith, he went to study for a term at Göttingen, under the famous Albrecht Ritschl. This venture left a lasting residue in his life, not only because of the influence of Ritschl, whose views he later modified in his own thought, but because he mastered the German language and acquainted himself with German scholarship with which he kept abreast throughout his life. He became so fluent in German that he was once mistaken for a native! He finally came, more often than not, to follow other theological paths than those broken by the Germans, but he did it against the background of his thorough knowledge of their scholarship, which gave to his thought an international and ecumenical quality. Aside from his final passionate adherence to the evangelical faith, he never could be identified with any narrow school or party. He belonged to the whole church.

Upon his return from Germany, he enrolled in the fall of 1872 in New College, London, to study theology. His health prevented his regular attendance at classes. His daughter suggests that reading between the lines indicates that he was not happy there. Whether for this reason, or solely because of his health, he resigned from the college in 1874 before completing his course. Two results of his days at New College were permanent, however. He met the girl to whom he was later married, and was deeply influenced by a Congregational preacher, J. Baldwin Brown, who shared with Forsyth a common admiration for F. D. Maurice, whose lengthened shadow over his life Forsyth never escaped. The next two years are a biographical blank. It may have been that his liberal views at that time made it difficult for him to get a call to a pulpit.

He emerged from total obscurity in response to a call to the Congregational Church at Shipley, a suburb of Bradley, in Yorkshire, in 1876. A year later he was married to Minna Magness, to whom was born his only child. Neither he nor his church was admitted into the local Congregational Union. Forsyth aligned himself with a group of younger ministers who were championing freedom from what they thought was the dead hand of orthodoxy. He took a strong part in the famous Leicester Conference which shook the entire Congregational Union in a theological convulsion. His youthful vigor of personality manifested itself in many ways, not the least of which was his appearing in his pulpit with plaid trousers and brilliant neckties. He attracted a congregation of such unorthodox sympathies that his church was nicknamed "The Cave of Adullam."

After four years, he moved to Hackney, a suburb of London, where he found wide outlet for his interests in art, music, literature, the theatre and politics. Here, too, particularly to his Sunday evening lectures, he attracted a congregation "of heretics and suspects" from all denominations and no denomination and all walks of life.

A third call came in 1885, to Cheetham Hill, in north Manchester. Once again, along with his preaching and pastoral duties, he entered vigorously into public life, both political and cultural, giving a series of lectures to workingmen on a collection of paintings gathered for the Manchester Exhibition of 1887, which were published in *Religion in Recent Art*. A deep interest in children led him to devote one full Sunday service a month to the children, which eventuated in the publication of *Pulpit Parables for Young Hearers*.

When, in 1888, Forsyth took up a fourth pastorate at

Clarendon Park, Leicester, he continued his cultural and political activities, becoming involved in a strike of dock workers, and making his influence felt on election platforms. During this period, however, a new note began to creep into his preaching and writing, reflecting his great theological conversion, of which more later. As the result of his contribution to a volume entitled *Faith and Criticism*, he attracted the notice of Dale and others as a solid theologian who was beginning to make a unique contribution to the thought of the church.

The arduous labors of his six year pastorate in Leicester left him in wretched health. When a call came for him to remove to the Emmanuel Church in Cambridge in 1894, he was hesitant to accept it, but did so mainly at the urging of several of the most influential leaders of his denomination. Eager to be represented in Cambridge by one of his intellectual gifts and theological acumen, they urged him to decide not by a "mere balancing of the church at Cambridge with the church at Leicester," but to consider not only "the interests of a local church, but of the Congregational churches in the country."

In the hope of regaining his health, he took a three months leave of absence before assuming his duties, with no results. Added to his physical weakness came the blow of his wife's death within a week of his arrival in Cambridge. For three years he labored on in a state of nervous exhaustion, too weak even to make the trip to Aberdeen to receive the doctorate his Alma Mater conferred on him. His congregation furnished him transportation to the church services, and people came to his home for pastoral care in lieu of his pastoral visitation. It was during this period that he preached his famous sermon "Holy Father" at a meeting of the Congregational Union which embodied the settled convictions to which his theological pilgrimage had brought him, stressing the holiness

of God, the sin of man and the centrality of the Cross in
solving the tension between the two. His remarriage in 1898
to Bertha Ison wrought a profound change in him. Under her
careful guardianship of his always precarious health, and
through the influence of her charm, vitality and wit, he recovered his zest for life and entered upon the most fruitful
period of his career. It was at this time that he began to
gain international attention, largely through his electrifying
address at a world Congregational Assembly in Boston on "The
Evangelical Principle of Authority," when, instead of discus-
sing his address, the congregation rose and sang "In the Cross
of Christ I glory."

Forsyth's twenty-five years in the pastorate had ideally
prepared him for the final position he held as Principal of
Hackney College, now known as New College, London, which he
accepted in 1901. The college had been but recently accredited
as a Divinity School by the University of London, which gave
Forsyth opportunity to strengthen its intellectual integrity
and to give himself to the formation of the faith and ministry
of younger men in whose hands the future of the churches lay.
His own theology had been wrought out on the anvil of the
pastorate. He sought, therefore, to train men whose thought
would be the outgrowth of the strictest discipline of the intellect, but always warmed by the devotion of the heart and
directed not to mere speculative ends but to the confrontation
of men with the holiness and love of God uniquely active in
the Cross for the redemption of the world. The burden of
financing a struggling institution, along with his personal
concern for each of his students, was demanding. Yet during
this period he turned out a prodigious amount of theological
writing which are his invaluable legacy to the world, including his Yale Lectures on Preaching, *Positive Preaching and
Modern Mind*, and his greatest book, *The Person and Place of*

Jesus Christ.

The coming of the first World War in 1914, which caught
so many by surprise, deeply affected Forsyth but did not star-
tle him. He felt that it was, at least in great part, God's
judgment on many of the false expectations from the Christian
faith furthered by the old liberalism which had not taken the
measure of human sin nor the holiness of God's love. His response to it is to be seen in two books, *The Justification of
God* and *The Christian Ethic of War.* His final book, *This Life
and the Next,* appeared just as the war closed, in 1918.

The end of the war found him past seventy and measurably
weakened by the strain of the conflict, lifelong disease, and
incessant labors. His mental alertness, however, kept him at
his post for two further years, when, at the end of 1920, his
wasted powers of mind and body could be pushed no further.
After another year as a complete invalid, he "succumbed to a
superior spiritual attraction" on Armistice Day, November 11,
1921. As A. M. Hunter has remarked, no more apt tribute could
be paid to him than that inscribed on the memorial tablet in
New College Chapel: PER CRUCEM AD LUCEM - "through the Cross
to the Light."

Some attempt to unearth the mind and heart of the man
whose inner life lies deeply buried behind this brief biographical sketch must now be made.

II

His Theological Conversion

Perhaps something of the inner shaping of the man may be
sensed, by those of us who never knew him in the flesh, by
trying to trace the lineaments of the profound theological conversion which radically transformed both his thought and life.

As with Luther, Forsyth's mature theology was the outgrowth of a great spiritual struggle. It was the effort to give theological expression to his own evangelical experience of saving grace. Unlike Luther, however, his reticence to speak of this makes it difficult to trace with finality and clarity.

That change there was seems indisputable. Two statements, one from his early career and another from his mature days, reflect the transformation. In 1877, he wrote critically of the church: "We have been thrown back on Paul. We have yet, as a Church, to learn to lean simply on Christ." Thirty years later, in 1907, he wrote concerning his book *Positive Preaching and Modern Mind*: "If there be anything in the book which St. Paul, as the supreme devotee, organ, and expositor of Christ, would not have passed or paralleled, that I would at once withdraw and lament, whether it were in matter or tone." To pass from the much-loved device of driving a wedge between Jesus and Paul to the view that Paul understood Jesus better than any other is not a minor shift of emphasis. It is rather a radical transformation of his entire understanding of the Christian faith.

When, and how, did this transformation occur? One searches in vain for any precise dating of this theological conversion or any momentary experience which wrought it. Forsyth seemed to be extremely reluctant to speak of it. One of his closest friends, Principal Sydney Cave, revealed that Forsyth never once spoke of it to him in private. Indirect allusions to it, however, are made in various places in his writings.

Although he retained to the end the intellectual freedom and critical methodology which his more liberal days had given him, he progressively discovered that far more was involved in the historic Christian faith than that which freedom and methodology had fathomed. The faith was dealing with issues which struck deeper into human life and experience, both for the individual and society, than his early liberalism could take him. The life and death issues with which the faith was concerned were not mere matters of the schools which were to be faced in the arena of the intellect alone. They broke through the calm surface of the liberal optimism of his day to the tragic contradictions of personal and societal experience where sinister destructive forces raged against the holiness of God, and necessitated God's holy recoil against sin in a redemptive moral act on Calvary mighty enough to overcome it. "The whole race is not only weighted with arrears," he insisted, "but infected with a blight. The train of history is not simply late, but there has been an accident due to malice and crime. We struggle not only with misfortune but with a curse." Therefore, we need a Saviour, "a Saviour who is *final*, as Saviour from *absolute* perdition; the Saviour of our moral helplessness and not merely our backwardness." A liberalism which begins with "the modern mind" instead of the gospel, which has not taken the true measure of human sin, which understands Christ more through what he has in common with us than in where he differs from us, which reduces grace to the drawing out of something latent in mankind rather than a totally undeserved gift coming from the beyond, "is something that claims to be Christianity" but "most imperils Christianity." Forsyth grants that he "was brought up in the fine tradition of. . . liberal theology." He admits: "That liberalism had its work to do. I felt its force. I took part in it. And it has won-- I might say all along the line. . . . But the result of the general victory of religious liberalism has been disappointing on the whole. . . . It is a spent movement."

The lineaments of his shift of view may be traced in a few biographical revelations in his writings. In one decisive passage he tells us much:

> Our youth begins in surprised impatient
> joy. We are all reformers and our sires were
> fools. We discover soon that even the spirit
> of the age can fail, and that many of our con-
> temporaries are not wise. For they will not
> at our bidding part with the folly of the
> creeds. A little longer and we misdoubt our
> own complete wisdom. Still longer and we are
> troubled most with the *sin* of our fathers and
> brethren. And at last we give in. No sin has
> hampered us like our own. We were on too good
> terms with our own conscience. We can never
> trust our breezy selves again. We have all
> our world and all our hope to reconstruct at
> the foot of the Cross. Our new views must
> arise from our new selves. And the Kingdom
> can only come by the humbled valour of those
> who have entered in, and who witness of a for-
> giveness they have seen, and heard, and known.

Here, it is plain, maturity and personal growth were part of the process of change. As his mind and experience of life expanded, his theology deepened. Even more decisive, however, was the deep discovery of his own sin which demanded a more radical cure than his liberalism could effect. Adolescent enthusiasm could make him see others' sins. Maturity could make him doubt his own wisdom. But that which dealt a death-blow to his easy conscience was that he saw something at the foot of the Cross which he had earlier missed. He spoke of this directly at another time: "It also pleased God by the revelation of his holiness and grace, which the great theologians taught me to find in the Bible, to bring home to me my sin in a way that submerged all the school questions in weight, urgency, and poignancy." It was thus, he said, that "I was turned from a Christian to a believer, from a lover of love to an object of grace."

A third element which drove him deeper into the faith was his pastoral experience of responsibility for the faith of others. He writes:

> There was a time when I was interested
> in the first degree with purely scientific
> criticism. Bred among academic scholarship
> of the classics and philosophy, I carried
> these habits to the Bible. . . . But, for-
> tunately for me, I was not condemned to the
> mere scholar's cloistered life. I could not
> treat the matter as an academic quest. I
> was kept close to practical conditions. I
> was in a relation of life, duty, and respon-
> sibility for others. I could not contemplate
> conclusions without asking how they would
> affect these people, and my word to them, in
> doubt, death, grief, or repentance. I could
> not call on them to accept my verdict on
> points that came so near their soul. . . .
> In a word, I was driven to a change of front,
> though not of footing--to the preacher's and
> the pastor's treatment of the situation,
> which is also the New Testament view, and
> which is very different from the scholars.

To those who argue that truth should be followed scientifically, no matter to what conclusions it leads, Forsyth
would reply that his own and his people's evangelical experience of the faith are facts of which even scientific theology
must take account.

> What! Am I really forbidden to make
> any use of my personal experience of Christ
> for the purposes even of scientific theology?
> Should it make no difference to the evidence
> for Christ's Resurrection that I have had
> personal dealings with the risen Christ as
> my Saviour, nearer and dearer than my own
> flesh and blood? Is his personal gift of
> forgiveness to me, in the central experience
> of my life, of no value in settling the ob-
> jective value of his Cross and Person?

This brief tracing of his theological conversion strongly
suggests the profound relation of his thinking to his believing.
The theology is the man.

III

His Style

Another revealing aspect of the man is his style of
writing. This has frequently occasioned comment, often un-
favorable. One critic describes his writing as "crowded with
strangely formed sentences, full of antithesis and epigram,
sprinkled with newly coined words." Others have described his
style as "needlessly obscure and involved," "ponderous and com-
plicated," "too literary," filled with "bizarre forms of expression," "a shower of sky rockets," "fireworks in a fog,"
"a series of electric flashes which did not succeed in dispel-
ling the obscurity that gathered about the subject." Even his
close friend and admirer, James Denney, expressed the wish that
"Dr. Forsyth could accommodate himself to the dull, and meet
him (if possible) half-way."

These criticisms bear some weight. But they seem paltry
in the light of the total impact Forsyth's style makes on any
thoughtful reader who is willing to put forth the effort to
swim in the depths to which Forsyth is trying to lead him.
Often, when reading Forsyth, I have felt rather like one
standing beside Niagara Falls with a tin cup, gathering in a
bit of the spray while the main stream flowed by. The reason
for this is, however, that my cup is too small. The limitation
is more mine than his. He is stretching me beyond the limit
of my capacity. Should I wish him to shut off the majestic
stream to a trickle so that I could take it all in? And is
not the bit of spray that I get better than the entire stream
of many others? He once remarked: "There is nothing more
obscure to common sense than the personal experience of faith

which believes in present grace, real judgment, and final good
amid a world that lies in wickedness." It is difficult, if not
impossible, to phrase things seen at the foot of the Cross for
others who have never stood there with bared heads or the shoes
removed from their feet. As Forsyth put it: "Only the bene-
ficiaries of the Cross can effectively discuss the Cross."

Granted, Forsyth's vocabulary abounds in unusual expressions, some of which he coined. But terms he coined, such as
"kerygma" and "crisis theology," soon became common coin.
Forsyth had the Celtic love of words. Why should he spurn an
enriched vocabulary? Another author of rich English prose,
when questioned about his unusual vocabulary replied that he
used no words that were not in the dictionary!

Presumably, words found in the dictionary were originally
devised to bear some useful meaning and their use is not amiss.
Forsyth felt also that the lust for simplicity of theological
expression arose perhaps less from a true desire for clarity
than from the reduction of the grandeur and paradoxical nature
of Christian thought to inane moral simplicities which skim
only the surface of truth. Romans and Galatians are hardly
examples of modern *Reader's Digest* style. But could they possibly be put in that style without watering down their meaning?
Forsyth felt that the deepest things in Christianity can be
grasped only from within the faith. He, therefore, used
faith-language to express them. The difficulties with his
style may lie in the strangeness of the experiences of faith
to which he was pointing. Add to these considerations the
fact that some passages in Forsyth have a literary power and
beauty which are hard to equal. Methodism's great theologian,
the late Edwin Lewis, once remarked that the last chapter in
Positive Preaching and Modern Mind is the most powerful piece
of theological writing done in our century. Forsyth would
hardly have been described as "the most quotable of theolo-

gians" had his style, though difficult at times, been as deficient as some suggest. Hermann has said of him: "In nine cases out of ten, nebulosity of style hides looseness if not shallowness of thought; Dr. Forsyth is the tenth case. Moreover, his culture of brilliant phrasing has given us a thousand and one. . .characterizations enshrining a whole body of almost uncommonly penetrating criticism within a few neat words."

In my judgment, the difficulties in Forsyth's style may be accounted for by the fact that his grasp of the Christian faith soared to ineffable sublimities where words break down. He was struggling to say what cannot be said. Like his mentor, Paul, he was caught up to such heights that "he heard things that cannot be told, which man may not utter." He unconsciously bears witness to this in the closing words of his *Holy Father*:

> That bows us. It takes us into the Holy Place. . . . It is all beyond thought, beyond poetry, beyond Scripture, beyond speech. God Himself in that mighty joy refrains from words. He could utter it only in act, in raising Christ from the dead by the spirit of holiness. . .Deep answered deep. We can feel it and worship it at the last only in the power and silence of the same Holy Ghost.

He had been so deeply touched by "an inscrutable and searching grace by which the most righteous and loving soul of man is but scarcely saved" that human language could not quite be fashioned to capture it. It is little wonder then, that, as his daughter tells us, in "wrestling with thoughts almost beyond human expression. . .he wrote with a physical and nervous intensity which shook the desk, and which after an hour or two left him utterly spent, stretched out white and still upon his study couch." If his theology was the expression of the man, even so his style was the man.

IV

The Depth of His Mind and the Breadth of His Interests

The range of Forsyth's mind, and the breadth of his interests, place him in a class which some would call "genius."
T. R. Glover's appraisal of Paul as a many-sided genius whom
smaller minds sometimes find contradictory, inconsistent and
baffling may account for the difficulty many have with Forsyth.
He was uncommonly brilliant and creative. He took other men's
ideas and gave them the stamp of his own enrichment, and frequently pioneered new terrain where others had not trod. One
difficulty he had in expressing his thought lay in the fact
that his mind worked faster than his pen. Ideas came tumbling
out so fast, and in such profusion, that it was difficult for
him to tidy up each thought before another overtook it. He
sought ever to state truth in terms related to the need of the
hour, thus keeping his thought, although always anchored to
the central fact of what he had seen in the Cross, supple and
mobile. He could engage in the same war, yet change fronts
and adapt himself to the tactics of the enemy. After he found
his center, he remained orthodox without the deadening influence of a theoretical orthodoxy more concerned about ordered
systems than with living truth. He sought ever to bring the
great Fathers of the Church and the Reformers up to date, to
use the ammunition of their truth in weapons cast for the conflict of our time. The "new" for him was not the shallowness
of the novel and the untested. It was rather the rediscovery
of the truth about Christ who is "the same yesterday and today
and forever" in fresh categories suited to the forms and needs
of the hour. When, however, the forms and needs of the hour
became the arbiters of truth, rather than the channels of ex-

pressing truth, he preferred even the old forms if no better
could be found. He welcomed and furthered the ethical aspects
of Christian doctrine which were to the fore in his day, but
saw the dangers to which this led. He wrote:

> It is the ethical rather than the
> strictly evangelical aspect of Christianity
> which it has been the function of our day
> to turn to light. A time may come, I admit,
> and may not be distant, when we shall have
> to do what Paul did. . .he pressed the ex-
> piatory aspect of the work of Christ. It
> formed the substance of his protest as it
> formed the essence of Luther's. And a pro-
> test may be forced on us which will cause
> us to renew our emphasis on some theory of
> the Atonement for the sake of a true view
> of Incarnation. We may have to go back on
> the more strictly evangelical aspect of
> Christ's work to save us from a one-sided
> morality, from a despotism of propriety, a
> deification of 'conduct,' and an ethical
> pharisaism which is all law and no Gospel,
> all practical, with no food or kindling for
> the living spirit at all.

He feared that "the New Evangelicalism" of his time was in danger of ceasing "to be evangelical at all. . .for that word
loses its meaning when the love of God takes the place in religion which is due to His holiness, and when the divine justice is conceived to be more engaged with wrongs than in the
war with sin." We see in these statements a mind which refused
to be straight-jacketed in any partial aspect of truth. His
thought had what Ruskin called "the balance of harmonious op-
posites." He saw dangers in half-truths which excluded
equally valid counterparts and sought to grasp truth as a living
whole.

The breadth of his interests may be seen in a multiplicity
of issues which claimed his attention. A glance at his bibliography astounds one with the range of his concerns. He

dealt with subjects theological, biblical, historical, ecclesiastical, ecumenical, and practical. He wrote on art and music and literature, on the cure of souls, on worship, on preaching, on denominational and interchurch problems, on New Testament theology, on Christology, on Soteriology, on the Christian life, on eschatology and the life to come, on politics, on the problem of the poor, on marriage, on the relation of the faith to the hypothesis of evolution, on public education, on prayer, on miracles, on Socialism and Capitalism, on the justification of God in time of war, on ethics, on the right way to use the Bible, on Christian Missions, on the problem of authority, and more. His interests were as broad as life.

Forsyth's wide knowledge of theology, philosophy, literature, history, art, music, science, politics, is revealed more often subtly than openly. He did not use learning for the sake of display. He seldom quotes, almost never identifies the source of his quotations, and more often alludes to or paraphrases the thought of others. But each reference indicates that he has thoroughly mastered the thought of the writers to whom he refers and the issues he discusses. In such sentences as the following he often reveals his grasp of another's thought:

> Does not Kant confess as a moralist the radical evil in man, and Carlyle speak of his infinite damnability? There is many a living Mephistopheles in Europe.

> Nothing is more remarkable in *Parsifal* than the return to European culture of the sense of sin, the need of forgiveness, and the faith in its possibility.

> The greatest Socialist thinkers, like Marx, are properly reticent on details, and this, instead of being a weakness, is a strength. It shows that they are not wholly doctrinaire, but have some sense of political perspective.

The French socialist thinkers treat
society much as Renan treats Jesus--with
sentimental rationalism.

It is no wonder. . .that Mr. G. B. Shaw,
with his literary skill and grotesque wit, has
much vogue with the Socialism that feels
things to be wrong without heart enough to
feel how wrong, without heart, in the Bible
use of the word, with a heart for man's suffering from man but none for God's.

The Saviour knew the evil in the world,
even as Schopenhauer did not.

There is much. . .to remind us of McLeod
Campbell and the whole school he represents. . .
This it shares with Maurice, but lacks his keen
ethical and social interest.

Now we are to beware of emptying the reconciliation idea of the idea of the atonement,
whether we do it philosophically with Hegel or
theologically with Ritschl.

Augustine's rediscovery was this, justification by grace alone; Luther's side of the
rediscovery was justification by faith alone--
faith in the Cross, that is to say, faith in
grace.

It is not an outgrown notion, a relic of
moral immaturity, like the patristic idea of
Christ cheating Satan by His death, or even the
Anselmic satisfaction of God's honour.

Sentences like these which unobtrusively reveal Forsyth's
broad mastery of dozens of the thinkers who have left their
mark on history, could be quoted endlessly. Few writers on
theology have had minds which ranged so broadly and so profoundly through the riches of other men's scholarship as did
his. But, as W. L. Bradley remarks, to read those who influenced Forsyth is not to arrive at his own thought. "He assimi-
lated the thoughts of others, then produced something distinc-
tively his own. The range of his interests and the depth and

originality of his thought make him always fresh. Theologically, he is a "man for all seasons." Hence, his thought,
when neglected during any one period, may be recovered at
various times through future generations.

Another thing revelatory of the man was Forsyth's amazing
output of work. He had published 8 books, countless essays,
magazine articles, sermons, addresses and book reviews during
his busy days as a pastor. During the twenty years of his
principalship of Hackney College, when somewhat more time was
available for writing, he published 17 books, most of them
solid works, 9 essays in works edited by others, approximately
53 magazine articles, about 24 sermons, addresses and newspaper articles, in addition to various lengthy book reviews.
When it is remembered that the last year of this period was
spent as a complete invalid, that the period included the
dislocations of four years of the First World War, that he
was involved in many public and church commitments, along
with the burdensome task of keeping afloat a poorly financed
theological college, this output of work for a man never
strong and constantly plagued with illness is eloquent of a
never-flagging commitment to duty and a capacity for creative
toil which are uncommon. Hunter tells us that his extraor-
dinarily quick mind could work under pressure "at almost de-
monic speed."

V

The Quality of His Life

His personal qualities as a man can only be drawn for
those of us who never knew him from reminiscences of others
and reflections of his personality in his writings. His
daughter tells us that he was the most considerate of fathers

and the most loyal of friends to his intimates. A streak of
mischievousness often broke through his usual reserve which
sometimes surprised students who had looked upon him as somewhat of a retiring saint. He had a sharp tongue at times, but
always in the defence of what he thought to be truth. He did
not hesitate to offend those whom he thought to be dilettantes
in their dealing with truth, or pompous or superficial in their
personal relations, or triflers who cleverly manipulated the
faith to justify an undisciplined life. Even in his early
years, before his theological conversion, he denounced those
who used his liberal views to justify moral laxity. In his
farewell sermon at his second pastorate in Hackney, London, he
looked up from his manuscript and said caustically: "I hope I
have offended such men. I think I see some of them here tonight." He never used such tactics, however, for purposes of
self-aggrandizement. Although circumstances involved him frequently in theological conflict, such as his famous defense of
the gospel against the New Theology of R. J. Campbell, he disliked it immensely and entered the arena only when he felt that
issues were involved which, in his judgment, were fatal to
Christianity. There was no personal malice in his theological
attacks, and when Campbell modified his views, Forsyth was immediately reconciled to him. He reached out to men of all denominations, and was particularly understanding of those who
seriously grappled with the faith through the dark night of
honest doubt. It was said of him that even though he "did not
always temper heat with light and light with sweetness. . .he
stood so disinterestedly and purely for the loftiest and most
imperative issues that few thoughtful opponents ranged themselves against him without some degree of regret."

The final measure of a man is his inner life. This can
be assessed in one as reticent to speak of himself as Forsyth
only through those occasional barings of the soul which reflect

the inner moral realism on which his thought was founded.
The key to Forsyth's inner life is here: "It also pleased God
by the revelation of his holiness and grace. . .to bring home
to me my sin in a way that submerged all the school questions
in weight, urgency, and poignancy." Once again: "I was all
the time being corrected and humiliated by the Holy Spirit."
This is echoed elsewhere: "No sin has hampered us like our
own. We were on too good terms with our own conscience. . . .
We have all our world and all our hope to reconstruct at the
foot of the Cross. Our new views must arise from our new
selves." "For God's sake," he urges, "do not tell poor prodigals and black scoundrels that they are better than they
think, for the conscience that is in hell is the first to be
angered at ingenuities and futilities like these." In com-
menting on the petition of the father of the epileptic for
healing for his son, he says:

> I seize the answer of the Lord, 'I will
> come down and heal him.' The words are life
> to my sick self. . . . On the wings of
> that word he moves. . .restless in search of
> me--me sick, falling, lost, desperate. He
> comes and he finds me and heals me in these
> words of the gospel. I do not ask the critics
> for assurance that the incident took place
> exactly as recorded. I will talk of that
> when I am healed.

Elsewhere, in stressing the necessity of God's atoning act in
Christ, he says:

> We sin--and for us inexpiably--against
> our own souls. How much less, then, can we
> atone to our injured, neglected, sin-stung
> God. If our theology would let us, our
> conscience would not. The past cannot be
> erased, cannot be altered, cannot be re-
> paired. No man can save his brother's soul--
> no, nor his own. . . . Man's debt no man
> can pay. . . . God alone could fulfil for
> us the holy law He never broke, and pay the
> cost He never incurred.

Such statements as these hint at the level of spiritual integrity at which Forsyth lived.

But perhaps the final vision of the quality of a man's life is to be seen at the level of his prayer life. A spiritually perceptive person may tell more about a man through hearing him pray than almost any other way. But public prayers may be a "pose." And it is impossible to observe a man's private prayer. Yet in Forsyth's writing about prayer, without consciously being autobiographical, many of his comments have about them the quality of Jacob's wrestling with the angel. They reflect the hidden struggle of the soul with God, and show us Forsyth at his deepest. As another has suggested, they help us to "realize that the hands that wage such ruthless war against what appears to him as a shallow liberalism are pierced hands." To give but one example:

> How is it that the experience of life is so often barren of spiritual culture for religious people. . . . Is it not because they have never really had personal religion? That is, they have never really prayed with all their heart;. . .They have never 'spread out' their whole soul and situation to a God who knows. . . . They do not face themselves, only what happens to them. They pray with their heart and not with their conscience. They pity themselves, perhaps they spare themselves, they shrink from hurting themselves more than misfortune hurts them. They say, 'if you knew all you could not help pitying me.' They do not say, 'God knows all and how can he spare me.'. . .We are not humble in God's sight, partly because in our prayer there is a point at which we cease to pray, where we do not turn everything out into God's light. It is because there is a chamber or two in our souls where we do not enter in and take God with us. We hurry Him by that door as we take Him along the corridors of our life to see our tidy places or our public rooms. We ask from our prayers too exclusively com-

fort, strength, enjoyment, or tenderness and graciousness, and not often enough humiliation and its fine strength. We want beautiful prayers, touching prayers, simple prayers, thoughtful prayers; prayers with a quaver or tear in them, or prayers with delicacy and dignity in them. But searching prayer, humbling prayer, which is the prayer of the conscience, and not merely of the heart or taste, prayer which is bent on reality, and to win the new joy goes through new misery if need be--are such prayers as welcome and common as they should be?

One feels, as he reads this, that the man who asks this question of others, has first asked it of himself. There is as much of confession here as of admonition. We see a soul baring itself to God.

There is much of indirect autobiographical light to be shed on the moral realism of Forsyth's own spiritual struggle in his love for John Newton's hymn, "Prayer Answered By Crosses." Forsyth refers to it as "one of the greatest and most realistic utterances of Christian experience," and elsewhere confesses that he looked upon it "as almost holy writ." The hymn opens with a prayer to "grow in faith, and love, and every grace." But the One to whom the prayer was addressed answered it in a surprising way--a way that, as the writer confesses, "almost drove me to despair." He had hoped that in one high moment the "constraining power" of God's love would subdue his sins and give him rest. Instead of this,

> . . . .He made me feel
> The hidden evils of my heart,
> And let the angry powers of hell
> Assault my soul in every part.

And then the woe was aggravated. The "fair designs" he schemed were "blasted," he was laid low.

> Lord, why is this? I trembling cried,
> Wilt Thou pursue Thy worm to death:
> 'Tis in this way,' the Lord replied
> 'I answer prayer for grace and faith.
>
> Those inward trials I employ
> From self and pride to set thee free;
> And break thy schemes of earthly joy
> That thou may'st seek thy all in Me.'

This was the man who looked at life with all its joys and its sorrows, its demands and its opportunities, its burdens and its pleasures, its tears and its smiles, its advances and its reverses, its nobleness and its sins, its innocence and its guilt, its triumphs and its tragedies, and could sum it all up at last:

> . . .I should count a life well spent,
> and the world well lost, if, after testing
> all its experiences, and facing all its prob-
> lems, I had no more to show at its close, or
> carry with me to another life, than the ac-
> quisition of a real, pure, humble, and grate-
> ful faith in the Eternal and Incarnate Son of
> God.

Such was the man whose heart and mind find expression through *Positive Preaching and Modern Mind* hereby reintroduced to the English reading world.

NOTES

1. The sources I have used are the delightful Memoir by his daughter, Jesse Forsyth Andrews, published in the reprint of her father's *The Work of Christ* (London: Independent Press, 1938); W. L. Bradley, *P. T. Forsyth: The Man and His Work* (London: Independent Press, 1952); Robert McAfee Brown, *P. T. Forsyth: Prophet For Today* (Philadelphia: The Westminster Press, 1952); A. M. Hunter, *P. T. Forsyth: Ad Crucem Lucem* (London: SCM Press, 1974); *Encyclopedia Britannica,* 11th ed., s.v. "Forsyth, Peter Taylor." *New Catholic Encyclopedia,* 1967 ed., s.v. "Forsyth, Peter Taylor," by William Walton Thomson Hannah; *The New Encyclopaedia Brittanica,* Micropaedia, Ready Reference and Index. 1974 ed., s.v., "Forsyth, Peter Taylor;" "Death of Principal Forsyth, Peter Taylor," *The London Times,* November 1921. E. Hermann, "Peter Taylor Forsyth, D.D.," *Homiletic Review,* 66(1913), 179-185; and countless of Forsyth's own works. Inasmuch as the purpose of this article is to induce readers to read Forsyth for themselves, in the interests of simplicity I have refrained from cluttering it with footnotes to each reference. I can vouch for the genuineness and accuracy of each quotation I have used. An extensive bibliography of works by Forsyth and on Forsyth is appended to the articles in this volume.

P. T. FORSYTH: THE PREACHERS' THEOLOGIAN--
A WITNESS AND CONFESSION

Browne Barr *

The year was 1944. A young minister was moving into a
high-ceilinged parsonage just off the wide main street of a
small New England city. The high dark brick house with interior shutters had deep bay windows, one group gracing the back
living room and another stacked directly over it for the large
back bedroom. There were three fireplaces and an ancient fur-
nace which once swallowed 36 tons of coal in a single winter.
The young incoming pastor would soon struggle in zero January
nights to haul the ashes and the cinders from the cellar, up
through the trap door and out over the icy snow to the street
for collection.

Everywhere the year was 1944. American soldiers were
sweating out imprisonment in the Philippines and dying in the
China Sea, the minister's brother-in-law among them, a volun-
teer in the Coast Artillery. In Europe the hinge of history
had not yet shown which way it was going to swing its door.
Anne Frank still was hiding out. The furnaces of the Nazis
belched their stink and smoke of human hair and flesh.

The young minister had been reared in the aftermath of
the First World War, the "war to end all wars." He had attended

---

*Browne Barr is Dean of San Francisco Theological Seminary,
San Anselmo, California.

church youth conferences addressed in alternate seasons by
prophets of prohibition and prophets of peace. As a Freshman
in high school he signed a pledge never to smoke or drink; as
a Freshman in college he signed a pledge never to go to war.
He was convinced by the prophet-preachers of the Chattauqua
circuit that if all Christian people would follow the example
of Jesus wars would end on the face of God's green earth and
the Kingdom of God would be ushered in. This earnest preacher
had finished college a few months before George VI, that hap-
less stuttering King, had taken to the radio to announce to
his far-flung empire that war had come. In college he studied
contemporary poets and excelled in a popular philosophy course
called "Behaviorism." But he had not read Shakespeare nor
heard of Ibsen. Kierkegaard would have fared poorly in a religion course dominated by "normative psychology" where salvation was defined as the "integration of personality."

A splendid university Divinity School welcomed him as a
student. No one there ever suggested he or any other "ministerial student" should study Hebrew or Greek. St. Paul was
absorbed in a survey New Testament course and the Book of
Romans was obscured by the dust lifted heavenward in the earthly
search for the historical Jesus, the real person. The saintly
scholar who taught systematic theology had become captive to
the scientific method. In gentle and imaginative fashion he
worked Christian doctrine out in algebraic-like equations in
order to address the "modern mind" with theology defined as an
empirical science.

The formal education this aspiring cleric had received by
his 27th year did not include any required work in art or music,
let alone architecture. In his cultural ignorance he had no
means to appreciate the parsonage he now encountered. He
laughed at it as a monstrosity out of the Victorian Age. Not
until professors of architecture from neighboring universities

brought classes to see it did he learn that it had been designed by Richardson. He didn't even know who Richardson was,
although he had seen the angel touching Phillips Brooks beside
Boston's Trinity Church. All he knew was that each of the
five bedrooms had a wash bowl in the corner to supplement the
one bathtub which sat grandly on fancy legs in the one bath-
room far down the back hallway.

He also knew that on the third floor under the massive
grey slate roof was a tremendous room at the front of the
house with a trio of close set windows looking out over and
around nearby housetops. To the left could be seen the entrance to the Community hospital, to the right the YMCA was
clearly in view, straight ahead was the steeple of the church
in which he was "to preach the Word, administer the sacraments,
and bear rule in Christ's Church." Due to a slight jog in
"the widest Main Street in New England," this exceptionally
graceful church building appeared to preside over the city and
catch up all the busyness of the thoroughfare and funnel it up
past the belfry and the bell, on up into the spire which narrowed as it lifted higher and higher until with a magnificent
concentration it seemed to thrust the whole little city into
the aching outstretched arms of God.

The earnest new parson stood a long time at that window in
the large room at the front of the attic when he was inspecting
the house and deciding into which of the many rooms he would
divide his few possessions. A few feet back from the window
which commanded the scene of street and spire was an improvised
reading desk. Or could it be a pulpit?

This large room had been his predecessor's study. There
were bookshelves everywhere. Some were still crammed with old
books. The former minister was now an *old* man--almost *sixty*
years old--and had suffered a debilitating stroke. (New
Englanders in 1944 called them "shocks" and at first the young

minister reared far inland where his New England ancestors had
pioneered among native Americans and missionaries and fur
traders, had found it difficult to imagine how a "shock" could
be so intense as to prompt retirement.) The stricken man had
been minister of this congregation for a quarter of a century
and the young man felt that it showed. The church needed re-
furbishing, the large pulpit could easily be moved to one
side and with some velour drapery and a few candles "a worship
center" could be easily created. The Church School needed a
movie projector to take advantage of the new "visual aids"
which his predecessor apparently had not heard about. The
young people sorely needed more than the Bible study the old
man had led on Sunday evenings in the parsonage, a ski-trip,
perhaps, or a drama club. Even a discrete neon sign at the
street corner would be an improvement over the little gold
leaf plaque near the front door which told the name of the
church, the date of its organization, 1747 (George Whitefield
had preached on the Green and the Great Awakening had sired
this congregation). That little sign also gave the name and
address of the minister who lived right around the corner and
across the street. The young man's name had not yet replaced
the old man's name, but that would come in time.

The new minister stood at the improvised pulpit for a long
time and looked out over the city. He wondered what his first
sermon should be about. This room was obviously where his
predecessor had studied and prepared his sermons. He had left
many of his books on the shelves. His wife had written the
young man when she learned of his call:

> We hope you will enjoy the big house. You
> will soon want to get married and fill it up.
> It is painful to leave it after 26 years, but
> more painful to leave the people. Someday, you,
> too, may learn what I mean.

It seemed best to come here to this
small house where I can care for my husband
as well as the house. He left many of his
books in the old parsonage. Our sons may
want some of them but the theological books
are yours if you want them. My husband is
sorry he cannot write or speak with you. I
am sure he is praying for you and our dear
people.

Then she added as a postscript:

If you give the radiator in the living
room a good bang with your fist or with a
book, the heat comes on better. But do get
a new stove in the kitchen before you marry.
Imagine asking a bride in 1944 to cook on a
coal stove. But I loved it. Especially the
warming ovens. I think the ladies in the
Union Society might help.

What should he preach on that first Sunday? The war? It
was hard to say much about Christian pacifism and what Christians really *should do* when most of the young men in the congregation were V-5 or V-12 students from the nearby college.
Besides, there was already one gold star in the Church's flag.
The integration of personality? It was also hard to say much
about that to a congregation absorbed with news of the nightly
bombing of London and weary with their work on airplane pro-
pellors and parachute cloth. They really appeared fairly well
integrated.

He was certain he would not preach about smoking or
drinking for he had long since abandoned those "moralisms,"
but he did hope he could say something "inspirational." He
had an old sermon entitled, "The Holy Spirit Laughs." It
dealt with humor under adversity. Maybe he should use it. In
any event it would be cheerful and positive and he would save
his prophetic words about the evils of war and nationalism and

capitalism and the whoring press until later—perhaps until the war was over. He hoped his first sermon would be inspiring and well-delivered. He stood behind the improvised pulpit in the attic study. He wondered why his predecessor practiced his sermons here in front of the attic window overlooking the street. Would it not have been better before a full length mirror where he could catch any distracting mannerisms?

He stepped away from the pulpit to glance at the titles on the bookshelves. The books looked old. Few of them had jackets any more. Most of them must have come from England where his predecessor had been reared and educated. The young man reasoned that the church was in such poor shape—no worship center, no 16mm projector, no personality games in the youth society or new signs on the front lawn—because the old minister, the stricken one, was a Britisher who simply was not up-to-date, modern. It was obvious he did not understand American needs nor use contemporary methods. There wasn't a single flannel cloth board in the whole church or parsonage, but he certainly had a lot of books!

The young man glanced at the titles and his eye fell on one about "preaching" and the "modern mind." He picked it up and flipped a few pages into it:

"A true sermon is a real deed," he read. A few lines further on these words had been underlined, "If you remember what men of affairs think about the people who make set speeches in committee you will realize how the preacher loses power whose sermons are felt to be productions, or lessons, or speeches. . . ."

"Wait a minute," the young man thought. "Productions? Lessons? Speeches? What else can they be? Is the sermon not to inspire them? A production! Is it not to teach them? A lesson! Is it not to address them? A speech! Did I not study "speech" in order to be a preacher?"

He read on: Sermons lose power if they are not felt to be "real acts of will, struggles with other wills, and exercises of effective power. The Gospel means something done and not simply declared. For this work Christ existed on earth. And to give this work effect Bible and Church alike exist."

He hardly realized how cold that attic study was, with its shelves lined with books and the pulpit overlooking the street. He remained there transfixed for a long time. He read on. "It is not with truth we have to do but reality. And reality is a moral thing, a matter of a person, and his will and his act." And "It is not the teaching of Jesus that interprets the cross; it is the cross that interprets the teaching of Jesus." He read until darkness and cold woke him to the hours' passing.

He tucked that single volume under his arm and went down out of the attic and through the cold house and into the street. He had found the place where he was to study and practice to be a preacher for the next years of his life. He had also found the man, then dead 23 years, who was to be his instructor. He had under his arm P. T. Forsyth's Beecher Lectures entitled, *Positive Preaching and Modern Mind*.

As the weeks and months lengthened into years that young preacher came to appreciate his predecessor for many things. P. T. Forsyth was one of them. But he would not have worked through P. T. Forsyth if the practice pulpit set up by his predecessor had not faced the street. It was facing the world rather than his own subjective state that made P. T. Forsyth necessary if that young man were to continue to preach. From that practice pulpit he saw the daily trips of ambulance and hearse to and from the hospital next door, as well as the constant parade of the crippled and hurting in and out of the corner delicatessen and liquor store. Many in that procession had long since given up the effort to reach the pool offered

by the church, because no one came to help them and more agile
prosperous assertive souls beat them to the healing waters.
That reality drove the preacher to Romans and there he would
have been lost without Forsyth, the homiletician's theologian,
taking him by the hand or, more accurately, by the scruff of
the neck!

Standing at that attic pulpit he saw the soldiers come
home and he saw the ghost of his brother-in-law who did not
come home. He had to deal with his own guilt for a Christian
pacifism he held intellectually when he was no pacifist at
heart, a moral intellectualism which absented him from the
struggle of his generation against incarnate evil in the body
politic. Forsyth, the preacher's forerunner of Barth and
Niebuhr, enabled him to keep preaching when he recognized the
corruption of his own will.

"If Forsyth had been known," another claims, "Barth,
Brunner and Niebuhr would have become irrelevant." It was
quite the opposite for this young man in his attic study. Because he had picked up Forsyth, a preacher to preachers, he
was able to hear Barth and Brunner, but especially the Niebuhrs,
who rescued sin from smoking and sex and restored to it its
capital "S" and hence opened the way into the lives of many
moralistic or psychologized Christians for Forsyth's "Salvation,"
--the Saving Deed.

This young preacher found through Forsyth the spiritual
reality of the first chapters of Genesis as well as Romans 5.
There he began to have feeling as well as understanding for
Paul and Luther and Camus' plague. The Scripture was opened
to depths beyond Lloyd Douglas or Henry Link or even the cou-
rageous pacifist prophets. The ambiguities of war and nationalism and capitalism and the whoring media which rightly
troubled him remained, but Forsyth helped set him free from
the arrogance of the moralist and the destruction of the

moralist's ultimate despair.

This essay is written to encourage preachers, as far removed from 1944 as that preacher was removed from the year of Forsyth's lectures, to study them afresh. In a decade when the new moralist is proud of his morality and his/her majority, the steady preaching of the Church, Catholic and Reformed alike, had best be informed by a new encounter with Forsyth, but more, far more, by the opening to Scripture and Gospel which he commands.

Other Christians--theologians, laypersons, politicians, teachers--may find the needed word elsewhere. Certainly there are others who write more fluently. One critic suggests that many of Forsyth's books must have been easier for the author to write than for his readers to read. Not so for the preacher because of the immediate relevancy of his writing to the preaching task. When eighty years of the Beecher Lectures were surveyed by Edgar DeWitt Jones in 1951, he entered this footnote to his summary of Forsyth's addition to that distinguished series:

> In talking with scores of ministers about the Lyman Beecher Lectures, I found without exception that those whose opinions are most highly valued, rated Forsyth's series at Yale as unrivaled of their kind, and a 'must' book for alert, studious preachers everywhere. This is superlative praise, for distinguished preacher-scholars also rated highly the Lectures of Andrew M. Fairbairn, George Adam Smith, and Reinhold Niebuhr, in the same series.[1]

The young preacher who was grasped by Forsyth in 1944 was confronted with the insignificance of his preaching which used the Bible to reinforce some moralistic observation about human behavior, personal or corporate. He was also confronted with the consequential triviality of the Church. Almost forty years later, Forsyth sounds contemporary on that score also:

"I will say then the Church suffers from three things," he wrote--not in 1944 but in 1907:
1. From triviality (with externality).
2. From uncertainty of its foundation.
3. From satisfaction with itself.

"And to cure these the Gospel we have to preach prescribes:
1. For our *triviality*, a new note of greatness in our creed, the note that sounds in a theology more than in a sentiment.
2. For our *uncertainty*, a new note of wrestling and reality in our prayer.
3. For our *complacency*, a new note of judgment in our salvation."[2]

When Peter T. Forsyth died in November, 1921, the *London Times* printed a lengthy obituary. The writer noted not only that Forsyth was a prolific writer, but also difficult to read. His words "were crowded with strangely formed sentences, full of antithesis and epigram, sprinkled with newly coined words, but they rewarded patient study for the erudition and thought they contained." Now at the other end of the century a professor hesitated to require the reading of Forsyth for these reasons and also because many of the ablest students in the class were women and Forsyth is full of the sexisms common in our language until this decade.

A bold feminist took up the challenge. In the report of her reading she confessed that after the first few pages she was not even hindered by the sexisms because of the natural power of Forsyth's thought and expression. "Let no student, man or woman, miss this contemporary thinker," she wrote to her teacher. "Hear him for example, 'The evolutionary idea is especially attractive to a scientific age. We have certainly no quarrel with that idea till it is lifted from being a method and elevated into a dogma. . . . It is a philosophy which explains much, and makes us patient of much, and hopeful of more. But it cannot give us the goal of its own movements any more than their real cause. And a religion has to do rather with the source and the goal than with the path, with the meaning rather than the method.' This book on preaching," she concluded, "has changed my life. . .and made my ministry possible!"

Thus from a very different perspective, in a very different time, this young woman, seeking to be a preacher in the church, reported the transforming power of Forsyth through the printed page. Her year is not 1944. It is not 1907. It is today. She will probably preach far into the 21st Century. Yet Peter Taylor Forsyth, whose verbal thrusts were not always chivalrous, and who may have been a hypochondriac, and who died in 1921 in very mortal fashion, because of the evidence of the truth he phrased, in that common frail mortality and fortitude, for all preachers: "To be ready to accept any kind of message from a magnetic man is to lose the Gospel in mere impressionism. It is to sacrifice the moral in religion to the aesthetic. And it is fatal to the authority either of the pulpit or the Gospel. The Church does not live by its preachers, but by its Word."[3]

NOTES

1. Jones, Edgar DeWitt, *The Royalty of the Pulpit* (New York: Harper & Bros., 1951), p. 134.

2. *Positive Preaching and Modern Mind,* pp. 169ff.

3. *Ibid.*, p. 60.

P. T. FORSYTH:

PROPHET FOR THE TWENTIETH CENTURY?

*Robert S. Paul**

"If one book more than another preluded the coming of a
new era," wrote the late J. K. Mozley, "it was *Positive Preaching and Modern Mind* by P. T. Forsyth", and the same writer
went on to point out that "very much of what is of special
value in the work of Dr. Karl Barth was anticipated by P. T.
Forsyth."[1] That is so. Readers of the present volume can
test it for themselves by comparing Forsyth's protest against
the liberal reduction of Christianity to "a perennial principle" (p. 66), or against the limitations of philosophy (pp.
265ff., 371), or the distinction he drew between Christian
faith and "religion" (p. 330), with almost identical passages
in the *Church Dogmatics.* Much more fundamentally Forsyth made
the saving work of Jesus Christ central and rejected any "religion whose genius is in thought or idea instead of historic
event" (p. 211), and he affirmed that "nothing can make us free
which does not secure the freedom of God" (p. 142). One does
not need to move out of the pages of Barth's *Church Dogmatics*,
I, 1 to find striking parallels and fundamental accord between
his theology and that of Forsyth.[2]

The perceptive reader will discover other emphases in

---

*Robert S. Paul is Professor of Ecclesiastical History and
Christian Thought, Austin Presbyterian Theological Seminary,
Austin, Texas.

Forsyth that have become significant in twentieth century theology. For example, he recognized the distinction that Die-
trich Bonhoeffer drew between the strength and the weakness of
a civilization (pp. 329ff.), although he was perhaps not quite
as sanguine about the strengths or as disdainful of the weak-
nesses as the later theologian.3 He certainly understood the
difference that Bonhoeffer stressed between cheap grace and
costly grace. In one of Forsyth's earlier writings he said of
the Puritans that they "grasped what makes God the Christian
God--not only a free grace but a costly. It is not only the
freedom of His grace, but its infinite price to Him that makes
God God."4 The same insight is developed in this present volume in his strictures against easy forgiveness as sufficient
for any adequate doctrine of Atonement: "a free forgiveness
flows from moral strength, but an easy forgiveness only means
moral weakness" (p. 295).

But although these foreshadowings of later theologians are
interesting enough and might enhance our respect for Forsyth
as an astute reader of the signs of the times or as a scholar
with an uncanny knack of recognizing the trends, they are not
in themselves sufficient justification for considering him a
prophet for the twentieth century. The salience of Peter Taylor Forsyth's work is much broader and much more profound. It
is to be seen in his critique of the 20th century Western civilization, and in his recognition that the fundamental problems
of that society were due to the erosion of authority at the
center of human experience. *That* points the significance of
his theology, for it was his conviction that the deepest needs
of society could not be met without putting the Christian gospel back at the center of human life.

It is as we recognize this overriding concern that the
importance of his own theological position may be recognized,
for that which Barth and his followers arrived at during the

trauma of World War I, or after several decades of Western
materialism, or while the Nazis were proclaiming an open challenge to Western Christendom, Forsyth had seen clearly in the
first decade of the century: the problems of humanity were
fundamentally spiritual, and they could be met only by taking
with absolute seriousness the claims of Jesus Christ.

I

Civilization in the Twentieth Century

Positive Preaching and Modern Mind was one of the first of
Forsyth's major works, and the subject allowed him to present
a conspectus of his theology in a congenial framework: he
speaks as a preacher to future preachers about the basic nature
and content of their message. Today that would be regarded as
a relatively innocuous occupation with an extremely modest
prospect of influencing any large part of the population; but
it is worth reminding ourselves that at the beginning of this
century the pulpit in both Britain and America still represented an influential form of the mass media, challenged by
the press but certainly no less powerful, although Forsyth
himself documented the signs and sources of the rapid decline
which was already noticeable. *Positive Preaching* was, however,
offered to young men at Yale who could expect to become persons of weight and respect not only in churches but also within local and even national society, and whose words would be
addressed not only to believers in the pews, but also to the
society in which the churches were set.

The book was published in 1908, and in Britain a year
before that the Liberal Party, with the support of the Nonconformist churches of which Forsyth was a leading representative,
swept into political power with the largest majority the House
of Commons had seen in its history.[5] Many Nonconformists in-

cluding Forsyth were wholly sympathetic to the radical social movement that was struggling to improve the lot of the common worker in the name of a *Christian* society:[6] Forsyth's plea that the gospel must be "ethicized", as this book clearly shows, cannot be restricted to the civil and political arena, but it had a very obvious application.

Forsyth's position in the relationship of Church and society was an example of what he would have regarded as an *essential* paradox. As a Free Churchman he believed that the Church and the State should remain separate, but he was far from believing that the Church should therefore restrict its activities to nurturing the spiritual perceptions of the individual, or that the State could therefore afford to ignore the Church's prophetic word to society. On the contrary, Church and Society have a separate but integral relationship in which each side has responsibility towards the other. As he expressed the issue in other places, Church and State were to remain separate but *not* neutral.[7]

It is in his critique of twentieth century Western culture, however, that Forsyth speaks with particular aptness for us, because in recognizing the characteristics that were beginning to appear in the first decade he shows us how we got where we are. "Do we not feel," he said, "that amid our unexampled wealth of broad interests, new departure, swift change, teeming variation, and external mobility life is flattening and starving for want of the eternal stay of Christ, as a gorgeous tent slowly subsides to the dust as the pole decays? All our escape from tradition and from bondage, the roses and raptures of romance, or even the heroisms of the great, do not permanently lift the tone or dignity of life. Where are we to take our bearings and find our true north?" (p. 229). That was the basic question he addressed to the new age and its culture, and if he addressed that question first to the Church it was

because he saw how fundamental the Church is to the age and
its culture.

He recognized the strengths of the new society. In all
but one aspect of life--the *moral*--it was stronger than ever
in history. "Never," he declared, "was man's mastery of the
world so complete. Never had he such resources in dealing
with it, and compelling it to his purpose"; but he went on to
say that the weakness of modern society was precisely in its
lack of any real purpose. "Our trouble," he said, "is the
paganism of the age, with its moral hollowness and its shell
of self-confidence" (pp. 329f.), and he then castigated
equally the ennui and indifference of Europe and the feverish
activity of America. Americans were so busy that "they have
neither the leisure nor the power to note the crumbling of
their moral interior." Because of this fundamental moral
failure everything else in Western society was threatened.

Just as the Church of pagan Rome had suffered from its
association with the empire, so, because "the world-power of
to-day is the money power the Church to-day suffers from the
plutocracy" (p. 169). People were threatened by a kaleidoscope
of new interests: "what marks the modern man is the mobility
and dispersion of his interest. And what does this mean but
weakness of will, the lack of power to attend, to decide, to
choose. . . . Men are stupified morally by all the thousand
impressions of the hour" (pp. 130f.). As a result, a relativity had entered into life which meant that there was no
need to make hard decisions, particularly hard moral and
spiritual decisions.

There had been a radical shift from belief in God to belief in man. It was relatively easy for critics of the Church
to denounce or poke fun at the earlier doctrines of predestination or reprobation held by the believers in previous centuries,
"because we believe in man (if we do) where they believed in

God. We are supremely concerned about human happiness where they were engrossed with the glory of God. We are preoccupied with human freedom, and are not interested (as they were above all) in the freedom of God" (p. 142). This passage and others like it might very well be dismissed as the rhetoric of religious and social conservatism, until we realize that Forsyth counted himself to be a theological liberal, and he was a political radical with strong attachments to the early Socialist movement in England. Moreover, he was living at a time when British Nonconformity was active politically more than it had been since the time of Oliver Cromwell.

Forsyth was saying that the twentieth century was getting its priorities muddled. "The age, and much of the Church, believes in civilization and is interested in the Gospel, instead of believing in the Gospel and being interested in civilization" (p. 194). It was really being afflicted with the old heresy of Gnosticism, the belief that salvation is to be obtained from superior knowledge, and yet underneath the apparent success and sophistication there was deep unease and a sense of guilt that he found in contemporary writers such as Ibsen. "If we get deep enough with the public mind," he said, "we shall find men are less satisfied with success than would appear from the plaudits of the day, less the victims of things as they are than the press would indicate, and more preoccupied with their inward moral failure than their bravado will admit" (p. 149). They feared judgment, but it was not the judgment of God but of society and the standards of respectability held up by their peers. Of course, from our vantage point in the last quarter of the century, we may feel that the sense of conscience that Forsyth discerned in his contemporaries has practically disappeared. But at least we may detect a residual influence.

Some of Forsyth's most interesting comments on society

were those he addressed directly to America. He obviously admired the dynamism of America in comparison with the "moral
fatigue" of Europe (p. 330), but he thought the activism of
Americans was equally defective, and he bluntly told his audience, "You are too Pelagian." He recognized that the cultured
but effete Europe of his day was moving into an eclipse, but
he then went on to ask the pertinent question:

> Do you think that the situation is
> to be saved by the spontaneous resources
> of human nature, or the entrance upon the
> *Weltpolitik* of a mighty young people like
> America? Is there no paganism threatening
> America? What is to save America from her
> colossal power, energy, self-confidence and
> preoccupation with the world? Her Chris-
> tianity no doubt. But a Christianity which
> places in the centre not merely Christ but
> the Cross and its Redemption, in a far more
> ethical way than America is doing; a Chris-
> tianity which is not only set in the pres-
> ence of Christ's person but caught into the
> motion of Christ's work, which is not only
> with Christ but in Him by a total moral
> and social salvation" (pp. 323f.).

Did Forsyth have anything specific in mind when he suggested
that America could act more ethically? We do not know, but
we should remember that when he delivered his lectures at
Yale America was in the presidency of Theodore Roosevelt; it
was the era of speaking softly and carrying a big stick.
America had already flexed its muscles in the War with Spain
which had brought Cuba and the Philippines into her sphere of
influence, and this expansionism was continued under Roosevelt
in the diplomacy surrounding the Panama Canal, and in a show
of naval strength that sent the American navy around the world.
    This then was the new world of the twentieth century
that Forsyth saw. It was a world that was materialistic and
losing touch with the faith on which its civilization had been

founded. "It is a society that is sick to death, and not a stray soul. We have to deal with a radical evil in human nature, and spiritual wickedness in deep places. We have not only to restore the prodigal but to reorganize the household of the elder brother" (p. 341). Even at that date it was a real question whether the people of Western culture could be regarded as Christian any longer, for the "bulk of the civilized public of Europe, practically, either belong to no Church, or they are indifferent to which Church they belong. And most culture is rather with the world than with the Gospel. We are thus at the most critical time since the first centuries" (p. 121).

II

The Problem of Authority

People felt that there was no longer any ultimate ethical authority which could be universally recognized. In 1905 Forsyth had written that there was "no question so deep and urgent at this moment as that regarding the seat of authority and its nature,"[8] and although he would later offer an extended treatment of the issue,[9] there is a sense in which all his writings were addressed to that problem, just as there is also a sense in which all his books center in the Atonement.[10] As a later writer has noted, Forsyth's modernity "is nowhere more clearly evidenced than in his emphasis on the problem of authority," which he saw not only as a problem for theology but "as the basic problem of the West and even of mankind."[11]

That is the nub of what Forsyth had to say on this subject. In this present volume his insight is extended not only to include the troubled realm of twentieth century theology, but the whole uncertain cultural area of western society. "The question of ultimate authority for mankind is the greatest of

all questions to meet the West, since the Catholic Church lost
its place in the sixteenth century, and since criticism no
longer allows the Bible to occupy that place. Yet the gospel
of the future must come with the note of authority. Every
challenge of authority but develops the need of it" (p. 41).
Later on he declared that "a huge problem is set to the Gospel
in the present moral anarchy of western civilization. We have
not found for society the Word which the individual freely
finds, the Word to replace for the public the external authority of the medieval Church." We may think he was too sanguine
when he went on to suggest that as long as the individual was
free to discover the Word "there is no need to fear that
Society will not find it in due course for purposes of public
control" (pp. 259f.). Forsyth was perhaps too optimistic at
this point, because for all its decadence or its ebullient
materialism, Western society still counted itself to be
"Christian." It was not until the devastation of World War I
and World War II and the dictatorships of the right and of the
left had appeared, that this illusion was effectively smashed.

The importance of Forsyth's thinking on the problem of
Authority is not in the detailed answers he offered, but his
recognition of the problem, and in his insistence that the
ultimate answer for any society could be sought only in a con-
sensus that recognized an absolute moral authority external to
us but at the same time which is always open to us and recog-
nizable by us.

The fundamental problem within the human family demanded
an authority that was supremely ethical, and whose claims could
be universally recognized as ethical. "The great question,"
he said in his later book, "is not really as to the seat of
authority, but as to its nature."[12] He found this in the con-
cept of "holiness" that is revealed to us in the God of the
Bible, and whose nature is demonstrated supremely in the cross

of Jesus Christ. Certainly his answer was an answer centered in Christian theology, but that was because he believed that the God behind universal history was the God of Christian theology, and that the Church had responsibility for bringing the claims of that God home to the race. "The conviction of these pages," he wrote at the begining of *The Principle of Authority*, "is that the principle of authority is ultimately the whole religious question, that an authority of any practical kind draws its meaning and its right only from the soul's relation to its God, *that this is so not only for religion strictly so called, but for public life, social life, and the whole history and career of Humanity.*"[13]

Forsyth discerned that the twentieth century had ushered in a time unlike anything that had been seen in world history to that point; an older world was passing because the traditional grounds for the faith on which its basic authority had been grounded had been undercut. But beyond this he recognized, as Toynbee recognized in his *Study of History*, that no civilization can be sustained without an ideological or religious root, and Forsyth believed that what had happened was not reason for jettisoning the Christian faith but for recognizing that the grounds for that Christian faith were in the revelation itself: we had to get rid of the earthen vessels in order to preserve the truths within.

The basic criterion for Christianity was not its ethical result, which was simply a consequence of the reconciliation it proclaimed between God and man, but the evangelical response to that reconciliation. Whatever therefore met the human need for that reconciliation "is the final and sole authority of our race, from which all that claims authority must deduce. Set that right in every man by what sets right also the race, and right views and right relationships will follow as the night the day. The great creed and the great millenium must

be alike confessions of the living faith which is our contact
with Him who sits on the throne and makes all things new and
true" (p. 59). Forsyth was willing enough to recognize the
insights that could come from the comparative study of religion, but he would not make Jesus Christ and his cross a relative good, for that is where the nature of God's grace was
revealed in all its holiness: "God cannot be discovered in
either history or the rational processes except as we meet
Him at the point where it pleased Him to appear as Saviour"
(p. 103). Or we may express it as it is set down in this
volume when he speaks of "the final authority of grace." He
goes on to declare:

> The question of the hour, for all life,
> and not only for the religious, is that of
> authority--the true effective authority.
> Where is it? At last it is here. It is in
> God's eternal, perpetual act and gift of
> grace, met by the absolute obedience of our
> faith. Faith is absolute obedience to
> grace as absolute authority. Personal faith
> in the holy, gracious God of Christ's Cross
> is the one creative, authoritative, life-
> making, life-giving, life-shaping power of
> the moral soul (pp. 213f.).

III

Critique of the Church

Forsyth saw that there was a faith crisis in his world,
but the preacher was hampered by people who no longer knew
their Bibles and disdained the Church: "He meets impatient
reformers who take a tone of superior realism, and coarsely
speak of Church life and the edification of believers as a
mere "coddling of the saints." He lives in an age when the
Kingdom of God engrosses more Christian interest than the
Church of Christ, and Christian people are more devoted to the

busy effort of getting God's will done on earth than to the
deep repose of God's finished will in Christ" (p. 75). Yet
Forsyth the social radical was the last person to downplay or
ignore the social implications of Christianity. It was again
a question of priorities, because if the Bible was God's great
sermon to humanity, the Church was its missionary: "it is the
Church that is the great missionary to Humanity, and not apostles, prophets, and agents here and there" (p. 77). The Church
is the great preacher in history, and "the first business of
the individual preacher is to enable the Church to preach"
(p. 79).

No Catholic, Eastern, Roman or Anglican could claim to
have a higher sense of the Church and its Sacraments than P.
T. Forsyth, and it was a theme to which he was to return in
what must surely be one of his greatest books.[14] At the same
time he refused to be sectarian in his approach to the doctrine
of the Church. As he wrote in the preface to *The Church and
the Sacraments* his position was "neither current Anglican nor
popular Protestant"; he wrote "from the Free Church camp, but
not from any recognized Free Church position" and although
"the audience is Free Church. . .the treatment means to be
Great Church."

That term, "Great Church," occurs many times in his
writings, and is the mark of his ecumenical vision and his
truly catholic understanding of the Church. We see an example
of it in the present book when he said:

> The business of each preacher in charge
> of a flock is to translate to his small
> flock this message and content of the great
> Church, that he may integrate the small Church
> into the great, and that he and it together
> may swell the transmission of the Word in
> the world. That is the true Catholicism, the
> universalizing of the universal Word. That
> is the principle which makes a Church out of

> a sect or conventicle, and puts a preacher
> in the true apostolic succession. The true
> succession is the true inheritance of the
> eternal Word, and not the due concatenation
> of its agents. The great apostolate is one,
> not in heredity or a historic line but in
> solidarity of a historic Gospel, not in a
> continuous stream but in an organic Word
> (p. 105).

The position is Protestant, but the attitude and intention is
clearly catholic. Forsyth rejected what Edmund Burke once
called "the dissidence of dissent" and any form of sectarianism, and it was this that caused him to turn away from a narrow
biblical restorationism as an adequate basis for ecclesiology
(cf. pp. 143ff.). Whatever else his Congregational churchmanship implied, it went far beyond that.[15]

This is seen in his attitude to ecumenism,[16] which in
terms of theological perception went far beyond the purely
pragmatic or pietist approaches that were popular in the first
two decades of this century. We must remember that the first
conference to bring the churches together was the Edinburgh
Conference in 1910. It was called to solve the practical missionary need for comity among the churches, and it proved possible only on the explicit understanding that theological
questions of Faith and Order would be excluded. This was a
totally inadequate basis on which to attack the problems of
ecumenism, and it led to an ecumenical interest that produced
the International Missionary Council, the Universal Christian
Council for Life and Work and the World Conference of Faith
and Order. But the first of these (the I.M.C.) was not formally
constituted until 1921, the year of Forsyth's death.

The road to reunion for Forsyth was governed not by friendly feelings and still less by practical pressures, but by the
Church's essential theology. "The union of believers," he
declared in a lecture in 1917, "depends at last on the nature

of the trust they believe Christ has given them to administer,
and not on their desires. It is not a matter of idealism. . . .
It is a matter of revelation; and we must handle the subject-
matter of revelation according to its nature as God's will,
and not according to our wish or dream." The Church's unity
rested on the will of God as Sovereign and not on our pious
feelings as his subjects: "Is it required, is it inspired, by
the Gospel of Grace and the Kingdom of God? That is the decisive question."[17]

The same basic insight runs through the present volume.
A preacher is to reflect the faith of the *Great* Church, and
not the views and beliefs of his own congregation or of his
particular denomination. He is "the mandatory of the great
Church, which any congregation or sect but represents here and
now. And what he has to do is to nourish that single and accidental community with the essence of the Church universal. .
. ." (p. 94). So too he criticized the atomism--he called it
"granular autonomy"--of local congregations that had become for
many Congregationalists the cherished center of ecclesiology,
in the name of a far greater autonomy, the autonomy of God as
Sovereign of his Kingdom. "Local autonomy is only sound and
valid," he declared, "as it serves the supreme autonomy of the
Great Church amid the powers of this world. . . . Autonomy
can easily run down into anarchy if it is not a constant reflection of the *absolute* holiness and *free* grace of God in His
Kingdom. It must be created from that. It must live in the
autonomy, the self-determination, of the One God and His Grace."[18]

Forsyth saw that the Church is in a constant struggle that
relates not only to the world, but also to its own members, for
whereas in the sciences we enter into the inheritance of the
past and add to that knowledge, that is not true in the spiritual realm. "We have constantly to acquire what we inherit"
(p. 173, cf. p. 53); there is a sense in which the Church has

to convert every generation afresh.

That was where the churches were failing. Forsyth
pointed out that even at the beginning of this century preachers could no longer rely on believers knowing their Bibles,
nor could they expect members to have experienced the reality
of religious experience that enabled them to test and ratify
the truth in the preacher's words (pp. 33-8). Even in the
midst of the apparent success and popularity of the free
churches in the Britain of 1907, Forsyth saw that they had a
faith-crisis, and that the root cause was a theology that did
not do justice either to modern science on the one hand or the
realities of Christian faith on the other. His call was not
to bigger and better evangelistic campaigns, or a retreat to
the doctrinal positions of the sixteenth century, but to what
he called a "positive theology"--a theology that recognized
the centrality of God's absolute holiness and grace in Jesus
Christ's cross--sovereign grace .

The liberal theology that was becoming popular was
totally inadequate, because only a gospel of holiness and
saving grace could meet the reality of human sin, and unless
this basic human condition was recognized and met, there was
no real gospel and there was no real hope of social justice.
To "ethicize" the gospel meant not merely adding an ethical
dimension to the Church's social consciousness, but it meant
putting the *Holy* God and his action for us on the Cross at the
very center. He insisted that an objective expiatory idea of
Atonement "is necessary to do justice to the idea of God as
love, and to the closeness of His identification with us," not
because he was anxious to defend sixteenth century orthodoxies
but because he wanted to do justice to twentieth century realities. It "gives expression, by its searching moral realism,
and its grasp of both holiness and sin, to an element in Christianity which has a crucial effect on the depth, wealth, and

moral penetration of the preaching of the Gospel." Without
that, Forsyth declared, a liberal theology could not "carry
the full κηρυγμα of the Church" because it "is not sufficiently
charged with repentance and remission" (pp. 368-9). There have
been few more devastating critiques of twentieth century liberal theology than from this liberal theologian who was quick
to acknowledge his indebtedness to the critical disciplines
and who shared the liberal concerns for scientific integrity,
contemporary relevance and social justice. But like Karl Barth
after him, he declared that without a fundamental concern for
revealed truth the Church had no "Good News."

In the new situation of the twentieth century the Church
needed to rid itself of triviality, uncertainty and complacency;
and many of the things he said under these headings strike
home as truly today as they did when he uttered them. Indeed,
perhaps we are able to recognize the point of what he was saying more easily than his contemporaries, because they had not
experienced the chastening that has come to the Church in the
events of the next half century.

For example, in speaking of the triviality that was then
affecting the worship of the churches, he spoke of worship
being sacrificed to busyness:

> You have bustle all the week and bald-
> ness on Sunday. You have energy anywhere
> except in the Spirit. . .we are more anx-
> ious to cover ground than to secure it, to
> evangelize the world than to convert it.
> It is faithless impatience of the youngest
> thinnest kind.[19] A bustling institution
> may cover spiritual destitution, just as
> Christian work may be taken up as a narcotic
> to spiritual doubt and emptiness. The
> minister's study becomes more of an office
> than an oratory. Committees suck away the
> breath of power. Socialities become the
> only welcome sacraments. The tea-meeting
> draws people together as the communion

table does not. The minister may talk the
silliest platitudes without resentment,
but he may not smoke a cigar without causing an explosion" (pp. 171f.).

There is much more of the same, and it is extremely pointed.

He attacked the complacency with which the Church accepted
the position that an indulgent society was willing to grant to
it. Religion, he said, had been debased "to a mere means of
human happiness, to a social utility"; it had once been "a
political pawn, it is now a social facility," and he went on
to declare:

> And the result is unfaith, or, worse,
> an affectation of faith. We are so healthy,
> so poetical, so kindly, so optimistic, God's
> love and patience and mercy are all so much
> in line with life's innocent charm, all so
> much a matter of course and of congratulation.
> And we are so strange to heart-hunger, or
> soul-despair, or passionate gratitude. Whole
> tracts of our religion are bare of spiritual
> passion, or spiritual depth. Christinaity
> speaks the language of our humane civiliza-
> tion; it does not speak the language of
> Christ" (pp. 193f.).

Against those who tended to make too much of the means of conversion, he said "we need an experience of Christ in which we
think everything about the Christ and not about the experience
. . . . Our great need is not ardour to save man but courage
to face God--courage to face God with our soul as it is, and
with our Saviour as he is" (p. 195).

The problem always comes back to the crisis in faith.
The twentieth century's uncertainty rather reminds me of the
humorous verse written about one of the modern schools of
philosophy:

I wish my room had a floor,
I don't mind so much for a door,
But this floating around
Without touching the ground
Is becoming a bit of a bore.

Forsyth had the spiritual perception to recognize the mood in the first decade of our century when there seemed little reason to take anything but an entirely optimistic view about the churches. He had the even more profound insight to recognize that if this lack of grounding continued our civilization was likely to face something more ominous than boredom, for there would be nothing to prevent it from the abyss of meaninglessness and ultimate despair.

This he saw clearly. "The soul of the age asks us to help it to footing," he observed, but the churches' response was vague and inept. Their tendency was always to look around to see what kind of support they could get for religion from the sciences or pseudo-sciences, from the psychology of William James to the parapsychology of Sir Oliver Lodge. "So," he said, "we will turn to men of science, to men often who evidently never in their lives read a theological classic or an authority on moral philosophy." This showed how unsure the churches were of their own faith, and it had allowed "all kinds of occultism [to] exploit this groping hunger of the age in the interests of their own hobby" (pp. 183, 184f.). It seems strange that the religious situation at the turn of the century should run so parallel to our own, but it is incredible to hear Forsyth, writing in a period which has been regarded as the heyday of British Nonconformist influence, stating categorically that the pulpit had lost authority "because it has lost intimacy with the Cross, immersion in the Cross "[20] (p. 188). Only a gospel that freed the conscience of man--"not his thought, or his theology, but his conscience"--could meet the need by carrying within itself the power of forgiveness and absolution:

> Only with this Gospel, authoritative because evangelical, can we make the spiritual life a world power, take it out of corners and coteries, give it control of the world and its resources, and save it from convent, conventicle and college alike, to be ecumenical, practical, and final. Our lack of authority is mainly due to our lack of piercing moral realism, the radicalism of the Cross" (p. 188).

Power and authority in the preacher are not effective without prayer, "laborious prayer, as the concentration of mind and will." He then told his audience of future ministers that ministers were both the despair and the hope of the Church, and warned them that a preacher "whose chief power is not in studious prayer is, to that extent, a man who does not know his business," for prayer "of the serious, evangelical, unceasing sort is to faith what original research is for science—it is the grand means of contact with reality" (p. 190). As with so many of the issues touched upon in this book, the place of prayer in the Christian life would receive treatment in a later book.[21]

Because of its gospel the Church held a crucial place in civilization. "In the last matters of the soul," he wrote, "it is the Church that gives the law to the world; it is not the world that gives the law to the Church." But he went on to warn against any inflated view of this ecclesiastical responsibility, for "it is the Church as prophet, not as King. It is not the imperial Church but the serving Church, the Church not as a judge but as witness. . .as the meek mighty apostle of the Redeemer, not as the gorgeous vicar of Christ" (p. 148).

62

IV

"From a lover of love to an object of grace"

We can no longer postpone recognition of the place that
his own religious experience had in the development of Forsyth's theology, and for this there could be no better work
than the present volume. Anyone reading his work for the first
time ought to begin by reading pages 281-5, because there he
gives us a firsthand account of how he arrived at the convictions and the commitment that forced him to look at the theological question from a totally new perspective. It is un-
necessary to quote that passage here; it should be read in its
entirety.

One of the things that must stand out as a major factor
in his change of theological stance was his pastoral concern,
his concern for the people with whom he was in a special relationship "of life, duty and responsibility." He could not
ignore the effect his words would have on these people, and
again one is reminded of the striking parallel in the experience of Karl Barth as minister of the little Swiss village of
Safenwil. So Barth testified to his own dilemma as a pastor:

> Once in the ministry I found myself
> growing away from those theological habits
> of thought and being forced back at every
> point more and more upon the specific *minis-*
> *ter's* problem, the sermon. I sought to find
> my way between the problem of human life on
> the one hand and the content of the Bible on
> the other. As a minister I wanted to speak
> to the *people* in the infinite contradiction
> of their life, but to speak the no less in-
> finite message of the Bible, which was as
> much a riddle as life. . .who shall, who can
> be a minister and preach?[22]

It was out of this dilemma and struggle that Forsyth and Barth were able to forge a fresh (that is, for the twentieth century) approach to theology which would be biblically grounded but not biblically bound. They become representatives of that line of seminal theologians that stretches from Paul, through Augustine, Anselm, Luther, Calvin, the Federal Theologians, and on through Schleiermacher and Reinhold Niebuhr, who have discovered their most profound theological insights in their attempt to bring the gospel pastorally to people. Forsyth would probably have disliked the idea of applying the word "creative" to any theology, yet we might say that insofar as it describes the discovery of fresh insights into the ancient faith, the pastorate is the most likely place for creative theology to happen.

But for Forsyth this was not simply an intellectual readjustment. He came into a new relationship with the One he knew as Jesus Christ. He wrote, "I never knew my sin so long as I saw Christ suffering for me--never until I saw Him under its judgment and realized that the chastisement of my peace was upon Him" (p. 369). It was this personal entry into the meaning of the Atonement that turned Forsyth "from a Christian [i.e. a person on the books of a Christian community] to a believer, from a lover of love to an object of grace." And apparently he arrived at that position after reading the older classical theologians and being driven to study the Bible anew.

This led him to realize that although theology is always intellectual, if it is true to the New Testament it never arises primarily as an intellectual exercise, but as the intellectual response to faith. Christian theology had begun in the early Church because of the Church's experience of God's grace in Jesus Christ, and specifically through the events of Good Friday, Easter Sunday and Pentecost. If there had been no faith there would have been no theology. So Forsyth recognized that St. Paul "was no dogmatician in the sense of Aquinas

or Melanchthon," and that the apostle was "comparatively careless about the correct form of his belief" because "he was
lost in the great experimental reality of it. He was the first
of Christian theologians only because he was the greatest of
Christian experimentalists" (p. 18).

Therefore the Bible should be best understood by the
preacher, because its revelation does not exist to deliver communications *about* God, but to convey the fundamental grace
that God gives us in the gospel. "The final criticism of the
Bible," he said, "is not the 'higher criticism' but the highest, the criticism whose principle is God's supreme object in
the Bible, Church, or even Christ--the object of reconciling
grace. The final criticism of it is neither literary nor
scientific but evangelical, as the preacher must be" (p. 18).

He was positive about the new areas of knowledge that had
been opened up by science, but he recognized the threats the
new disciplines posed to humanity when they claimed an absolute
authority for human reason. This ambivalence between genuine
appreciation for scholarship on the one hand and unwillingness
to grant the results of human reasoning a final authority on
the other, is particularly seen in his attitude to the historical criticism of scripture. He supported the new methods and
was even enthusiastic about the freedom that they could bring
to theological studies--in that he was fully in line with the
liberal methods that have dominated theology in the twentieth
century--but the faithful preacher could never permit those
methods to erase or obscure the scriptural testimony to God's
grace in Jesus Christ: "the Bible is the greatest sermon in
the world" (p. 10).

Forsyth's position was unique at that time. It caused
him to criticize not only the sterile orthodoxies in the Church,
but also to be even more stringent against the Liberal reconstruction that was to govern most of our century. Indeed, in

comparison with what was being perpetrated in the name of modern theology, he forthrightly declared that in spite of all that could be said against the older orthodox theologians, at least they had the essential gospel: "I am compelled to recognize often," he declared, "that the most deeply and practically pious people in the Church are among those whose orthodox theology I do not share. I even distrust it for the Church's future. But they have the pearl of price" (p. 357).

V

The Mighty Acts of God, and the Reality of Judgment

The essential quality of the God revealed in the Bible was, for Forsyth, the quality of holiness, but the presence of God in history--the evidence, if you will--was to be seen not in reasons worked out by philosophers and metaphysicians, but revealed to faith through God's actions in history. Forsyth took the biblical emphasis on the *magnalia dei* with ultimate seriousness: the divine was essentially the divine *action*, and it was revealed to faith supremely in the positive action of Jesus Christ upon the Cross.[23] The story of this divine activity runs throughout the Bible, in the events of Israel's history, the incarnation, Christ's death on the cross, the resurrection, and the coming of the Holy Spirit to the Church.

The Church exists only to continue that divine action. "The Gospel means something done and not simply something declared," he said. "For this the work of Christ existed on earth. And to give this work effect Bible and Church exist. We treat the Church as plastic to that work and its fulfilment . . . . That is the true Church, and the true form of the Church, which gives best effect to the Gospel" (pp. 22f.). There is a whole twentieth century ecumenical ecclesiology contained in that statement. As the *acts* of the apostles were evidence of the Holy Spirit, so the Church in history gave evidence of that same Spirit in the quality of its own life within society and in the saving action revealed within its sacraments. "The essence of the Sacrament is the common *act*, the act of the community, inhabited by the 'common person' of Christ. . . . It is the Church rising with its Lord to the height of *action*--active reception of his gift who is acting in its midst with the utmost that God could do. . . . The holy sacrament is the sacrament of the holiest act and not simply of the most sacred essence or even presence."[24] Forsyth clearly believed that the meaning of the sacraments centered in the Atonement, and would probably have endorsed my view that "Protestant Christians who know something of their atonement-centered theology and value it should be the most sacramental of all Christians."[25]

In the final issue, however, God acted in the world *for the world*. Forsyth saw with great clarity that Christian faith is not concerned only with the fate of individuals but also with the fate of human society. For him the whole of Western civilization in the twentieth century hung on the solution to its moral dilemma. This caused him to come to grips with the very unpopular subject of judgment that was well on its way to being completely excised from liberal theology. He recognized the problems we have when this doctrine is preached crudely as "the last day," the "great assize," or "quenchless fire," and he insisted that "it is useless to put judgment at the close of history if it have not a decisive place at the centre of history." We have to maintain the reality of divine judgment because it has already taken place in the cross: the ultimate judgment "draws its true solemnity of meaning from the judgment day in Pilate's hall. To repudiate as mere theology this element of judgment in the Cross, to eliminate the awe of it from our practical habit of piety, is to subside in

due course into nonethical religion, which finally becomes but
a sweetened paganism" (pp. 316f.).

He told the young candidates for ministry not to concentrate upon some future Assize outside the experience of their
congregations, but to concentrate on the reality of God's judgment here and now:

> Let your song be of mercy, but of the
> mercy of judgment. And learn not to say
> so much to your people of a day of Judgment
> sure though far. The farness destroys the
> sureness. Ethicize the reality of judgment.
> Moralize the eschatology. Couple it up to
> the hour. Drop if need be the drapery of
> the remote assize. The judge is at the
> door. Everything comes home. It comes
> home in calamity if you do not take it home
> in repentance. Everything comes home (p. 153).

In this book Forsyth did not say much about the way in which
God's judgment on society can be seen in history, although I
believe it could have been developed.[26] Judgment in order to
be made real must be seen as *real* and inevitable, not only in
relation to what happened historically on the cross but also
here and now to the person or the society that deliberately
rejects it. Aldous Huxley put his finger on the problem when
he noted that a basic difference between the effectiveness of
the prophetic voice in the society of the seventeenth century
and in our own day is that twentieth century rulers unlike
their predecessors "do not lie awake at nights wondering if
they are damned."[27] The crude form of hell fire as accepted
by the middle ages and taken over by later Protestants may be
unacceptable today, but unless divine judgment against sin can
be *shown* to be implacable and effective, prophetic preaching
will be dismissed by our society as the jeremiads of those who
are paid to cry "Wolf!"

Forsyth recognized that God's judgment is here and now and

that society is not immune from it, but it was difficult to
bring this home to the complacency of Britain and the optimism
of America in 1907. That needed the trauma of all that has
happened since, and even yet there are few signs that the truth
has been understood. But in the middle of World War I Forsyth
saw it very clearly when he wrote *The Justification of God,*
and his words in those pages could be the warning to or the
epitaph of our civilization:

> World calamity bears home to us the
> light way in which, through a long peace
> and insulation, we were coming to take the
> problem of the world, and especially its
> moral problem. 'We do not now bother
> about sin' was said with some satisfaction.
> The preachers protested in vain against
> that terrible statement--those of them
> that had not lost their Gospel in their
> culture. But they were damned with the
> charge of theology. And now God enters
> the pulpit, and preaches in his own way
> by deeds. And his sermons are long and
> taxing, and they spoil the dinner. Clear-
> ly God's problem with the world is much
> more serious than we dreamed. We are
> having a revelation of the awful and des-
> perate nature of evil.[28]

Let me end with a brief personal note. I was baptized
and raised in the British Congregational churches to which P.
T. Forsyth gave his lifelong ministry, but it was not until
some time after I was ordained that I began to read his works.
This is my century and I too have struggled, as every faithful
minister must, to interpret the gospel to my own time; and yet
the more I have read Forsyth the more I have been impressed
with the humbling thought that all the ideas and the insights
which I had thought most peculiarly my own, he had already
seen clearly when the century was still in its infancy. For
me at least, the title of this essay is not a question.

NOTES

1. Canon J. K. Mozley was writing in the *British Weekly* of November 21, 1946, and is quoted by Gwilyn O. Griffith, *The Theology of P. T. Forsyth*, 1948, pp. 18f.

2. Eg. *Church Dogmatics* I/1, § 6.2.

3. Cf. Bonhoeffer's letter, April 30, 1944, in *Letters and Papers from Prison* (edited by Eberhard Bethge; E. T. by Reginald H. Fuller, 1954) pp. 121ff.

4. *The Church, the Gospel and Society* (1905), 1965 edn. p. 122.

5. In a House of Commons of 670 members, 127 were Nonconformists, many of them in the ranks of the victorious Liberal party or in the small Labour Party. The Liberals had 377 seats, and together with 53 Labour members, this gave a firm basis for the new social legislation which was introduced by Lloyd George.

6. James Kier Hardie, the founder of the Independent Labour Party, was a Congregationalist. He had been born into poverty and spent his life trying to improve the lot of the Scottish miners.

7. See Forsyth's "Reunion and Recognition" in *Congregationalism and Reunion* (1917), 1953, pp. 18ff., and also his book *Theology in Church and State* (1915).

8. "Authority and Theology," *The Hibbert Journal*, IV (October), 1905.

9. In *The Principle of Authority* (1913).

10. As I noted in *The Atonement in the Sacraments* (1960), p. 230. Cf. ibid., 227-40 for the treatment of Forsyth's view of the Atonement.

11. Willis B. Glover, Jr., *Evangelical Nonconformists and Higher Criticism in the 19th Century* (1954), p. 274.

12. *The Principle of Authority* (1913), 1952 edn., p. 10.

13. *Ibid.*, pp. 2f. [My italics.]

14. *The Church and the Sacraments* (1917).

15. See also the two lectures included in *Congregationalism and Reunion*.

16. See especially what he said about the "notion that the great Church was composed by the coagulation of a certain number of single Churches," in *The Church and the Sacraments*, pp. 68f.

17. "Reunion and Recognition," *Congregationalism and Reunion*, pp. 11, 13.

18. *Ibid.*, pp. 48, 49.

19. It should be remembered that many evangelicals at this time were enthused with the call "to evangelize the world in this generation."

20. The centrality of the cross of Christ to Forsyth's thought was expressed in one of his little classics, *The Cruciality of the Cross* (1909).

21. *The Soul of Prayer* (1916).

22. Karl Barth, *The Word of God and the Word of Man* (1928; E. T. by Douglas Horton, 1957), p. 100.

23. He insisted that Christ was actively involved in the cross; cf. *Positive Preaching*, pp. 358ff.

24. *The Church and the Sacraments*, pp. 237, 274, 297. I developed a similar emphasis in *The Atonement and the Sacraments* (1960).

25. *The Atonement and the Sacraments*, p. 309.

26. I tried to develop this in the little book, *Kingdom Come!* (1974).

27. Cf. Aldous Huxley, *Grey Eminence* (1941), pp. 156f.

28. *The Justification of God* (1916), pp. 22f.

APPENDIX

An Excerpt from the Address
Delivered at Commemoration, 1977

The Rev. H. F. Lovell Cocks, M.A., D.D.

A speaker sometimes begins his address by wondering why
he has been invited to give it--a risky gambit which only too
often sets his hearers wondering too! But I know and you know
why I have been asked to address you today. It is because I
am a museum piece, not a rare collector's item, perhaps, but
still an exhibit whose undoubted authenticity may make a modest
contribution to the story of this College by helping you to
imagine what life was like at 527 Finchley Road in those far-
off days before the first World War.

* * * * *

But for me and my contemporaries in Hackney College the
supreme experience was our contact with *Peter Taylor Forsyth*.
When I entered Hackney in 1912 Forsyth was at the peak of his
powers. It is not true, as some have supposed, that he was
neglected in his lifetime and discovered only later as "a
Barthian before Barth". Not only discerning Anglicans like
J. K. Mozley, but his fellow Congregationalists were well
aware of his stature. Whenever a theological issue was before our denominational assemblies, the cry of "Forsyth!"
shouted from all parts of the hall, would summon him to the
platform. We students were proud of our Principal and pitied
men who studied in other colleges under teachers who, however

71

competent in their way, were not to be compared with P. T. F.
I know a lot of nonsense was talked, then and afterwards,
about Forsyth's "fireworks in a fog". There was certainly fog
about in those days. We used to meet ministers, patently fog-
bound, who asked us whether we could really understand Forsyth.
"Understand him?", we replied, "of course we understand him!"
And we did! Thank God, we did! He was a brilliant and excit-
ing teacher. His lectures were luminous. But for all the
power and profundity of his formal teaching, what is impressed
most deeply on my memory is our Wednesday evening session,
when, after prayer, Forsyth would prop a few scraps of paper
against the big pulpit Bible, and for forty-five minutes would
think aloud on a theme--sometimes biblical, sometimes literary
or philosophical--which he would expound, "winding into his
subject like a serpent", as Goldsmith said of Burke, opening
to us new vistas of truth and setting the whole within the
context of the Gospel. "He being dead yet speaks." As an old
Forsythian my heart is warmed to know that here and there all
over the world theological students are still discovering
Forsyth and finding that he speaks to their condition, as long
ago he spoke to ours. During my lifetime I have learned much
from many teachers, but it is to Peter Forsyth that I owe my
theological soul and my footing in the Gospel.

P. T. FORSYTH BIBLIOGRAPHY

1877-1980

The Bibliography is divided into two parts: published writings of Forsyth, and writings about or relating to Forsyth. The entries in Part One are ordered initially by year of publication. Within each year books, pamphlets, and contributions to symposia are placed first; articles and letters are arranged chronologically under the titles of the journals in which they appeared, these being in alphabetical order. In several instances, new editions of Forsyth's books are indicated. In addition, an attempt has been made to identify journal articles which were reprinted as pamphlets, books, or as chapters in books. When a book was published simultaneously in the United Kingdom and the United States, the UK edition is cited.

The entries in Part Two are arranged by type of material. The various types appear in alphabetical order as follows: books, contributions to books and journals, dissertations, reports in journals, reviews, and unpublished material. The books are subdivided into monographs and selections. Entries under the first three major headings are arranged alphabetically by author. Reports in journals, highlighting aspects of Forsyth's ministry, are arranged chronologically under the titles of the journals in which they appeared, these being in alphabetical order. Reviews are divided into two sections: reviews of Forsyth's writings, and reviews of writings relating to Forsyth. Within each section the works being reviewed are listed

74

in alphabetical order, and reviews are arranged by the titles
of the journals in which they appeared, these also being in
alphabetical order. The unpublished material is arranged by
location and file number when applicable.

A separate Title Index of Forsyth's Writings, arranged in
alphabetical order, has been appended to the bibliography and
should facilitate access to Forsyth's works. Books by Forsyth
are indicated by large type and references are to the year of
publication. While this bibliography is not intended to be
exhaustive or critical, the compilor's hope is that it will be
of value to those who have an academic or pastoral interest
in Forsyth.

I would like to acknowledge the contributions of the following persons. Dr. W. L. Bradley of the Edward W. Hazen
Foundation; Rev. Dr. Charles S. Duthie, former principal of New
College, University of London; and Dr. C. S. Pitt of Oakwood
College graciously supplied materials and made valuable suggestions. Mr. John V. Howard of New College Library, University of Edinburgh kindly answered my queries and forwarded
relevant material. I am especially indebted to Mr. Dikran Y.
Hadidian of the Pickwick Press for his suggestion that this
bibliography be compiled and for his encouragement and advice.
Deficiencies in design, content and style are my responsibility
alone.

University of Hawaii   Robert Benedetto

1. WRITINGS OF P. T. FORSYTH

1877

Letter. *English Independent* (Nov. 1): (re: "Religious Communism") 1202-3.

 English Independent (Nov. 8): 1230ff.

1878

Maid, Arise! Bradford: T. Brear.
 Pamphlet.

The Weariness of Modern Life. n.p.
 Pamphlet.

1881

"The Obligations of Doctrinal Subscription." *Modern Review* 2:273-281.

1883

"Pfleiderer's View of St. Paul's Doctrine." *Modern Review* 4:81-96.
 Published as a pamphlet.

"Auguste Bouvier, 'Le divin d'apres les apôtres'" et "Paroles de foi et de liberté." *Modern Review* 4:410-413.

1884

"A Tribute, a Reminiscence, and a Study." In *In Memoriam: James Baldwin Brown.* Edited by Elizabeth B. **Brown**. London: James Clarke.

"Pessimism." *Christian World Pulpit* 25 (Jan. 16):42-44.

"Nouvelles paroles de foi et de liberté." *Modern Review* 5:379-381.

1885

The Pulpit and the Age. His installation sermon at **Cheetham** Hill Congregational Church, Manchester. Manchester: Brook and Chrystal.
 Pamphlet.

"The Argument for Immortality is Drawn from the Nature of Love." *Christian World Pulpit* 28 (Dec. 2):360ff.

1886

Socialism and Christianity in Some of Their Deeper Aspects. Manchester: Brook and Chrystal. Pamphlet.

Pulpit Parables for Young Hearers (with J. A. Hamilton). Manchester: Brook and Chrystal.

1887

Religion in Recent Art: Being Expository Lectures on Rossetti, Burne-Jones, Watts, Holman Hunt, and Wagner. Manchester: Abel Heywood and Son. 3rd ed. London: Hodder and Stoughton, 1905.

"Sunday-Schools and Modern Theology." *Christian World Pulpit* 31 (Feb. 23):123ff.

1888

"The New Year." *Congregational Monthly* 1 (Jan.):13.

"The Relation of the Church to the Poor." *Congregational Monthly* (March).

1890

"Preaching and Poetry." *Expository Times* 1 (Sept.):269-272.

1891

The Old Faith and the New. Manchester: Brook and Chrystal. Pamphlet.

"Teachers of the Century: Robert Browning." *The Modern Church* (Oct. 15):451.

1892

Letter. *Congregational Monthly* 5 (Jan.):2.

"Faith and Charity." *Congregational Monthly* 5 (Jan.):13.

1893

"Revelation and the Person of Christ." In *Faith and Criticism:* Essays by Congregationalists. 2nd ed. London: Sampson Low, Marston. 95-144.

"Words for the Times." *Congregational Monthly* 6)July):167.

1894

"Mystics and Saints." *Expository Times* 5 (June):401-404.

"A Pocket of Gold." *Independent and Nonconformist* (Mar. 8): 187.

1895

"The Divine Self-Emptying." *Christian World Pulpit* 47 (May 1):276ff.
Published in *The Taste of Death and the Life of Grace*.

1896

The Charter of the Church: Six Lectures on the Spiritual Principle of Nonconformity. London: Alexander and Shepheard.

Intercessory Services for Aid in Public Worship. Manchester: John Heywood.

Letter. *British Weekly* 20 (Sept. 24):356.

"Holy Father." *British Weekly* 21 (Nov. 19, 26):74, 94-95.
Published in *The Holy Father and the Living Christ*.

"The Holy Father." *Christian World Pulpit* 50 (Oct. 7):225-229.
Published in *The Holy Father and the Living Christ*.

1897

The Holy Father and the Living Christ. Little Books on Religion. Edited by W. R. Nicoll. London: Hodder and Stoughton.
Reprinted in *God the Holy Father*.

"The Living Christ." *British Weekly* 22 (July 22):228.
Published in *The Holy Father and the Living Christ*.

"The Conversion of Faith by Love." *British Weekly* 23 (Oct. 28):22.

1898

The Happy Warrior: A Sermon on the Death of Mr. Gladstone. London: H. R. Allenson.
Pamphlet.

"Sacramentalism and the Remedy for Sacerdotalism." *Expositor* 5th ser. 8 (Aug., Oct.):221-233, 262-275.

1899

Christian Perfection. Little Books on Religion. Edited by W. R. Nicoll. London: Hodder and Stoughton.
Reprinted in *God the Holy Father*.

Rome, Reform and Reaction: Four Lectures on the Religious Situation. London: Hodder and Stoughton.

Priesthood and Its Theological Assumptions. Free Church Tracts for the Times, no. 3. London: National Council of Evangelical Free Churches, n.d.
Pamphlet. Published c. 1899-1900.

"A Hymn to Christ." *British Weekly* 26 (June 1):133.

"The Atonement in Modern Religious Thought." *Christian World.*

"The Cross as the Final Seat of Authority." *Contemporary Review* 76 (Oct.):589-608.
Appears in *Living Age* (Boston) 233:671-687; also published in *Proceedings of the Second International Congregational Council.*

"Dr. Dale." *London Quarterly Review* 91 (April):193ff.

1900

Essay in *The Atonement in Modern Religious Thought: A Theological Symposium.* London. James Clarke.
See pages 69-88.

Essay in *Different Conceptions of Priesthood and Sacrifice: A Report of a Conference.* Edited by W. Sanday. London: Longmans, Green. 174ff.

Proceedings of the Second International Congregational Council. Boston: Usher.
Contains "The Cross as the Final Seat of Authority."

"God as Holy Father." *Homiletic Review* 33:234-236.

"The Way of Life." *Wesleyan Methodist Monthly* 120:83-88.

"Prayer." *British Weekly* 27 (Feb. 22):424.

"Farewell Counsels to Students." *British Weekly* 28 (June 14): 179-80.

"A Simple Gospel." *British Weekly* 28 (Oct. 11):504.

"The Empire for Christ." *Christian World Pulpit* 57 (May 16): 303-311.

"The Taste of Death and the Life of Grace." *Christian World Pulpit* 58 (Nov. 28):296ff.
Published in the book of the same title.

Aphorism quoted. *Congregational Monthly* n.s. 1 (April):8.

"Does the Third Beatitude Fit the Englishman?" and "The Moral Peril of the Frontier Life." *Congregational Monthly* n.s. 1 (April):11.

"Things New and Old in Heresy." *Examiner* (July 12):399.

"The Slowness of God." *Expository Times* 11 (Feb.):218ff.

"Dr. Martineau." *London Quarterly Review* 93 (April):214ff.

1901

The Taste of Death and the Life of Grace. Small Books on
Great Subjects, 21. London: James Clarke.
Reprinted in *God the Holy Father.*

"Dr. G. A. Smith's Yale Lecture." *British Weekly* 30 (April
25):51-53.

"Treating the Bible Like Any Other Book." *British Weekly* 30
(Aug. 15):401-402.

"Notes from Pisgah." *British Weekly* 30 (Oct. 3):551.

"The Significance of the Church Fabric." *Christian World Pulpit* 59 (June 26):415ff.

"The Power of the Resurrection." *Examiner* (April 11):26.

1902

Holy Christian Empire. London: James Clarke.
Pamphlet. First published in the *Christian World Pulpit,*
this address also appears in *Missions in Church and
State,* Chapter 10.

"An Allegory of the Resurrection." *Christian World Pulpit*
61 (May 14):312ff.
Published as a pamphlet: *Holy Christian Empire* and in
Missions in State and Church, Chapter 10.

"Judgment." *Christian World Pulpit* 62 (Oct. 1):209ff.
Published in *Missions in State and Church,* Chapter 2.

"The Evangelical Basis of Free Churchism." *Contemporary Review* 81 (May):680-695.

"Preachers and Politics." *Examiner* (Feb. 6, 13):107, 129.

1903

"Forgiveness: A Problem of the Lord's Prayer." In *The Sermon
on the Mount: A Practical Exposition of St. Matthew* 6:9-
13, vol. 2. Manchester: James Robinson, 181-207.

"Bring us not into Temptation." In *The Sermon on the Mount:
A Practical Exposition of St. Matthew* 6: -9-13, vol. 2.
Manchester: James Robinson.

The Courage of Faith. Glasgow: Wm. Asher.
Pamphlet.

"The Charter of Missions." *Christian World Pulpit* 63 (May 20):
305ff.

Published as a pamphlet: *The Glorious Gospel* and in *Missions in State and Church,* Chapter 3.

"The New Congregationalism and the New Testament Congregationalism." *Examiner* (June 4, 11):551ff., 575ff.

"The Church, the State, the Priest, and the Future." *Examiner* (July 9, 16):27ff., 55ff.

"Sanctity and Certainty." *Examiner* (July 23):86.

"The Spiritual Reason for Passive Resistance." *Examiner* 2 (Oct. 8):2.

"Our Need of a Positive Gospel." *Examiner* (Nov. 5, 12):462, 86.

1904

Letter. *Examiner* (Jan.):5.
On Kierkegaard and Denny.

"The Scotch Church Case." *Examiner* (Aug. 18):144ff.

"The Need for a Positive Gospel." *London Quarterly Review* 101 (Jan.):64-99.

"The Paradox of Christ." *London Quarterly Review* 102 (June): 111ff.

1905

A Holy Church the Moral Guide of Society. London: Congregational Union of England and Wales.
Pamphlet. Also appears in the *British Weekly,* the *Congregational Year Book,* 1906, and in *The Church, The Gospel and Society.*

The Grace of the Gospel as the Moral Authority in the Church. London: Congregational Union of England and Wales.
Pamphlet. Also appears in the *Congregational Year Book,* 1906, and in *The Church, the Gospel and Society.*

Letters. *British Weekly* 37 (Mar. 23, 30):614, 638.

"A Holy Church the Moral Guide of Society." *British Weekly* 38 (May 11):129.
Published as a pamphlet.

Letter. *British Weekly* 38 (May 18):143.

"Message from Principal Forsyth, D.D." *Congregational Monthly* n.s. 6 (July):74.

"The Evangelical Churches and the Higher Criticism." *Contemporary Review* 88 (Oct.):574-599.

"A New Year Message to the Churches." *Examiner* (Jan. 5):7ff.

Letter. *Examiner* (June 29).
 "Our Colleges."

Letter. *Examiner* (Nov. 9):434.

"Authority and Theology." *Hibbert Journal* 4 (Oct.):63-78.
 Also appears in *Living Age* (Boston) 248 (1906):18-27.

"Some Christian Aspects of Evolution." *London Quarterly Review* 104 (Oct.):209-239.
 Also appears in *Living Age* (Boston) 247:323. Published separately, London: Epworth Press, 1950.

1906

"When We Were Boys." In *Bon Record. Records and Reminiscences of Aberdeen Grammar School.* Edited by H. F. M. Simpson. Aberdeen: D. Wylie and Son. 259-260.

Congregational Year Book.
 Contains "A Holy Church the Moral Guide of Society" and "The Grace of the Gospel as the Moral Authority in the Church." 15-97.

"Church and University." *British Congregationalist* (Sept. 26):201-202.
 Also appears in *Quartercentenary* of Aberdeen University.

"The Ideal Ministry." *British Congregationalist* (Oct. 18).

"Virgin Birth." *British Congregationalist* (Oct. 25).
 Remarks on a conference.

"Dr. Forsyth on the Education Crisis." *British Congregationalist* (Nov. 8):369.

Letter. *The British Weekly* 40 (July 12):344.

"The Place of Spiritual Experience in the Making of Theology." *Christian World Pulpit* 69 (Mar. 21):184-187.

"The Catholic Threat of Passive Resistance." *Contemporary Review* 89 (April):562-567.

"Church, State, Dogma and Education." *Contemporary Review* 90 (Dec.):827-836.

"The Chairman's Mantle." *Examiner* (Jan. 11):28.

"A Rallying Ground for the Free Churches -- the Reality of Grace." *Hibbert Journal* 4 (July):824-844.

"The Church's One Foundation." *London Quarterly Review* 106 (Oct.):193-202.
 Also appears in *Living Age* (Boston) 251:351-356.

Letters. *Times* (Jan. 18, 20, 25, 26, 29):4, 12, 11, 7, 7.
 On Chinese labor.

1907

Positive Preaching and Modern Mind: The Lyman Beecher Lecture
on Preaching, Yale University, 1907. London: Hodder and
Stoughton. 3rd ed. London: Independent Press, 1949.

"Church and University." In *Record of the Celebration of the
Quartercentenary of the University of Aberdeen.* Edited
by P. J. Anderson. Aberdeen: University of Aberdeen.

"Immanence and Incarnation." In *The Old Faith and the New
Theology.* Edited by C. H. Vine. London: Sampson Low,
Marston. 47-61.

Alma Mater, Aberdeen University (Dec. 18):110ff.

"The New Theology. Immanence and Incarnation." *British Congregationalist* (Jan. 24).
Published in *The Old Faith and the New Theology.*

"The Apostolate of Negation." *British Congregationalist* (Mar.
21):271.

"The Pastoral Duty of the Preacher." *British Congregationalist*
(Mar. 28):297.
Part of the Yale Lecture, *Positive Preaching and Modern
Mind.*

"Address from the Chair." *British Congregationalist* (May 16):
489.

"The Minister's Prayer." *British Congregationalist* (June 6).
Published in *The Soul of Prayer* and in *The Power of Prayer.*

"Sentiment and Sentimentalism." *British Congregationalist*
(July).

"Some Aspects of Spiritual Religion." *British Congregationalist* (Aug. 15):134.

"Motherhood." *British Congregationalist* (Sept. 26):255.

"National Purity Crusade." *British Congregationalist* (Oct. 3):
273.

"The Union and the Railway Dispute." *British Congregationalist*
(Oct. 24):361.

"Sociality, Socialism, and the Church." *British Congregationalist* (Nov. 28; Dec. 5, 12, 19):487, 509, 534, 561.
Published in *Socialism, the Church and the Poor.*

"The Newest Theology." *British Weekly* 41 (Mar. 7):581-582.

"God, Sin, and the Atonement." *British Weekly* (Mar. 28):669-
670.

Letter. *British Weekly* 43 (Oct. 31):83.

1908

Missions in State and Church. London: Hodder and Stoughton.

Socialism, The Church and the Poor. London: Hodder and Stoughton.

"Forgiveness Through Atonement the Essential of Evangelical Christianity." *Proceedings of the Third International Congregational Council.* London: Congregational Union of Wales.

Gibson, J. Munro. *The Inspiration and Authority of Holy Scripture.* Christian Faith and Doctrine Series, 1. London: Thomas Law.
With an introduction by Forsyth. vii-xviii.

"The Faith of Congregationalism" (with A. E. Garvie). *British Congregationalist* (June 18):593.

"Forgiveness Through Atonement the Essential of Evangelical Christianity." *British Congregationalist* (July 2):2.
Published in the *Proceedings of the Third International Congregational Council,* and revised in *The Cruciality of the Cross.*

"What is Evangelical Faith." *British Congregationalist* (Sept. 10, 17, 24):217-218, 239-240, 257-258.

"Some Christmas Thoughts." *British Congregationalist* (Dec. 24):553.

"To the Congregational Churches of England and Wales." *British Weekly* 43 (Feb. 27):556.
An open letter from the former Chairman and the College Principals.

"Christ at the Gate." *Christian World Pulpit* 73 (Mar. 18):177-182.

"The Love of Liberty and the Love of Truth." *Contemporary Review* 93 (Feb.):158-170.
Also appears in *Living Age* (Boston) 256:771-780.

"What is Meant by the Blood of Christ." *Expositor* 7th ser. 6 (Sept.):207-225.
Published in *The Cruciality of the Cross,* Chapter 4.

"The Distinctive Thing in Christian Experience." *Hibbert Journal* 6:481-499.

"Prayer and Its Importunity." *London Quarterly Review* 110 (July):1-22.

1909

The Cruciality of the Cross. London: Hodder and Stoughton. 2nd ed. London: Independent Press, 1948.

The Person and Place of Jesus Christ. London: Hodder and Stoughton. 6th ed. London: Independent Press, 1948.

"Monism." London Society for the Study of Religions. Private Printing. Pamphlet.

"Nonconformity and Politics." *British Congregationalist* (Feb. 4):85.

"Miraculous Healing, Then and Now." *British Congregationalist* (Mar. 11):194.

"Lay Religion." *British Congregationalist* (Apr. 29):337. Published in *The Person and Place of Jesus Christ.*

"The Person and Place of Jesus Christ." *British Congregationalist* (May 6, 20, 27; June 10, 17, 24; July 1). Published as a book under the same title.

"Modernism, Home and Foreign." *British Congregationalist* (Oct. 14):303, 323-326.

"Authority and Religion." *British Congregationalist* (Dec. 23): 538.

"The Interest and Duty of Congregationalists in the Present Crisis. A symposium." *British Congregationalist* (Dec. 23):539.

"The Modern Ministry: Its Duties and Perils. Interview with Dr. Forsyth." *British Congregationalist* (Dec. 30):559.

"Sir Joseph Compton Rickett's New Book." *British Weekly* 46 (May 13):122.

"Theological Reaction." *British Weekly* 46 (May 13):150.

"An Open Letter to a Young Minister on Certain Questions of the Hour." *Christian World* (May 27):11.

"The Roman Road to Rationalism." *Christian World* (Aug. 26; Sept. 2):6, 3.

"Milton's God and Milton's Satan." *Contemporary Review* 95 (April):450-465. Also appears in *Living Age* (Boston) 261:519-530.

"The Faith of Jesus." *Expository Times* 21 (Oct.):8-9.

"The Insufficiency of Social Righteousness as a Moral Ideal." *Hibbert Journal* 7 (April):596-613. Also appears in *Living Age* (Boston) 261:779-789.

"The Evidential Value of Miracles." *London Quarterly Review* 112 (July):1-7.

1910

The Work of Christ. London: Hodder and Stoughton. 2nd ed. London: Independent Press, 1938. Rpt. London: Collins: Fontana Library, 1965.
Second edition contains a forword by John S. Whale and a Memoir by Jessie Forsyth Andrews.

The Power of Prayer (with D. Greenwell). Little Books on Religion. Edited by W. R. Nicoll. London: Hodder and Stoughton.

"The Attitude of the Church to the Present Unrest." *British Congregationalist* (Mar. 17):214.

"War and Charity." *British Congregationalist* (Nov. 25):439. A letter on war and welfare.

"Messages from the Progressive Leaders." *British Weekly* 47 (Jan. 6):421.

"The Word and the World." *British Weekly* 47 (Feb. 10):533-534.

"Theological Liberalism v. Liberal Theology." *British Weekly* 47 (Feb. 17):557-558.

"God Takes a Text and Preaches." *British Weekly* 48 (April 14): 36.

Letter. *British Weekly* 48 (May 19):172.

"Missions the Soul of Civilization." *Christian World Pulpit* 77 (May 4):273ff.

"Calvinism and Capitalism." *Contemporary Review* 97 (June): 728-741; 98 (July):74-87.

"Orthodoxy, Heterodoxy, Heresy, and Freedom." *Hibbert Journal* 8:321-329.

"Intellectual Difficulties to Faith." *Record* (July 22):708ff.

1911

Christ on Parnassus: Lectures on Art, Ethic, and Theology. London: Hodder and Stoughton. Rpt. London: Independent Press, 1959.

"Christ and the Christian Principle." In *London Theological Studies.* London: University of London Press 133-166.

Revelation Old and New. Edinburgh: Blackwood. Pamphlet.

A United Free Church of England (with J. H. Shakespeare). London: F. B. Meyer.
Pamphlet. Contains Forsyth's "The United States of the Church," which also appears in *The Church and the Sacraments.*

The Story of the Scottish Congregational Theological Hall 1811–
    1911. Edinburgh: Morrison and Gibb.
    Pamphlet. See pages 20–22.

"Is Anything Wrong with Our Churches? A Symposium." *British
    Congregationalist* (Jan. 19):46.

"The Majesty and Mercy of God." *British Congregationalist*
    (May 4):367.

"The Duty of the Christian Ministry." *British Congregational-
    ist* (July 13):27.

"The Goodness of God." *British Congregationalist* (Aug. 10):97.

"Marriage, Its Ethic and Religion." *British Congregationalist*
    (Nov. 30):403.
    Published as a book under the same title.

Letter. *British Weekly* 51 (Oct. 26):100.

"Plebiscite and Gospel." *Contemporary Review* 100 (July):60–76.
    Published in *The Principle of Authority*, Chapter 13.

"Revelation and the Bible." *Hibbert Journal* 10 (Oct.):235–252.

"The Soul of Christ and the Cross of Christ." *London Quarterly
    Review* 116 (Oct.):193–212.

1912

Faith, Freedom and the Future. London: Hodder and Stoughton.
    Rpt. London: Independent Press, 1955.

Marriage, Its Ethic and Religion. London: Hodder and Stoughton.

*The Principle of Authority in Relation to Certainty, Sanctity,
    and Society*. London: Hodder and Stoughton. 2nd ed.
    London: Independent Press, 1952.

"New Year Messages." *British Congregationalist* (Jan. 4):3.

"Tribute to Andrew Martin Fairbairn." *British Congregational-
    ist* (Feb. 15):116.
    Reprinted from the *Westminster Gazette*, Feb. 12.

"The Doctrinal Method." *British Congregationalist* (Feb. 15):
    114.

"The Home Rule Bill." *British Congregationalist* (April 18):259.

"The Divorce Commission Report. Opinions of Prominent Congre-
    gationalists." *British Congregationalist* (Nov. 21):847.

"Tributes to Principal Fairbairn." *British Weekly* 51 (Feb. 15):
    568, 574.

"Liberty and Its Limits in the Church." *Contemporary Review*
    101 (April):502–512.

Published in *The Principle of Authority*, Chapter 14.

"Self-Denial and Self-Committal." *Expositor* 8th ser. 4 (July): 32ff.

"The Pessimism of Mr. Thomas Hardy." *London Quarterly Review* 118 (Oct.):193-219.
Also appears in *Living Age* (Boston) 275:458-473.

"Faith and Mind." *Methodist Review* (Oct.):627ff.

"Tribute to Andrew Martin Fairbairn." *Westminster Gazette* (Feb. 12).

1913

"The Religious Strength of Theological Reserve." *British Weekly* 53 (Jan. 13):576-577.

Letter. *British Weekly* 54 (May 15):169.

"The Fund and the Faith." *British Weekly* 54 (May 29):219.

"The Church and Society--Alien or Allied?" *British Weekly* 55 (Oct. 9):43.

"The Late Rev. C. S. Horne--A Tribute." *British Weekly* 56 (May 7):140.

"Christianity and Nationality." *British Weekly* 56 (July 9): 385-386.

"Things New and Old." *Christian World Pulpit* 84 (Oct. 29): 273ff.

"Congregationalism and the Principle of Liberty." *Constructive Quarterly* 1 (Sept.):498-521.

"Land Laws of the Bible." *Contemporary Review* 104 (Oct.):496-504.

"Intellectualism and Faith." *Hibbert Journal* 11 (Jan.):311-328.

"The Church and Society." *Westminster Gazette* (Sept. 6, 13, 20).

1914

"Principal Forsyth on 'Wedded Churches.'" *British Congregationalist* (Feb. 26):156.
Review of an article by Forsyth in the *Daily Chronicle*, Feb. 21.

"The Effectiveness of the Ministry." *British Congregationalist* (Mar. 12)1-20.
Also published in the *London Quarterly Review* and in *The Church and the Sacraments*, Chapter 7.

"The Church and the Nation." *British Congregationalist* (May 14):383.

"Principal Forsyth on 'Church and State.'" *British Congregationalist* (July 9):40.
Extracted from an article in the *Westminster Gazette*.

"Music and Worship." *Homiletic Review* 67:18-22.
Reprinted in the *Congregational Quarterly* 33(1955), 339-344.

"The Man and the Message." *London Quarterly Review* 121 (Jan.): 1-11.

"The Effectiveness of the Ministry." *London Quarterly Review* 122 (July):1.

"Regeneration, Recreation, and Miracle." *Methodist Review* (Oct., Nov.):627ff, 89ff.

"Progress of the Free Churches." *Times* (May 25):30.

"The Church and the Nation." *Westminster Gazette* (May 12):1ff.

"Church and State." *Westminster Gazette* (July 6).

1915

Theology in Church and State. London: Hodder and Stoughton.

Letter. *British Weekly* 59 (Nov. 4):93.

Letter. *British Weekly* 59 (Nov. 18):134.
On "The Colleges and Recruiting," signed by Forsyth, Garvie, Selbie, and Bennett.

"Lay Religion." *Constructive Quarterly* 3 (Dec.):767-789.

"Churches, Sects, and Wars." *Contemporary Review* 107 (May): 618-626.

"History and Judgment." *Contemporary Review* 108 (Oct.):457-470.
Published in *The Justification of God,* Chapter 11.

"The Preaching of Jesus and the Gospel of Christ." *Expositor* 8th ser. 9 (April, May):325-335, 404-421; 10 (July, Aug., Oct., Nov.):66-89, 117-138, 340-364, 445-465.

"Ibsen's Treatment of Guilt." *Hibbert Journal* 14 (Oct.):105-122.

"Veracity, Reality, and Regeneration." *London Quarterly Review* 123 (April):193-216.

"Prayer." *London Quarterly Review* 124 (Oct.):214-231.
Published in *The Soul of Prayer*.

"Faith, Metaphysic, and Incarnation." *Methodist Review* (Sept.): 696ff.

1916

The Christian Ethic of War. London: Longmans, Green.

The Justification of God: Lectures for War-time on a Christian
Theodicy. Studies in Theology, 23. London: Duckworth.
2nd ed. London: Latimer House, 1948.
The second edition omits the author's preface and includes
a foreword by D. R. Davies.

The Soul of Prayer. London: C. H. Kelly. 2nd ed. London:
Independent Press, 1949.
Includes Forsyth's contribution from *The Power of Prayer*.

Letter. *British Weekly* 59 (Jan. 6):284.

"The Spiritual Needs in the Churches." *Christian World Pulpit*
89 (May 3):251-255.

"The Conversion of the 'Good.'" *Contemporary Review* 109 (June):
760-771.

"The Truncated Mind." *Manchester Guardian* (Nov. 4).

1917

Lectures on the Church and the Sacraments. London: Longmans,
Green. 3rd ed. London: Independent Press, 1949.
The second (1947) and third editions include a preface by
J. K. Mozley and a note by Jessie Forsyth Andrews.

Letter. *British Weekly* 61 (Mar. 29):496.

"The Future of the Ministry." *The Christian World* (Aug. 23):4.

"The Need of a Church Theory for Church Union." *Contemporary
Review* 111 (Mar.):357-365.

"The Preacher and the Publicist." *London Quarterly Review*
127 (Jan.):1-18.

"The Moralization of Religion." *London Quarterly Review* 128
(Oct.):161-174.

1918

This Life and the Next: The Effect on this Life of Faith in
Another. London: Macmillan. 2nd ed. London: Independent Press, 1946.

"Reconstruction and Religion." In *Problems of Tomorrow*.
Edited by F. A. Rees. London: James Clark.

The Roots of a World Commonwealth. London: Hodder and Stoughton. 2nd ed. London: Independent Press, 1952.
Pamphlet.

"The Unborn, the Once Born, and the First Born." *The Christian
World* (Feb. 14).

"Evangelicals and Home Reunion." *The Churchman* 32 528-536.

"The Reality of God: A War-time Question." *Hibbert Journal* 16 (July):608-619.

"Testamentary Ethics." *London Quarterly Review* 129 (April):169-179.

1919

"Unity and Theology." In *Towards Reunion*. Church of England and Free Church Writers. London: Macmillan. 51-81.

Congregationalism and Reunion. London: Congregational Union of England and Wales.
Pamphlet. Reprinted in *Congregationalism and Reunion, Two Lectures*.

A Few Hints About Reading the Bible. New York: Association Press.
Pamphlet.

The Validity of the Congregational Ministry (with J. V. Bartlett and J. D. Jones). London: Congregational Union of England and Wales.
Pamphlet. Contains Forsyth's "Church, Ministry and Sacraments."

"The Inner Life of Christ." *Constructive Quarterly* 7 (Mar.): 149-162.

"Religion and Reality." *Contemporary Review* 115·(May):548-554.

"The Foolishness of Preaching." *Expository Times* 30 (Jan.): 153-154.

"Religion, Private and Public." *London Quarterly Review* 131 (Jan.):19-32.

Letters. *Times* (May 28, 29; June 6, 16):8, 8; 8, 8.
On the Church of England National Assembly Bill.

Letter. *Times* (Aug. 30):6.
On the interchange of pulpits between the Church of England and the Free Churches.

1920

Selbie, W. B. *The Life of Charles Silvester Horne*. London: Hodder and Stoughton.
See pages 302ff.

"Does the Church Prolong the Incarnation?" *London Quarterly Review* 133 (July: Oct.):1-12; 204-212..

1922

Hunter, Leslie S. *John Hunter, D.D. A Life.* 2nd ed. London:
Hodder and Stoughton.
See pages 289ff.

1943

The Glorious Gospel: An Abridgement of a Sermon Preached for
the London Missionary Society, May, 1903. London Missionary Society. Triple Jubilee Papers, no. 3. London:
Livingstone Press.
Pamphlet. Appears as "The Fatherhood of Death" in *Missions in State and Church.*

1950

Christian Aspects of Evolution. London: Epworth Press.
Pamphlet. Reprinted from the *London Quarterly Review.*

1952

Congregationalism and Reunion, Two Lectures. London: Independent Press.
Contains two lectures originally delivered in 1917 and
1918 under the titles "Reunion and Recognition" and "Congregationalism and Reunion."

1955

"Music and Worship." *Congregational Quarterly* 33:339-344.
Reprinted from the *Homiletic Review.*

1957

God the Holy Father. London: Independent Press. Rpt. Edin-
burgh: St. Andrews Press (pb), 1978.
Contains *The Holy Father and the Living Christ, Christian
Perfection* and *The Taste of Death and the Life of Grace.*

1962

The Church, the Gospel and Society. London: Independent Press.
Contains *A Holy Church the Moral Guide of Society* and *The
Grace of the Gospel as the Moral Authority in the Church.*

Undated Material

Coleridge's *"Ancient Mariner."* An Exposition and Sermon from a
Modern Text. Bradford: Wm. Byles and Sons.
Pamphlet.

The Minister's Prayer. London: National Council of Evangelical Free Churches.
Pamphlet.

Pfleiderer's View of St. Paul's Doctrine. London: W. Speaght. Pamphlet.

2. WRITINGS RELATING TO P. T. FORSYTH

BOOKS

Monographs

Bradley, W. L. *P. T. Forsyth: The Man and His Work,* London: Independent Press, 1952.

Brown, R. M. *P. T. Forsyth, Prophet for Today.* Philadelphia: Westminster Press, 1952.

Griffith, Gwilyn C. *The Theology of P. T. Forsyth.* London: Lutterworth Press, 1948.

Hunter, A. M. *P. T. Forsyth: Per Crucem ad Lucem.* London: SCM Press, 1974.

Rodgers, J. H. *The Theology of P. T. Forsyth.* London: Independent Press, 1965.

Selections

Anderson, Marvin W., ed. *The Gospel and Authority:* A P. T. Forsyth Reader. Minneapolis: Augsburg, 1971.

Escott, Harry. *P. T. Forsyth and the Cure of Souls:* An Appraisement and Anthology of his Practical Writings. Rev. and enl. ed. London: George Allen and Unwin, 1970. First published as *Peter Taylor Forsyth: Director of Souls.* London: Epworth Press, 1948.

Huxtable, John, ed. *Revelation Old and New:* Sermons and Addresses. London: Independent Press, 1962.

Mikolaski, Samuel J., ed. *The Creative Theology of P. T. Forsyth.* Grand Rapids: Wm. B. Eerdmans, 1969.

CONTRIBUTIONS TO BOOKS AND JOURNALS

"Agro" and "The Watch Tower." *Record* (Dec. 1, 1944):479.

94

Anderson, Marvin W. "P. T. Forsyth: Prophet of the Cross." *Evangelical Quarterly* 47 (1975):146-161.

Andrews, Jessie F. Memoir in Forsyth's *The Work of Christ*. 1938, 1946, eds.

Barth, Markus, "P. T. Forsyth: The Theologian for the Practical Man." *Congregational Quarterly* 17 (Oct., 1939):436-442.

Bishop, John. "P. T. Forsyth: 'Preaching and the Modern Mind.'" *Religion in Life* 48 (1979):303-308.

Bradley, W. L. "Forsyth's Contributions to Pastoral Theology." *Religion in Life* 28 (1959):546-556.

Brown, R. M. "The 'Conversion' of P. T. Forsyth." *Congregational Quarterly* 30 (1952):236-244.

Cave, Sydney. "Dr. P. T. Forsyth: His Influence in Congregationalism." *Christian World* (Nov. 24, 1921).
Clipping in New College Library (N.C.L.), London.

_____. "Dr. Forsyth: 'A Student Tribute'." *Christian World* (Dec., 1921).
Clipping in N.C.L.

_____. "P. T. Forsyth: The Man and his Writings." *Congregational Quarterly* 26 (Apr., 1948):107-119.

Child, R. L. "P. T. Forsyth: Some Aspects of His Thought." *Baptist Times* (June 3, 1948).
Clipping in N.C.L.

Cocks, H. F. L. "P. T. Forsyth, 'A Voice from a Better Future'." *British Weekly* (May 6, 1948):7.

_____. "The Message of P. T. Forsyth." *Congregational Quarterly* 26 (July, 1948):214-221.

_____. "P. T. Forsyth's *The Person and Place of Jesus Christ*." *Expository Times* 64 (Apr., 1953):195-198.

Coggan, F. D. "P. T. Forsyth's *Positive Preaching and the Modern Mind*." *Expository Times* 72 (Aug., 1961):324-326.

Cunliffe-Jones, H. "P. T. Forsyth's *Principle of Authority*." *London Quarterly and Holborn Review* 172 (1947):316-324.

_____. "P. T. Forsyth: Reactionary or Prophet." *Congregational Quarterly* 27 (1950):344.

Garvie, A. E. "Placarding the Cross. The Theology of P. T. Forsyth." *Congregational Quarterly* (Oct. 1943):343.

_____. "A Cross-Centered Theology." *Congregational Quarterly* 22 (1944):324.

_____. Letter to the Editor. *Congregational Quarterly* 12 (1945):96.

Glegg, A. J. Tribute to Forsyth. *Christian World* (Nov. 17, 1921):4.

Gossip, A. J. "P. T. Forsyth." *Expository Times* 60 (Mar., 1949):149.

Green, Alan. "Personal Memories of P. T. Forsyth." *British Weekly* (May 13, 1938):11.

Gummer, Selwyn. "Peter Taylor Forsyth: A Contemporary Theologian." *London Quarterly and Holborn Review* 173 (Oct., 1948):349-353.

Hamilton, Kenneth. "Love or War? Nels Ferré Versus P. T. Forsyth." *Canadian Journal of Theology* 8 (1962):299-336.

Hermann, E. "Sketch of His (Forsyth's) Work in Theology." *Homiletical Review* 66 (1913):179-185.

Higginson, P. T. "The Authentic Word: A Study in Forsyth's Attitude to the Bible." *Churchman* (June, 1946):82-86.

Hughes, P. E. "Forsyth: Theologian of the Cross." *Christianity Today* (Dec., 1957):5-7.

Hughes, T. Hywell. "A Barthian before Barth?" *Congregational Quarterly* 12 (July, 1934):308-315.

_____. "Dr. Forsyth's View of the Atonement." *Congregational Quarterly* 18 (Jan., 1940):30-37.

Hunt, G. "Interpreters of our Faith." *A.D.* (May, 1975):39.

Hunter, A. M. "P. T. Forsyth Neutestamentler." *Expository Times* 73 (Jan., 1962):100-106.
Originally a Presidential Lecture given to St. Mary's Theological Society, St. Andrews, November 3, 1961.

_____. *Teaching and Preaching the New Testament*. London: SCM Press, 1963.
Contains a study of Forsyth's theology.

Jackson, G. D. "P. T. Forsyth's Use of the Bible." *Interpretation* 7 (1953):323-337.

Jowett, J. H. "Dr. P. T. Forsyth." *British Weekly* (Nov. 17, 1921):146.

Lambert, D. W. "A Great Theologian and his Greatest Book: *The Work of Christ*." *London Quarterly Review* 173 (1948):244-247.

_____. "The Missionary Message of P. T. Forsyth." *Evangelical Quarterly* (July, 1949):203-208.

_____. "The Theology of Missions: The Contribution of P. T. Forsyth." *London Quarterly and Holborn Review* (Apr., 1951):114-117.

96

Leembruggen, W. H. "The Witness of P. T. Forsyth, a Theologian of the Cross." *Reformed Theological Review* (1945):18-46. Also published as a pamphlet with a Foreword by the Rev. Prof. John Giles, M. A., B. D. Melbourne: John Bacon n.d.

Mackintosh, R. "The Authority of the Cross." *Congregational Quarterly* 21 (1943). Annotated by Forsyth.

McMurray Adams, R. H. "Postman's Son Who Became Church Leader." *The Press and Journal* (May 21, 1948).

Meadley, T. D. "The 'Obscurity' of P. T. Forsyth." *Congregational Quarterly* 24 (Oct., 1946):308-317.

Mikolaski, S. J. "P. T. Forsyth on the Atonement." *Evangelical Quarterly* 36 (1964):78-91.

_____. "The Theology of P. T. Forsyth." *Evangelical Quarterly* 36 (1964):27.

_____. *Creative Minds in Contemporary Theology*. Edited by P. L. Hughes. Grand Rapids: Wm. B. Eerdmanns, 1966. Contains a chapter on Forsyth.

Mozley, J. K. "The Theology of Dr. Forsyth." *Expositor* (Jan., Mar., 1922):81, 161. Published in *The Heart of the Gospel*. London: S.P.C.K., 1925.

_____. "Preface to Forsyth's *The Church and the Sacraments*. 2nd ed., 1947.

Peake, A. S. *Recollections and Appreciations*. Edited by W. F. Howard. London: Epworth Press, 1938. See "P. T. Forsyth", pages 192ff.

Robinson, N. H. G. "The Importance of P. T. Forsyth." *Expository Times* (Dec., 1952):76-79.

Rosenthal, Klaus. "Die Bedeutung des Kreuzesgeschehens für Lehre und Bekenntnis Nach Peter Taylor Forsyth. *Kerygma and Dogma Zeitschrift für Theologische Forschung und Kirchliche Lehre* 7 (1961):237-259.

Ruhu, H. Vincent. Letter *British Weekly* (Nov. 24, 1921).

Rupp, Gordon. Preface to A. M. Hunter's *P. T. Forsyth: Per Crucem ad Lucem*. A quotation about Forsyth.

Scullard, H. H. "Principal Forsyth." *London Quarterly Review* 137 (Jan., 1922):104-106.

Shaw, J. M. "The Theology of P. T. Forsyth." *Theology Today* (Oct., 1946):358.

Simpson, A. F. "P. T. Forsyth: The Prophet of Judgement." *Scottish Journal of Theology* 4 (1951):148-156.

Thomas, H. Arnold. "Preacher I Have Known." *Congregational Quarterly* (Jan., 1923):60.

Warschauer, J. "Liberty, Limited: A Rejoinder to Dr. Forsyth." *Contemporary Review* 101 (1912):831-839.

Webster, D. "P. T. Forsyth's Theology of Missions." *International Review of Missions* 44 (1955):175-181.

Whale, J. S. "Foreword to Forsyth's *The Work of Christ*." 1938, 1946, eds.

Wiersbe, W. W. "Theologian for Pastors." *Moody Monthly* (May 1975):97-101.

Worrall, B. G. "The Authority of Grace in the Theology of P. T. Forsyth." *Scottish Journal of Theology* 25 (Feb., 1972): 58-74.

DISSERTATIONS

Allen, Ray. *The Christology of P. T. Forsyth*. Duke University, 1953.

Bradley, W. L. *The Theology of P. T. Forsyth, 1848-1921*. University of Edinburgh, 1949. Published as *P. T. Forsyth, the Man and His Work*. London: Independent Press, 1952.

Brown, Robert M. *P. T. Forsyth and the Gospel of Grace*. Columbia University, 1951. Published as *P. T. Forsyth: Prophet for Today*. Philadelphia: Westminster Press, 1952.

Gardner, Harry M. *The Doctrine of the Person and Work of Jesus Christ in the Thought of Peter Taylor Forsyth and Emil Brunner*. Boston University, 1962.

Jackson, Georg D. *The Biblical Basis of the Theology of P. T. Forsyth*. Princeton Theological Seminary, 1952.

McKay, Clifford A. *The Moral Structure of Reality in the Theology of Peter Taylor Forsyth*. Vanderbilt University, 1970.

Newman, Guy D. *The Theology of P. T. Forsyth with Special Reference to His Christology*. Southwestern Baptist Theological Seminary, 1953.

Pitt, C. S. *Church, Ministry and Sacraments: A Critical Evaluation of the Thought of Peter Taylor Forsyth*. New College, London, 1977.

Simpson, A. F. *Certainty Through Faith: An Examination of the Religious Philosophy of Peter Taylor Forsyth.* New College, London, 1949.

Stewart, Winthrop R. *The Biblical Foundations and Insights of P. T. Forsyth's Theology.* Aberdeen, 1965.

Thompson, Robert F. *Peter Taylor Forsyth: A Pre-Barthian.* Drew University, 1940.

Wismar, Don R. *A Sacramental View of Preaching as Seen in the Writings of John Calvin and P. T. Forsyth and Applied to the Mid-Twentieth Century.* Pacific School of Religion, 1963.

Wismar, Reginald A. *The Problem of Religious Authority in Contemporary Theological Thought with Particular Reference to the Interpretations of John Oman, P. T. Forsyth, and A. E. J. Rawlinson.* Columbia University, 1960.

REPORTS IN JOURNALS

Aberdeen Press and Journal

    May 12, 1948. "Postman's Son Who Became Church Leader: Fought Deadly Menace to Christianity."

Aberdeen University Review

    1921-22, Vol. 9, p. 186. Obituary.

British Congregationalist

    Jan. 16, 1908, p. 51. Forsyth to preach at Mansfield College.
    July 9, 1908, p. 33. His Edinburgh address.
    Oct. 8, 1914, p. 323. His recent illness.

British Weekly

    Feb. 25, 1887, p. 2. "Church Life in Manchester."
    Mar. 8, 1894, p. 322. He accepts call to Cambridge.
    Sept. 20, 1894, p. 364. Begins his ministry at Cambridge.
    Oct. 4, 1894, p. 380. Death of his wife.
    Apr. 14, 1898, p. 492. Description of a sermon in Dulwich.
    Sept. 28, 1899, p. 411. Forsyth in Boston.
    Oct. 5, 1899, p. 431, 437. Forsyth in Boston.
    Feb. 14, 1901, p. 459. Forsyth's call to Hackney College.
    Mar. 7, 1901, p. 530. "Dr. P. T. Forsyth of Cambridge," by Lorna (Miss Jane Stoddart).
    Mar. 21, 1901, p. 582. He accepts call to Hackney College.
    Mar. 21, 1901, p. 587. "Dr. Forsyth and Aberdeen," a letter.

April. 11, 1901, p. 664. "Dr. Forsyth in Hackney," a
letter.
Dec. 12, 1901, p. 239. A portrait.
May 22, 1902, p. 136. Forsyth's resolution on the Educa-
tion Bill.
June 19, 1902, p. 242. "Dr. Forsyth at New College."
Mar. 17, 1904, p. 611. "Principal Forsyth among the Wes-
leyans."
May 12, 1904, pp. 107ff. Election of Forsyth as Chairman
of the Congregational Union; his speech on Chinese
labor.
Sept. 8, 1904, p. 511. "Rev. Dr. Forsyth on Christ's
Teaching in Economics."
May 18, 1905, p. 147. "Dr. Clifford on Principal For-
syth's Address."
Oct. 12, 1905, pp. 3, 4. "Dr. Forsyth's Burden;" a re-
port of Forsyth's address from the Chair of the Union.
Oct. 19, 1905, pp. 35, 36. "Dr. Forsyth's Plea to the
Archbishops;" "Dr. Forsyth on Passive Resistance."
Oct. 26, 1905, p. 59. "The Bishop of Bristol and Dr.
Forsyth."
Apr. 19, 1906, p. 31. Interview with Forsyth on the
Education Bill.
May 10, 1906, p. 104. Forsyth at the Assembly.
July 19, 1906, p. 370. "Dr. Forsyth," a letter.
Oct. 4, 1906, p. 617. "The Correspondence of Claudius
Clear," a report of Forsyth's Aberdeen University
sermon.
Nov. 29, 1906, p. 211. "The Congregational Union and the
Education Bill," quotes Forsyth's address.
Mar. 14, 1907, pp. 634. "Dr. Forsyth's Position," a
letter. "The Leicester Conference and the New The-
ology," a letter.
Apr. 25, 1907, pp. 57ff. "Principal Forsyth's Impres-
sions of America."
Mar. 17, 1910, p. 480. Forsyth's address at the National
Free Church Council.
May 12, 1910, p. 132. R. J. Campbell's reference to For-
syth at the Assembly.
Oct. 19, 1911, p. 90. The contention between Forsyth and
Campbell.
Nov. 2, 1911, p. 132. "Dr. Forsyth and Mr. Campbell,"
two letters.
Nov. 9, 1911, p. 170. Three further letters about their
disagreement.
Nov. 16, 1911, p. 196. Another five letters on the same
subject.
Sept. 4, 1913, p. 549. "Principal Forsyth: The Roose-
velt of Modern Theology."

Mar. 19, 1914, p. 730. "Dr. Forsyth's Address at Norwich."

Nov. 11, 1915, p. 108. "Dr. Forsyth and Mr. Campbell," a letter.

Nov. 16, 1916, p. 128. "Principal Forsyth at Westminster Chapel."

Nov. 17, 1921, p. 146. "Principal Forsyth," by W. R. Nicoll.

Nov. 24, 1921. Tribute to Forsyth.

Dec. 1, 1921. Tribute to Forsyth.

May 18, 1922. Memorial Tablet to Dr. Forsyth unveiled at Hackney College.

The Christian World

Nov. 17, 1921, p. 3. "Death of Principal Forsyth."

The Congregational Monthly

Mar. 1888, vol. 1, p. 64. Mention of an address by Forsyth.

June 1888, vol. 1, p. 180. Forsyth's call to Leicester.

July 1888, vol. 1, p. 201. Forsyth's address noted.

Oct. 1892, vol. 5, p. 289. Mention of address by Forsyth on the growth of population in large towns.

Feb. 1893, vol. 6, p. 51. Forsyth appointed College Pastor at Oxford.

Dec. 1893, vol. 6, p. 326. Forsyth appointed to Leicester Museum and Art Gallery Committee.

Mar. 1894, vol. 7, p. 93. Forsyth accepts call to Cambridge.

Sept. 1899, vol. 12, p. 205. Forsyth sails for Boston.

Apr. 1901, n.s., vol. 1, p. 3. Forsyth accepts call to Hackney College.

July, 1901, n.s., vol. 2, p. 3. Forsyth's address at Lancashire Independent College.

Oct. 1903, n.s., vol. 4, p. 229. "Peter Taylor Forsyth, The Life-Story of the Principal of Hackney College."

June, 1905, n.s., vol. 5, p. 107. "P. T. Forsyth, M.A., D.D., The New Chairman of the Congregational Union."

Literary Digest

Aug. 23, 1913, pp. 288-289. "Principal Forsyth: The Roosevelt of Modern Theology."

The Times

Feb. 26, 1906, p. 12. Accepts Lyman Beecher Lectureship.

Mar. 9, 1806, p. 10. At Birmingham, "Evangelical Free Churches Council."

Nov. 28, 1906, p. 7. At City Temple, on Education Bill.

Feb. 13, 1909, p. 9. At University College, "The Study of the Bible."

May 14, 1909, p. 14. At Congregational Union conference. On Christianity.
Mar. 11, 1910, p. 4. At "The Free Church Council."
Apr. 28, 1910, p. 4. At Bloomsbury Chapel, "The Baptist Anniversaries."
Mar. 10, 1911, p. 4. At Evangelical Free Church Conference, "Free Church Council, Religious Reunion."
Oct. 12, 1911, p. 12. At Congregational Union Conference on Christianity.
Oct. 4, 1913, p. 8. At Southhampton, "Church Congress, Problems of Property and Rural Life."
May 13, 1914, p. 6. At Memorial Hall, "Church and Nation, Dr. Forsyth on Spiritual Independence."
Oct. 10, 1914, p. 11. His health.
May 9, 1918, p. 3. At Memorial Hall, "Christian Union, Dr. Forsyth on a New Phase."
Oct. 12, 1919, p. 12. At Congregational Union Conference.
Nov. 12, 1921, p. 14. "Death of Principal Forsyth, an Original Thinker."
Nov. 16, 1921, p. 13. Description of his funeral.

REVIEWS

Reviews of Forsyth's Writings

The Charter of the Church

British Weekly (May 21, 1896):65.
London Quarterly Review (Jan., 1897):205.

Christ on Parnassus

Church Quarterly Review (Oct., 1912):226.
Church Quarterly Review 162 (1961):387-388. By G. Cope.
Expository Times (Nov., 1911):74.

The Christian Ethic of War

Expository Times (Nov., 1916):55.
Times Literary Supplement 15 (1916):426.

Christian Perfection

London Quarterly Review (Apr., 1899):383.

The Church and the Sacraments

Expository Times (Aug., 1917):497.
Journal of Theological Studies 19 (Oct., 1917):91.
London Quarterly and Holborn Review (Jan., 1910):145.
London Quarterly and Holborn Review (Oct., 1948):377.
London Quarterly Review (July, 1917):131.

The Church, the Gospel and Society

    Modern Churchman n.s., 6 (1963):245-246. By R. Preston.

Congregationalism and Reunion

    Baptist Quarterly 15 (1953):46-47. By G. W. Hughes.

The Cruciality of the Cross

    Baptist Quarterly 13 (1949):44-45.
    Expository Times (Nov., 1909):84.
    London Quarterly Review (Jan., 1910):145.

Faith and Criticism

    London Quarterly Review (Oct., 1893):1.

Faith, Freedom, and the Future

    Congregational Quarterly 67 (1956):202-203. By C. S.
      Duthie.
    Congregational Quarterly 36 (1958):270. by J. Huxtable.
    Expository Times (June, 1912):411.
    Journal of Theological Studies 15 (1913):132.

The Holy Father and the Living Christ

    Expository Times (Apr., 1898):269.

The Justification of God

    Anglican Theological Review 35 (1953):63-64. By F. W.
      Dillistone.
    Boston Transcript (Sept. 12, 1917):6.
    Expository Times (Jan., 1917):177.
    Journal of Bible and Religion 20 (1952):44-45. By J.
      Gardner.
    New York Times 22 (Nov. 25, 1917):500.

Marriage, Its Ethic and Religion

    Expository Times (Nov., 1912):79.

Missions in State and Church

    British Weekly (Oct., 1908):50.
    Church Quarterly Review (Apr., 1910):208.
    Expository Times (Nov., 1908):86.

"The Old Faith and the New"

    Congregational Monthly 4 (Dec., 1891):320.

The Person and Place of Jesus Christ

    American Journal of Theology 14 (1910):313. By C. A.
      Exley.
    British Weekly (Oct. 21, 1909):57.
    Expository Times (Apr., 1910):320.

Expository Times (Apr., 1953):195.
Hibbert Journal 8 (May, 1910):686.   By Arthur Boutwood.
Independent 69 (July 28, 1910):197.
Nation 91 (Oct. 20, 1910):367.
New York Times 15 (July 16, 1910):400.

Positive Preaching and the Modern Mind

Baptist Quarterly 13 (1949):190-191.   By I. J. Barnes.
Biblical World 31 (May, 1908):400.
British Weekly (Oct. 24, 1907):57.
Expository Times 72 (Aug., 1961):324-326.   By F. D.
   Coggan.
Independent (Aug. 20, 1908):436.
London Quarterly Review (Jan., 1908):1.
London Times 6 (Dec. 20, 1907):387.
Modern Churchman 40 (1950):166-167.   By W. G. Fallows.
Nation 86 (Mar. 26, 1908):284.
New York Times 13 (May 9, 1908):267.
Outlook 7 (Mar., 1908):560.
Public Opinion (May, 1949):333.
Saturday Review 106 (July 4, 1908):24.
Springfielder 30 (1966):67-69.   By G. Aho.
Times Literary Supplement 6 (Dec. 19, 1907):387.

The Principle of Authority

Baptist Quarterly 14 (1952):378-379.   By. A. W. Argyle.
Congregational Quarterly 31 (1953):75-76.   By H. F. L.
   Cocks.
Expository Times (Feb., 1913):213.
Hibbert Journal (July, 1914):936.
London Quarterly Review (Apr., 1913):340.

Religion in Recent Art

London Quarterly Review (Jan., 1902):201.
New York Times (June 7, 1902):379.
Outlook 72 (1902):463-464.

Rome, Reform and Reaction

British Weekly (Jan. 11, 1900):306.
London Quarterly Review (Apr., 1900):352.

The Soul of Prayer

London Quarterly Review (Jan., 1917):130.

The Taste of Death and the Life of Grace

Expository Times (June, 1901):367.

Theology in Church and State

American Journal of Theology 20 (1916):615.   By F. A.
   Starratt.

Biblical World 47 (May, 1916):341.
Boston Transcript (June 17, 1916):6.
Congregational Quarterly 35 (1957):297-310. By J. Huxtable.
Expository Times (May, 1916):276.
New York Times 21 (Aug. 6, 1916):312.
Springfield Republican (Mar. 5, 1916):15.
Times Literary Supplement 14 (Dec. 30, 1915):495.

This Life and the Next

American Library Association Booklist 14 (1918):313.
Baptist Quarterly 13 (1949):44-45. By R. L. Child.
Bookman 47 (1918):653. By Tertius Van Dyke.
Boston Transcript 24 (Aug., 1918):3. By Tertius Van Dyke.
London Quarterly Review (Apr., 1918):121.
Springfield Republican (Aug. 27, 1918):6.
Times Literary Supplement 17 (Sept., 1918):175.

"Wedded Churches"

British Congregationalist (Feb., 1914):156.

The Work of Christ

Expository Times (Nov., 1910):84.
London Quarterly Review (Jan., 1911):151.

Reviews of Writings Relating to Forsyth

The Creative Theology of P. T. Forsyth (Mikolaski)

Christianity Today (Aug. 1, 1969):16, By W. C. Robinson.
Evangelical Quarterly 42 (1970):247-248. By A. S. Wood.
Journal of American Academy of Religion 38 (Sept., 1970): 342-343. By C. A. McKay, Jr.
Reformed Review 23 (Fall, 1969):29-30. By W. H. Bos.
Westminster Theological Journal 33 (Nov., 1970):111-112. By A. M. Harman.

The Gospel and Authority: A P. T. Forsyth Reader (Anderson)

Choice 9 (1972):660.

P. T. Forsyth: The Man and His Work (Bradley)

Church Quarterly Review 153 (1952):516-520. By W. F. Lofthouse.
Congregational Quarterly 31 (Jan., 1953):73-74. By S. Cave.
Interpretation 8 (Oct., 1954):490-491. By C. Gamble.

P. T. Forsyth: Per Crucem ad Lucem (Hunter)

Anglican Theological Review 59 (July, 1977):349-350. By
F. M. McClain.
Church History 44 (June, 1975):274-275. By Neal C.
Gillespie.
Perkins School of Theology Journal 29 (Winter, 1976):45-
46. By Geoffrey D. Scott.
Theology 77 (Oct., 1974):544-545. By B. G. Worrall.

P. T. Forsyth, Prophet for Today (Brown)

Interpretation 8 (Jan., 1954):99-100. By K. B. Cully.
Scottish Journal of Theology 9 (Dec., 1956):447. By G.
W. Bromiley.
Theology Today 10 (Oct., 1953):429-431. By J. M. Shaw.

The Theology of P. T. Forsyth (Griffith)

Theology Today 7 (July, 1950):268-269. By J. N. Thomas.

The Theology of P. T. Forsyth (Rodgers)

Canadian Journal of Theology 12 (Apr., 1966):141-142.
By R. F. Aldwinckle.
Christianity Today 9 (Sept. 25, 1965):20-21. By J. Daane.
Churchman 80 (Mar., 1966):49-50. By J. P. Baker.
Expository Times 77 (June, 1966):268-269. By D. Ebor.
Journal of Religious Thought 23, no. 2 (1966-67):187-188.
By J. D. Roberts.
Journal of Theological Studies n.s. 18 (Apr., 1967):288-
289. By N. H. G. Robinson.

UNPUBLISHED MATERIAL

London.   New College Library*

File 182/3/2/1. Letter from J. F. Andrews to J. B.
Binns regarding Forsyth, 7 October 1948.

File 182/3/2/2. Letter from J. B. Andrews to J. B.
Binns regarding Forsyth, 10 October 1948.

File 182/3/2/4. Letter from J. F. Andrews to Dr. Cave
regarding Forsyth, 30 June 1948.

File 182/3/2/5. Letter from J. F. Andrews to J. B.
Binns regarding Forsyth, 13 October 1948.

----

*New College, University of London ceased to exist in
1977, but continues as a Foundation which helps theological
students preparing for ministry.

File 182/3/9. References to Forsyth's health in Minutes of New College, London.

File 182/3/12. References to Forsyth's health in Minutes of New College, London.

File 244/2. Midsummer examination in Apologetics set by Forsyth, 1902.

File 536/22. Letter to Forsyth from J. K. Mozley, 20 January 1909.

Forsyth's Letter from Gwalia Hotel in Llandrindod Wells, Wales to James Shepheard of Lyndhurst Rd., Congregational Church, saying he could not give an address because of the pressure of work, 23 July 1913.

"The Addresses delivered at the unveiling of the Tablet erected in the College Library, to the memory of-- Rev. Peter Taylor Forsyth--," 11 May 1922.

Program for 275 Commemoration of the founding of the Harmondsworth Charity (which later became New College, London) containing a reference to Forsyth as a "most distinguished alumnus" of New College, 10 June 1948.

Price, Charles. *Introduction to the Theology of P. T. Forsyth.* Notes of lectures given at the Protestant Episcopal Theological Seminary in Virginia, Alexandria, 1960.

TITLE INDEX OF FORSYTH'S WRITINGS

Address from the Chair, 1907.

Allegory of the Resurrection, An, 1902.

Apostolate of Negation, The, 1907.

Argument for Immortality is Drawn from the Nature of Love, The, 1885.

Atonement in Modern Religious Thought, The, 1899, 1900.

Attitude of the Church to the Present Unrest, The, 1910.

Auguste Bouvier, 'Le divin d'apres les apôtres' et "Paroles de foi et de liberté," 1883.

Authority and Theology, 1905.

Authority in Religion, 1909.

Baldwin Brown: A Tribute, a Reminiscence, and a Study, 1884.

Bring Us Not Into Temptation, 1903.

Calvinism and Capitalism, 1910.

Catholic Threat of Passive Resistance, The, 1906.

Chairman's Mantle, The, 1903.

Charter of Missions, The, 1903.

CHARTER OF THE CHURCH, THE, 1896.

Christ and the Christian Principle, 1911.

Christ at the Gate, 1908.

CHRIST ON PARNASSUS: LECTURES ON ART, ETHIC, AND THEOLOGY, 1911.

Christianity and Nationality, 1913.

CHRISTIAN ETHIC OF WAR, THE, 1916.

CHRISTIAN PERFECTION, 1899.

Church and Society, The, 1913.

Church and Society--Alien or Allied?, The, 1913.

Church and State, 1914.

Church and the Nation, The, 1914.

Church and University, 1906.

Church, Ministry and Sacraments, 1919.

Church, State, Dogma and Education, 1906.

CHURCH, THE GOSPEL AND SOCIETY, THE, 1962.

Church, the State, the Priest, and the Future, The, 1903.

Churches, Sects, and Wars, 1915.

Church's One Foundation, The, 1906.

Coleridge's *Ancient Mariner*. An Exposition and Sermon from a Modern Text, undated.

Congregationalism and Reunion, 1919.

CONGREGATIONALISM AND REUNION, TWO LECTURES, 1952.

POSITIVE PREACHING
AND MODERN MIND

By

P. T. FORSYTH, M.A., D.D

THE LYMAN BEECHER LECTURE ON
PREACHING, YALE UNIVERSITY, 1907

SECOND EDITION

THE PICKWICK PRESS
Pittsburgh, Pennsylvania
1981

τῷ ἀγαπήσαντί με καὶ παραδόντι ἑαυτὸν
ὑπὲρ ἐμοῦ

PREFACE

MAY I remind those who honour me by looking into this book that it consists of lectures, and that I have been somewhat careful not to change that form in print. Also, as the audience consisted chiefly of men preparing for the Ministry, it was inevitable that I should speak chiefly *ad clerum*. I trust this may help to excuse a shade of intimacy that might not befit address to a wider public, possibly something of a pulpit style at times, and a few repetitions. I need hardly add that the lectures were abbreviated in delivery.

I should also like to mention that as the lectures were given to a post-graduate audience I have taken more for granted in places than if I had been speaking to a more general assembly. While I am grateful for any who will listen to me, I confess I have kept in view rather students than mere readers—those who do not resent an unfamiliar word, who are attracted rather than impatient towards a dark saying, who find the hard texts the mighty ones, and who do not grudge stopping the carriage to examine a mysterious cave or to consider a great prospect.

It has cost the writer much to find his way so far. And he has yet a long way to go. But he believes he has found the true and magnetic North. And a voice is in his ears, καὶ σύ ποτε ἐπιστρέψας στήρισον τοὺς ἀδελφούς σου. This voice he would obey—humbly to it, respectfully to his brethren. How grateful he is to the great university of Yale for giving him such an opportunity of service, and providing him with a world-pulpit in such an apostolic succession as his predecessors make.

I have to thank my colleague, Rev. Prof. Bennett, D.D., Litt. D., for valuable assistance with proofs, and my pupil, Mr. Sydney Cave, M.A., B.D., for the table of contents.

CONTENTS

ix

Contents

Contents

II. Its recognition of modern principles. (1) The autonomy of the individual ; (2) The Social Idea ; (3) the development of personality ; (4) the distinction between practical and theoretical knowledge ; (5) the need of popularisation ; (6) the principle of Evolution ; (7) the passion for reality.

III. The issue not really critical but dogmatic—This illustrated in the case of the Bible and of Christ.

The vital need throughout of an experimental foundation in grace—A living, positive faith in a historic gospel.

VIII

The modern ethical note—An ethicized Christianity means a more positive doctrine of the Cross—The moral paradox of God's forgiveness—The primacy of the moral—The ethicizing of religion by the idea of the holy—The Cross as the consummation of holiness—Judgment as an essential factor in God's Holy Love—The analogy of Fatherhood and its danger—The Cross as the centre of the Kingdom—So Christianity, as supremely moral, appeals to a society intent on moral righteousness—But the preacher has his opportunity also in the moral weakness of society.

IX

The inadequacy of the common view of God's benignant Fatherhood—Popularity not the test of the Gospel—The complexity of the soul's situation—Sin as enmity to God —God's love brought home not by a spectacle but by a finished universal act—An ethicized Theology must emphasize holiness—Christ as God forgiving—The need of moral mordancy, of iron in our blood—The Cross not a martyrdom but God's decisive and creative act—Christ not only redeemed, He atoned—The element of judgment, the wrath of God—The Atonement to God—This aspect of propitiation essential to the final prospects of Christianity—Conclusion.

THE PREACHER AND HIS CHARTER

I

The Preacher and his Charter

It is, perhaps, an overbold beginning, but I will venture to say that with its preaching Christianity stands or falls. This is surely so, at least in those sections of Christendom which rest less upon the Church than upon the Bible. Wherever the Bible has the primacy which is given it in Protestantism, there preaching is the most distinctive feature of worship.

But, preaching a feature of worship! I will ask leave to use that phrase provisionally, till, at a later stage, I can justify the place of preaching as a part of the cultus, and not a mere appendix.

Preaching (I have said), is the most distinctive institution in Christianity. It is quite different from oratory. The pulpit is another place, and another kind of place, from the platform. Many succeed in the one, and yet are failures on the other. The Christian preacher is not the successor of the Greek orator, but of the Hebrew prophet. The orator comes with but an inspiration, the prophet comes with a revelation. In so far as the preacher and prophet had an analogue in Greece it was the dramatist, with his urgent sense of life's guilty tragedy, its inevitable ethic, its unseen moral powers, and their atoning purifying note. Moreover, where you have the passion for oratory you are not unlikely to have an impaired style and standard of preaching. Where your object is to secure your audience, rather than your Gospel, preaching is sure to suffer. I will not speak of the oratory which is but rhetoric, tickling the audience. I will take both at their best. It is one thing to have to rouse or persuade people to do something, to put themselves into something; it is another to have to induce them to trust somebody and renounce themselves for him. The one is the political region of work, the other is the religious region of faith. And wherever a people is swallowed up in politics, the preacher is apt to be neglected; unless he imperil his preaching by adjusting himself to political or social methods of address. The orator, speaking generally, has for his business to make real and urgent the present world and its crises, the preacher a world unseen, and the whole crisis of the two worlds. The present world of the orator may be the world of action, or of art. He may speak of affairs, of nature, or of imagination. In the pulpit he may be what is called a practical preacher, or a poet-preacher. But the only business of the apostolic preacher is to make men practically realize a world unseen and spiritual; he has to rouse them not against

a common enemy but against their common selves ;
not against natural obstacles but against spiritual
foes ; and he has to call out not natural resources
but supernatural aids. Indeed, he has to tell
men that their natural resources are so inadequate
for the last purposes of life and its worst foes
that they need from the supernatural much more
than aid. They need deliverance, not a helper
merely but a Saviour. The note of the preacher
is the Gospel of a Saviour. The orator stirs men
to rally, the preacher invites them to be redeemed.
Demosthenes fires his audience to attack Philip
straightway ; Paul stirs them to die and rise with
Christ. The orator, at most, may urge men to
love their brother, the preacher beseeches them
first to be reconciled to their Father. With
preaching Christianity stands or falls because it
is the declaration of a Gospel. Nay more—far
more—it is the Gospel prolonging and declaring
itself.

§

I am going on the assumption that the gift to
men in Christianity is the Gospel deed of God's
grace in the shape of forgiveness, redemption,
regeneration. *Im Anfang war die That.* But I
should perhaps define terms.

By grace is not here meant either God's general
benignity, or His particular kindness to our failure
or pity for our pain. I mean His undeserved and
unbought pardon and redemption of us in the face

6 The Preacher and his Charter

of our sin, in the face of the world-sin, under such moral conditions as are prescribed by His revelation of His holy love in Jesus Christ and Him crucified.

And by the Gospel of this grace I would especially urge that there is meant not a statement, nor a doctrine, nor a scheme, on man's side ; nor an offer, a promise, or a book, on God's side. It is an act and a power : it is God's *act* of redemption before it is man's message of it. It is an eternal, perennial act of God in Christ, repeating itself within each declaration of it. Only as a Gospel done by God is it a Gospel spoken by man. It is a revelation only because it was first of all a reconciliation. It was a work that redeemed us into the power of understanding its own word. It is an objective power, a historic act and perennial energy of the holy love of God in Christ ; decisive for humanity in time and eternity ; and altering for ever the whole relation of the soul to God, as it may be rejected or believed. The gift of God's grace was, and is, His work of Gospel. And it is this act that is prolonged in the word of the preacher, and not merely proclaimed. The great, the fundamental, sacrament is the Sacrament of the Word.

What I say will not hold good if the chief gift to the world is the Church and its sacraments, instead of the work and its word. Wherever you have the ritual sacraments to the front the preacher is to the rear, if he is there at all.

In Catholicism worship is complete without a sermon ; and the education of the minister suffers accordingly. So, conversely, if the preacher is belittled the priest is enhanced. If you put back the pulpit, by the same act you put forward the altar. The whole of Christian history is a struggle between the apostle, i.e. the preacher, and the priest. The first Apostles were neither priests nor bishops. They were preachers, missionaries, heralds of the Cross, and agents of the Gospel. The apostolic succession is the evangelical. It is with the preachers of the Word, and not with the priestly operators of the work, or with its episcopal organisers. Our churches are stone pulpits rather than shrines. The sacrament which gives value to all other sacraments is the Sacrament of the living Word.

I note that the Catholic revival of last century is coincident with complaints elsewhere of the decay of preaching. And if this decay is not in the preaching itself, there is no doubt of the fact in regard to the pulpit's estimate and influence with the public. Even if the churches are no less full than before, the people who are there are much less amenable to the preached Word, and more fatally urgent for its brevity.

This coincides with the Catholic revival on the one hand, as I say, and with something to which I have not yet referred, on the other—I mean the decay among our churches of the personal use of the Bible. Preaching can only flourish

8 The Preacher and his Charter

where there is more than a formal respect for the Bible as distinct from the Church, namely, an active respect, an assiduous personal use of it, especially by the preacher. But to this point I shall have to recur.

The Bible is still the preacher's starting-point, even if it were not his living source. It is still the usual custom for him to take a text. If he but preach some happy thoughts, fancies, or philosophies of his own, he takes a text for a motto. It was not always so ; but since it became so it is a custom that is fixed. And this from no mere conservatism. The custom received ready, nay inevitable, confirmation from the Reformers. It corresponded to the place they gave the Bible over the Church, on the one hand, and the individual on the other. It is the outward sign of the objectivity of our religion, its positivity, its quality as something given to our hand. Even when we need less protection against the Church, we still need it against the individual, and often against the preacher. We need to be defended from his subjectivity, his excursions, his monotony, his limitations. We need, moreover, to protect him from the peril of preaching himself, or his age. We must all preach *to* our age, but woe to us if it is our age we preach, and only hold up the mirror to the time.

And not only so, not only do we adhere to texts, but there is a growing desire for expository preaching —for a long text, and the elucidation of a passage.

The public soon grow weary of topical preaching alone, or newspaper preaching, in which the week's events supply the text and the Bible only an opening quotation. And the new scholarship is making the Bible a new book, a new pulpit for the old Word, a new golden candlestick for the old light. Preachers are inspired by the historic freshness of it, as the public are interested by its new realism. It is a great recent discovery that the New Testament was written in the actual business and colloquial Greek of the day. And less than ever is the textual style of preaching like to die, or the Bible to cease to be the capital of the pulpit. Preaching has a connexion with the Bible which it has with no other book. For the Bible is the book of that Christian community whose organ the preacher is. Like the preacher, it has a living connexion with the community. Other books he uses, but on this he lives his corporate life. It is what integrates him into the Church of all ages. Preachers may, for the sake of change, devote their expositions on occasion to Tennyson, Browning, or Shakespeare. They may extract Christianity from modern art, or from social phenomena. They may do so in order to lay themselves alongside the modern mind. But they will be obliged to come back to the Bible for their charter, if they remain evangelical at all. If they cease to be that, of course, they may be driven anywhere and tossed.

§

But the great reason why the preacher must
return continually to the Bible is that the Bible
is the greatest sermon in the world. Above every
other function of it the Bible is a sermon, a κήρυγμα,
a preachment. It is the preacher's book because
it is the preaching book. It is still a book with an
organic unity of idea and purpose. I admit all the
truth intended when the Bible is called a library,
and part of it a national library. It was quite
needful that that fact should be strongly urged on us.
But when we have recognized the Bible as the literature of a nation, and subject to its literary and historical conditions, we soon recognize that that nation
had a providential function. It was the people
of the Word. It arose at God's hands to be the
preacher among the nations—with the preacher's
perishableness, but also the preacher's immortality,
with the fugitiveness of the preacher, but with the
perpetuity of his message. And this message is
one, definite, and positive. It runs through the
whole literature of that nation (with one or two
exceptions, like Esther or the Canticles, which do
not destroy the general fact). The library is a
unity in virtue of this historic message and purpose. It is not nationalist. It is not a history
of Israel, but it is a history of redemption. It
is not the history of an idea, but of a long
divine act. Its unity is a dramatic unity of
action, rather than an aesthetic unity of struc-

ture. It is a living evolving unity, in a great historic crescendo. It does not exist like a library in detached departments. It has an organic and waxing continuity. It is after all a book. It is a library, but it is still more a canon. You may regard it from some points as the crown of literature, for it contains both the question and the answer on which all great literature turns. It is the book, as Christ is the person, where the seeking God meets and saves the seeking man.

The crown of literature is thus a collection of sermons. It is one vast sermon. It is so much more than literature, because it is not merely powerful; it is power. It is action, history, it is not mere narrative, comment, embellishment or dilution. It makes history more than it is made by history. There is no product of history which has done so much to produce history as the Bible. Surely that which had in it so much of the future had also in it more than the mere past. It had the Creator.

It is akin to the press on one side, as to the pulpit on the other. Its value is in its news more than in its style. It is news to the world from foreign parts—but, remember, from foreign parts unseen, which ought not to have been so foreign to us as they are. And it is akin to the world of action more than the world of sentiment. It deals more with men's wills than with their taste, with conscience more than with imagination. It is the greater literature because it never aimed at being literature, but at preaching something, doing something, or getting something done. It is so precious for the preacher because it is so practical. It is a " *Thatpredigt.*" It is history preaching.

§

How far is the Bible a record? It has been common of late to speak of the Bible, not as God's Word, but as the *record* of God's Word. The Word, it is said, is the living Word, Christ. There is much truth in this view also. It is another symptom of the great historical movement which has passed over religion, the great restoration of the person of Christ to its place in Christianity. It is one side of the movement which sends us back to the historical study of the Bible, as the Reformers went back to its grammar. But it is only a partial truth after all. It is only in a modified sense that we can speak of the books of the Bible as historical records. They are not records in the strict historian's sense of archives. They are not documents of the first value for scientific history. There is hardly a book of the Bible that is a document in that severe sense. And certainly the object of the Bible was not scientific history, as we know that science. Why is it that we find it hard, if not impossible, to write a biography of Christ? Because the object of the New Testament writers was not to provide biographical material but evangelical testimony. The New Testament (the Gospels even), is a direct transcript, not of Christ, but of the preaching about Christ, of the effect produced by Christ on the first generation, a transcript of the faith that worshipped Him. It is a direct record not of Christ's biography but of Christ's Gospel, that is to say of Christ neither as delineated, nor as reconstructed, nor as analysed, but *as preached*. The inmost life of Christ we can never reach. We cannot reconstruct the nights of prayer.

Well, is this not to say that the first value of the Bible is not to historical science but to evangelical faith, not to the historian but to the gospeller? The Bible is, in the first instance, not a voucher but a preacher. It is not a piece of evidence. The Gospels are not like articles in the dictionary of National Biography, whose first object is accuracy, verified at every point. They are pamphlets, in the service of the Church, and in the interest of the Word. They are engrossed with Christ, not as a fascinating character, but as the Sacrament, the Gospel, to us of the active grace of God. The only historical Christ they let us see is not a great figure Boswellised, but a risen eternal Christ preached, a human God declared by His worshippers. They are homiletical biography, not psychological; they are compiled on evangelical rather than critical principles. The stories told are but a trifling selection, not chosen to cast light on the motives of a deep and complex character, but selected entirely from a single point of view—that of the crucified, risen, exalted, preached Saviour. (See p. 38.) There is not an idyllic feature in them that is not imbedded in the great doom, and sobered by the supreme tragedy whose conquest made the Church. It is the Saviour born to die that is the burthen of the New Testament; it is the Redeemer, not the Messiah, not the champion of humanity, not the spiritual hero, not the greatest of the prophets, not the exquisite saint. The history is history with a purpose, history unto salvation, history unto edification, history made preacher, history whose object is to create not an opinion on our part but a determination. The story is on a theme. It is there for the Gospel. It is inferior as art, but it is mighty as action. It is a crisis of spiritual action. It is preaching, I repeat. The object is not proof, but life. The appeal is not to intelligence but to will. These things " are written that ye might believe that Jesus is Messiah and Son of God, and that believing ye might have life in His name." They spoke from faith to faith. They were not proofs to convince the world. Neither the miracles nor the Gospels were advertisements. They were not evidences. They were there to feed rather than to fascinate, to edify more than defend, and to confirm more than to convince. They were material to build up the Church. They spoke to believers. They appeal not to an estimate of evidence but to a fault of will, to our need of a Saviour and our experience of grace. They belong to the literature of power, not of knowledge. The news they bring is of an impressive creative act,

and not a cold cause, or a still fact. Their inspir
ation is not in regard to mere truth, but to
the truth as it is in Jesus, to Jesus as the Truth,
to truth as a personality, and a personality
gathered up in a universal redeeming act.

It is inspiration, therefore, which does not guarantee every statement or view, even of an apostle.
The inspiration is not infallible in the sense that
every event is certain or every statement final.
You may agree with *what* I say without agreeing
with *all* I say. The Bible's inspiration, and its
infallibility, are such as pertain to redemption and
not theology, to salvation and not mere history. It
is as infallible as a Gospel requires, not as a system.
Remember that Christ did not come to bring a
Bible but to bring a Gospel. The Bible arose afterwards from the Gospel to serve the Gospel. We do
not treat the Bible aright, we do not treat it with
the respect it asks for itself, when we treat it as a
theologian, but only when we treat it as an apostle, as
a preacher, as the preacher in the perpetual pulpit of
the Church. It is saturated with dogma, but its
writers were not dogmatists ; and it concerns a
Church, but they were not ecclesiastics. The Bible,
the preacher, and the Church are all made by the
same thing—the Gospel. The Gospel was there
before the Bible, and it created the Bible, as
it creates the true preacher and the true sermon
everywhere. And it is for the sake and service
of the Gospel that both Bible and preacher exist.
We are bound to use both, at any cost to

tradition, in the way that gives freest course to the Gospel in which they arose.

The Bible, therefore, is there as the medium of the Gospel. It was created by faith in the Gospel. And in turn it creates faith among men. It is at once the expression of faith and its source. It is a nation's sermon to the race. It is the wonder-working relic of a saint-nation which was the living organ of living revelation. What made the inspiration of the book? It was the prior inspiration of the people and of the men by the revelation. Revelation does not consist of communications about God. It never did. If it had it might have come by an inspired book dictated to one in a dream. But revelation is the self-bestowal of the living God, his self limitation in the interest of grace. It is the living God in the act of imparting Himself to living souls. It is God Himself drawing ever more near and arrived at last. And a living God can only come to men by living men. Inspiration is the state of a soul, not of a book—of a book only in so far as the book is a transcript of a soul inspired. It was by men that God gave Himself to men, till, in the fullness of time, He came, for good and all, in the God-man Christ, the living Word; in whom God was present, reconciling the world unto Himself, not merely acting through Him but present in Him, reconciling and not speaking of reconciliation, or merely offering it to us. He acted not only through Christ but in Christ. He who came was God the Son, and not a sinless saint dowered and guided by the Spirit. In Christ we have God Himself, and no mere messenger from God. That truth was the substantial victory gained by Athanasian theology for the Church once for all.

§

Now if this be so, that the Bible exists for the Gospel which created it, then this Gospel is the standard of all that the Bible contains. If the Bible is the great discourse, and may even be called a preacher above all else, then it is to be interpreted as a sermon is interpreted, and not as a dogmatic, nor as a protocol.

We do not treat a preacher fairly when we judge him by statements, logic, anecdotes, or phrases. We must judge him by his positive and effective message. The preacher claims to be thus understood. He protests bitterly against the mindless isolation of his *obiter dicta*, and the throwing up into large type of chance phrases. He asks that we will give much more attention to his message than to his methods. And if his methods eclipse his message he feels, or ought to feel, that he has failed. He has preached himself. His idiosyncrasy has stepped in front of his Gospel.

Well, what the preacher claims from the public in this way the Bible claims from the preacher. Measure it by its message, not its phrase, its style, its incidents, episodes, views, or faults.

The Bible is the preacher for preachers. It speaks

to them above all, and with a word and not a creed. It makes believers into preachers or agents in proportion as it lays hold of them. Its first congenial appeal is not to the scientific theologian. It handles his ideas, but it does not speak his methodic language. St. Paul, for instance, was no dogmatician in the sense of Aquinas or Melanchthon. He was comparatively careless about the correct form of his belief, what could now be called its orthodoxy (indeed he was the great heretic of his day) ; and he was lost in the experimental reality of it. He was the first of Christian theologians only because he was the greatest of Christian experimentalists. To express a reality so unspeakable he strained language and tortured ideas, which he enlisted from any quarter where he could lay hands on them. No, it is not to the scientific theologian, far less to the correct theologian, the orthodoxist, that the Bible first speaks. It is a preacher to preachers. And as the preacher's first concern is not dogma but Gospel, not creed but grace, so it is with the Bible. Every part of it is to be valued in the perspective of grace, in the proportion of faith in grace. It is all to be measured by its contribution to God's redeeming grace, by its effect as an agent of grace. The final criticism of the Bible is not the ' higher criticism ' but the highest, the criticism whose principle is God's supreme object in Bible, Church, or even Christ—the object of reconciling grace. The final criticism of it is neither literary nor scientific but evangelical, as the preacher must be. If the Bible is a preacher its first object is not to carry home divine truth but divine mercy. It is not formal but dynamic, not scientific but sacramental. The theologian has charge of the Gospel as truth, the preacher has it in his charge as grace. The very iteration of the word grace in my style only reflects the continuity, the dominance of the thing in our faith. The Bible, like its preacher, is not the organ of God to the scientific intelligence, but the sacrament of God to the soul, of the living God to living men, of the gracious God to lost men.

If we ask what is a modern Christian theology, it is the Gospel taking the age seriously, with a real, sympathetic and informed effort to understand it, in the interest of no confession, but always keeping a historic and positive salvation in the front, and refusing everything in any age that is incompatible with it. It takes its stand neither on the spirit of the age, nor on the Christian consciousness, nor on the Christian principle, but on the historic and whole New Testament Christ.

§

May I illustrate what I mean when I say that the final criticism of the Bible, as a preacher, is not the higher rationalism but the highest grace. The question of the Virgin Birth is one that already exercises many and is shortly bound to exercise many more. How is that question to be settled? It is generally admitted that if it were not for the opening chapters of Matthew and Luke no other parts of the Bible would leave it tenable, by direct evidence at least. Now the higher criticism claims the right to dismiss these early chapters, and to say whether they are integral with the rest of the Gospels in which they are incorporated ; or, if so, whether they represent the earliest truth, or a later tradition used by the evangelist. But supposing it came to be generally held that the story is integral to the literary whole of the book in which it occurs, that does not settle the question of fact. Such could only be the case if we agree beforehand that everything stated integrally in the Bible is historically true. Nor would the question be settled if we held that the story was believed by the Church at a stage earlier than the Gospels. That would settle it only if we agreed in advance that whatever was held by the Church of the first decades was true—including the explanation of epilepsy by demons. Or if, on the other hand, critics came to agree that the narrative was quite detachable from the rest of Matthew or Luke, that would not settle the question against its historicity. It could do so only if we agree in advance that nothing is historically true but what proceeded from the pen of a particular apostolic writer or writers. That is to say, the matter is not really to be settled by any decision of the literary critics, acting simply as critics. So also it might be shown not to be at the mercy of historical criticism either. The real settlement of the question lies farther within theological territory. It is really a theological question and not a

critical, as I hope later to show. The Virgin birth
is not a necessity created by the integrity and
infallibility of the Bible; it is a necessity created
(if at all) by the solidarity of the Gospel, and
by the requirements of grace. Was such a mode
of entry into the world indispensable for Christ's
work of redemption? If it was otiose to that work
then we can leave it to the methods of the critics.
But if it was essential to that work we must refuse
them the last word. If it was essential to the perfect
holiness of Christ's redeeming obedience, what is
unhappily called His sinlessness, then it must stand,
whatever the critics say. I am not here called on to
decide that question. I only quote it as an illustration of method, to show what is meant by saying that
there is a dogmatic criticism of the Bible higher
than what is called the higher. And it consists
in judging the parts of the Bible by its whole message
and action, in bringing every detail to this test—how
does it serve the one divine purpose which makes the
library a book and the book the Word—the purpose
of preaching saving grace?

This is actually Luther's test—does this or that
passage " ply Christ, preach Christ? " Is it in
solidary connexion, direct or indirect, with Him?
But the way I have ventured to put it, by saying the
Gospel instead of Christ, makes the issue a little
more distinct, perhaps, and the test more pointed.
As I said, we cannot have a biography of Christ.
We cannot easily tell what is or is not congruous with
a character of whose psychology we know so little

as the Gospels tell us. But we do know above all
other knowledge the scope, object, and act of Christ's
person. We do know the Christ of our faith better
than any Christ of our constructive imagination, for
all its precious results from modern methods. He was
gathered up for us, as for God, in the consummation
of the Cross. And the Cross is there as the agent
of God's grace in redemption. Christ was born to
die. To preach Christ really means to preach the
Cross where His person took effect as the incarnation
and the agent of the atoning grace of God. For this
therefore, I say that Christ Himself existed—not to
present us with the supreme spiritual spectacle of
history, but to achieve the critical thing in history.
The Gospel is an act of God, gathered in a point but
thrilling through history, and it calls for an act, and
inspires it. Its preaching must therefore be an act, a
" function " of the great act. A true sermon is a
real deed. It puts the preacher's personality into
an act. That is his chief form of Christian life and
practice. And one of his great difficulties is that he
has to multiply words about what is essentially a
deed. If you remember what men of affairs think
about the people who make set speeches in committee
you will realize how the preacher loses power whose
sermons are felt to be productions, or lessons, or
speeches, rather than real acts of will, struggles with
other wills, and exercises of effective power. The
Gospel means something done and not simply
declared. For this work Christ existed on earth.
And to give this work effect Bible and Church alike

exist. We treat the Church as plastic to that work
and its fulfilment, do we not ? That is the true
Church, and the true form of Church, which gives
best effect to the Gospel. So also we must treat the
Bible with much flexibility. The test and the trial
of all is the grace of God in Jesus Christ, and in
Him as crucified. Everything is imperishable which
is inseparable from that.

§

The Bible, I have said, is the preacher to the
preacher. But I shall be met perhaps by the observation that the preacher to the preacher is the Holy
Spirit. It is an observation quite just. But it
does not impair the force of what I have said. What
is the principle of the Spirit's action on men ? The
Spirit is so much the spirit of Christ that we find in
Paul's mouth the expression, " the Lord the Spirit "
—the Lord is the Spirit. I will not discuss the hard
question thus raised as to the relation between the
kingly Christ in Heaven and the Holy Spirit. For
my purpose I may speak of the Spirit's action as the
action of Christ in that heavenly kingship of His,
which is the completion of His work as prophet
and priest. The same Christ as on earth was both
prophet and priest is in Heaven king also, by His
finality and perfection in both. He does not sit on
a height apart, retired, and simply watch, with a
parental eye, the progress of the great kingdom He
set on its feet, the great concern He founded and left
to run. He still continues his prophetic and priestly
work in a supreme and kingly way. But how,

precisely ? Is it merely by the emission of waves of spiritual force, supplementary and propulsive to the fundamental work of His earthly life ? It is sometimes so viewed, as if the Spirit were a new and even a superior dispensation. We find the tendency both among the dogmatic pietists and among the undogmatic Christians who renounce theology in the interest of the Christian spirit or temper. In the history of the Church men and movements arise under a strong religious impulse which is either vague or extravagant. It is vague as being undefined by the positive principles of faith ; or it is extravagant as being uncontrolled by the authority of a historic revelation. Certain mystic movements have their very vogue by their independence of the Bible. They gratify our modernity, our subjectivity, our spurious spirituality, our impressionism. Some Christianized forms of natural piety manage to combine much human grace and religious sympathy with little personal use of Scripture. And other movements in the direction of a superior sanctity seem, at least at times, to associate sanctification much less directly with justification than the Bible does. But the action of the glorified Christ is always represented in the New Testament not as making new departures, or issuing fresh waves, but as giving fresh effect to His own historic work, keeping it a personal act, and preventing it from being a mere spiritual process. One of the greatest actions of the Spirit in modern thought is to preserve Christ's influence from being detached from his act and turned into a moral process. His spirit brings the act to remembrance ; or takes of the work of Christ and shows it to the Church. He leads the Church into all truth, but it is the truth as it is in the whole Jesus. And nothing is more shallow and pretentious than the attempt to reform Church or creed by giving the Bible the go-by, or pooh-poohing its theology in the interest of an aesthetic or an idealist construction of religion.

This return to history is especially shown at the great crises of the Church's career, whether you take Luther, Wesley, or Schleiermacher. The Lord from Heaven forces the soul of the Church into a closer contact with His historic person and work, and gives a deeper penetration of it. It is the only condition of real revival. It is the inspiration of evangelical preaching in the great sense of the word. It was particularly the case with Paul, from whom these other great names have their apostolic succession. He fastened on the Cross, if I might venture so to say, and pressed the whole divine life out of it for our healing. And the history is our great protection now against both an idealism and an extravagance which readily run down into aloofness, feebleness, and futility. It keeps faith from the sentimentalism which to-day so easily besets it, by keeping it in the closest contact with the focus of the world's moral realism in the Cross. Our aim must be an ever fresh immersion in the Bible, an immersion both scholarly and experimental. We see deeper into it than our deep fathers did, though on other lines ; for the new age

has new eyes. It has new needs, and need makes
wit. Through the ever-deepening need of man
Christ is pressing His one personal, fundamental, and
final work into our souls. He unfolds and freshens
its searching meaning and eternal power. New men
and new occasions do but elicit from Him fresh
wealth of resource. But it all comes from the Bible
Christ, from the Christ of the Cross. The more He
changes the more He is the same. Stability is not
stiffness. Jesus, the same yesterday, to-day,
and for ever, is not a dead identity, a monument that we leave behind, but a persistent personality that never ceases to open upon us. All
permanent work in the kingdom is His work, of
His initiative and not only in His succession. It
is because He acts on us from the other world that
that world is not a mist, a riddle, or a desert for us,
and we are not aliens there. But from there He
acts on us through what He was and did in history
once for all. Our real and destined eternity goes
round by Nazareth to reach us. What abides in
history is not the impression He made, nor a
Church's report. But it is His historic self, prophetic
and priestly still in the kingly way of eternity. He
is born again in each soul that is born anew.
And those who preach are the channels and agents
of the preaching, praying Christ, working from His
spiritual world, but working still through Jerusalem, through the Bible. If it is not so our
Protestant doctrine of Scripture, its constant use,
free function, and first necessity for every soul, is
a mistake and an unreality.

§

But if the Bible is the supreme preacher to the preacher, if it is through the Bible and its gospel above all that the Holy Ghost works upon him, how is the preacher to preach the Bible? Is his relation to it suggestive or expository? Is he to read in, or read out? Is he to preach whatever it may strike from his mind, or what his faith truly finds in it? Is he to treat it as a jewelled mass of facets of trembling lights, or as the living source of a positive revelation? Is it a huge brilliant, finely cut, afire with all kinds of rich and mystic hues, or is it a sun which issues the energy of the new world more even than its light? Is the preacher's work to lead the people into a larger modern world of suggestion which the Bible, without creating, has yet the power to stir, or shall he lead them into the Bible's own great renewing heart? There is no doubt the modern man inhabits a world larger in some ways than the Bible view of the cosmos or of man, a world of conception not due to the Bible but rather to art, science, exploration, industry and the like. And the Bible does possess on its part, in many words and phrases, that feature of inspiration which we might call glancing lights, as distinct from penetrative power, the flash rather than the force of the Spirit's sword. The book of Job, for instance, apart from its place in the history of moral revelation, has an extraordinary modernity both in theme and phrase. It is full of angles of reflection of the modern mind.

All that is true. But our whole view of the relation of the Bible to the Gospel must be changed if we hold that that *suggestive* power is the main feature of the Bible, or its main function, that the Bible is there like a work of art, *nimium lubricus adspici*, offering, like a bird's neck, a play of fleeting hues for every man to seize what he has affinity to find. The Bible does not appeal to our affinities so much as to our needs, nor to our ingenuity so much as to our penetration, nor to our spiritual fancy so much as to our faith. To treat the Bible chiefly in that casual way is to return by another route to the old textual, atomistic, individualist fashion of dealing with it, the old, unhistoric, and often fantastic Biblicism. Whereas one of the great tasks of the preacher is to rescue the Bible from the textual idea in the mind of the public, from the Biblicist, atomist idea which reduces it to a religious scrap book, and uses it only in verses or phrases. There is a true place for such a use, but it has monopolized the Bible with the general public ; and that is not right. The Bible is much more than a collection of spiritual apophthegms, or the gnomic *reliquiae* of moral sages. And a great part of the preacher's work is to rescue the Bible from this treatment, which is largely due to textual preaching, and is part of the price we pay for it. He must cultivate more the free, large, and organic treatment of the Bible, where each part is most valuable for its contribution to a living, evangelical whole, and where that whole is articulated into the great course

of human history. This is one of the benefits we
learn from the study of comparative religion, and
particularly from the work of the new religious-
historic school, when rightly used. But at first it
will be less popular than the more fanciful treatment
in which the public loves to roam and pick up the
stray gifts that belong to whoever can find. Their
right is not here denied if it be kept in its due place,
which is the second, not the first. Who can deny the
Bible's fragmentary and suggestive power ? Who
should refuse it in private meditation ? Who would
forbid textual preaching ? But for the public purposes of Church and ministry there is another and
higher point of view. The Bible is primarily there
for a single and public purpose, for a historic, social,
and collective purpose, for a purpose of the race.
It is there not as a fountain of stray suggestion
but as a channel of positive revelation and a source
of spiritual authority. Bible preaching means leading people into the Bible and its powers. It is
not leading them out of the Bible into subjectivities,
fancies, quips, or queries. The Bible has a world
and a context of its own. It has an ethos, if not
a cosmos, of its own. It cannot simply be assigned
a leading place among the literatures of the world,
or given the hegemony of those fine forces of the
human spirit " bound to get to God." It has a
place far beyond what it takes in the history of
religion, if we think of religion only as the Godward
projection of man. It has also a supreme, a
solitary, place of its own in the action of revelation,

thinking of revelation " as the manward movement of God." It not only stirs our opinion as
another religion might do : it demands our decision,
our selves. The ethos of the Bible is beyond our
cosmos, however largely you construe that cosmos,
though you extend it to all modern dimensions.
And not only so, but it represents the God of the
cosmos. If it is to be integrated with the cosmos
at all, it is as the final purpose always controls
the evolving process, and the drift the context.

When I speak of Biblical context I am not thinking
on the mere textual scale. I mean the context of the
whole spiritual order in which the Bible is imbedded.
It is necessary, of course, for any preacher who
would deal seriously with the verse of his text
to study and handle it in its context. But what is
true of a text from the Bible is truer still of the whole
Bible as a text. It can be truly and fruitfully
studied only in its moral context of history. And
by that again I do not merely mean either the context of each passage in the history of Israel, or the
whole book's context in the history of religion, in its
relation to other religions, other contemporary or
previous systems amid which it arose. Great is the
light that comes from that source, and it entails some
change in divers of our interpretations. But there is
such a thing as the Bible's evangelical context, its
organic moral relevancy to the conscience of Humanity, and I mean that. I mean its function in the actual
moral condition of the total perennial human soul,
in the great tissue and issue of human destiny. I

mean the whole moral situation which Christianity reveals in man as truly as it reveals the holy grace of God. I speak of the moral context of the Bible as a whole in the race's conscience—the human sin which the holy Saviour casts into the deeper shade, the lostness revealed by the Gospel that finds. In respect of the cosmos, whether of nature, the soul or society, the Bible may be very suggestive ; and it may give rise to many theologoumena, some speculative, some merely fantastic, as most amateur theologoumena are. The Bible is like the United States (will you pardon this glancing light ?), the richest ground in the world for every variety of " crank." But in respect of the ethos, in relation to the fundamental moral condition of the race, the Bible is much more positive for conscience than suggestive for fancy. It has a definite message and a central task. It has something imperative, which overrules all the suggestions of fantasy or ingenuity ; and something crucial which transcends the mere play of thought, or the mere practice of poetry. It compels an attitude, a choice, a line to be taken. Its reality appeals to our reality in will. It has at its core something which demands to be met actively, and crucially if need be, something that closes with history in moral conflict. It has a Gospel, nay *the* Gospel, for the worst condition of the whole energetic race. It has mankind's inevitable word and its eternal destiny.

§

It is that word that the preacher must bring to the

people. It is in that word he must himself live;
especially with historic study, avoiding the artificial
paradigms and surface "railways" that disfigure its
meaning to the untaught. The Dutch gardeners do
the Bible as much harm as the people who but
pick the flowers. Let the preacher's suggestion teem
by all means, as it will teem, in the quickened vitality
given to his personal resources by the Word of Life.
Let the gift of his fancy be stirred up, as well as all
his other gifts, by this life beyond all gifts. But let
every suggestion keep its true place in the economy
and proportion of faith. Let it wear the clear livery
of the Gospel, and conspire to lighten and magnify
that. For instance if, as the preacher reads the words
"He shall show you an upper room furnished," it
strikes him with a flash that Christ's Gospel not only
lights up the ideal world over him but stocks it with
a content of positive truth for our spiritual dwelling
and use, by all means let him preach a sermon to that
effect from the text. But let it be clear that he is
using some sacred fancy in so doing. And let him
realize that such a treatment of the Bible is on a
very different footing from that which he employs
if he preach on central words like these : " Being
justified by faith we have peace with God through
our Lord Jesus Christ." It is into the Bible world
of the eternal redemption, that the preacher must
bring his people. This eternal world from which
Christ came is contemporary with every age. To
every age it is equally near, and it is equally authoritative for every age, however modern. It is never

antiquated in its final principles and powers. The only preaching which is up to date for every time is the preaching of this eternity, which is opened to us in the Bible alone—the eternal of holy love, grace and redemption, the eternal and immutable morality of saving grace for our indelible sin.

It is not the preacher's prime duty then to find happy texts for the exposition of modern thought. Nor must he sink the Gospel to a revelation which puts people in a good humour with themselves by declaring to them that the great divine message is the irrepressible spirituality of human nature. It is an inversion of his work if he begin with Christ and enlarge into Goethe. Let him begin with Goethe, if he will, so that he go on to enlarge into Christ. Let him learn from the first part of Faust; he has nothing to learn from the second. Let him state the problem as powerfully as Shakespeare left it, but let him answer it with the final answer Christ left. No genius has or can have it but from Christ. For He is the answer that they but crave. And they but state, as only genius can, the human tragedy which it is Christ's to retrieve.

§

But the preacher who tries to follow this advice will find himself in one great difficulty. The Bible may be his text book, but it has ceased to be the text book of his audience. The Bible is not read by the Christian, or even by the churchgoing, public as a means of grace greater even than churchgoing. Our people, as a rule, do not read the Bible, in any sense which makes its language more familiar and dear to them than the language of the novel or the press. And I will go so far as to confess that one of the chief miscalculations I have made in the course of my own ministerial career has been to speak to congregations as if they did know and use the Bible. I was bred where it was well known and loved, and I have spent my ministerial life where it is less so. And it has taken me so long to realize the fact that I still find it difficult to adjust myself to it. I am long accustomed to being called obscure by many whose mental habits and interests are only literary, who have felt but a languid interest in the final questions of the soul as the New Testament stirs them, who treat sin as but lapse, God's Grace as if it were but love, and His love as if it were but paternal kindness. At first I believed I was obscure, and I took pains to be short in the sentence and unadorned in style. But I found my critics still puzzled. And I have come to think the obscurity is at least in some degree due to the fact that while I am attracted by such matters beyond all else, I am often dealing with people to whom they are not only strange but irritating. They have applied to religion what William Morris applied to life, " Love is enough." They have given a Christian varnish to what in him was mainly pagan, but they have not really stepped out of his natural world. They have risen to locate the affections in God ;

but they have not realized faith as the inroad, the uprise in us of a totally new world, Christianity as a new creation, and the new life as a new birth. Grace for them is only love exercised on the divine scale not in the divine style, not under the conditions of holiness and sin. They read in the heart more than in the Bible.

The old Protestant principle, therefore, no longer rules the relation of preacher and people. They are not spoken to from their Bible as they are from their preacher. Consequently they do not easily find the thing they like in the preacher who lives in his Bible. And, on the other hand, they are unable to exercise on the preacher the check of personal experience of the Bible and first-hand knowledge of it, as they did in the days of the great classic preachers. But that is the habit in the people which makes great preachers in the pulpit. And it is that principle that is the basis of the people's place, the place of the laity in a Protestant Church. Anything else is in principle Catholic. It is a Catholic treatment of the Bible to leave it in the hands of the minister alone. And, unless there be a change, it is to that that Protestantism is coming. Outside an evangelical Protestantism, amply construed, there is nothing for us but Catholicism. For general Atheism is permanently impossible. I trust you will not here think me extravagant. The final action of a principle, to those disaccustomed to principles, is sure to seem fanciful. And I am only stating the action of one of those deeper principles which in the end form the logic of history, and override all the tactics of the hour. And the principle is that where Protestantism falls into the Catholic treatment of the Bible, namely its disuse by the laity, we are rapidly getting ready for the Catholic idea of the Church, and the Catholic construction of the priest. To restore to the people an intelligent and affectionate use of the Bible is a service to Protestantism far more needed than those violent and ill-informed denunciations of the priest which are so easy and so cheap.

§

Bible preaching then means that we adjust our preaching to the people's disuse of the Bible. We have to regain their interest in it. It is, therefore, not the preaching of doctrine with proof passages. It is not preaching which does the Bible the lip homage of taking a text. Nor is it simply preaching historic facts on the one hand, or personal experience on the other. But it is the preaching of those facts and gifts of grace which are experimentally verifiable and creative of experience. It is only on points so verifiable that the Bible can be doctrinally used by the laity. A fact like the Virgin Birth is not at all on the same footing as the Resurrection of Christ, who is met as the risen Lord by His disciples to this day. Christianity is not the religion of a book, though it is a book religion. Nor is it the religion of a Church, though it is a Church religion. But it is the religion of a Gospel and a grace. These are the facts that make the Church. Doctrine as doctrine is a precious and indispensable possession of the Church, but it was not such doctrine that made the Church. Neither ideas nor truths could do that, but only persons and powers. Nor does such doctrine make the great changes of the Church. The Reformation was not a reformation of theology, but of faith. It is remarkable how little of the theology it changed in its first stage. It was the renewed action, not of truth, but of grace. It was the greatest of evangelical revivals. That is why it re-discovered the Bible. It was not the Bible that lighted up grace for Luther, but Grace to his needy soul lighted up the Bible. Biblical preaching preaches the Gospel and uses the Bible, it does not preach the Bible and use the Gospel.

For the Gospel the Bible must be used. The minister must so live in it that he wears it easily. One reason why people are repelled from it is that the preachers cannot carry it with easy mastery. They are in Goliath's armour. Now the ideal ministry must be a Bibliocracy. It must know its Bible better than any other book. Most Christians hardly know their Bible at first hand at all. They treat it with respect, no doubt. They keep a great Bible in the house ; but it is on a little table, not very steady, in the parlour window, and it has stiff clasps. It is in the room least used ; it carries a vase of once pretty flowers ; and it gets in the way of the rich lace curtains. Which is all an allegory. Some preachers know it only in the way of business, as a sermon quarry. But the true ministry must live on it. We must speak to the Church not from experience alone, but still more from the Word. We must speak from within the silent sanctuary of Scripture. We do not realize always how eager people are to hear preaching which makes the Bible wonderful by speaking from its very interior, as men do who live in it and wonder themselves. I do not believe in verbal inspiration. I am with the critics, in principle. But the true minister ought to find the words and phrases of the Bible so full of spiritual food and felicity that he has some difficulty in not believing in verbal inspiration. The Bible is the one Enchiridion of the preacher still, the one manual of eternal life, the one page that glows as all life grows dark, and the one book whose wealth rebukes us more the older we grow because we knew and loved it so late.

Note to p. 13.
"The first Church troubled about 'the real Jesus' only in so far as suited the Jesus living for their faith. . . . Had Mark attempted or achieved such a model biography of Jesus as historical science demands his work would have been useless for religion."—Jülicher, *Neue Linien*, p. 71.

THE AUTHORITY OF THE
PREACHER

II

The Authority of the Preacher

I VENTURE here to state at once what I will go on
to explain, that the preacher is the organ of the only
real and final authority for mankind. He is its
organ, and even its steward ; but he is not its vicar,
except at Rome.

The question of the ultimate authority for mankind is the greatest of all the questions which meet
the West, since the Catholic Church lost its place
in the sixteenth century, and since criticism no
longer allows the Bible to occupy that place. Yet
the gospel of the future must come with the note
of authority. Every challenge of authority but
develops the need of it. And that note must sound
in whatever is the supreme utterance of the church,
in polity, pulpit, or creed. It seems clear, indeed,
unless the whole modern movement is to be simply
undone, that the Church must draw in the range of
its authority, and even Catholicism must be modified
if it is to survive. But the Church can never part
with the tone of authority, nor with the claim that,
however it may be defined, the authority of its

message is supreme. That is the very genius of an evangelical religion; for it declares that that which saves the world shall also judge the world, and it preaches the absolute right over us of the Christ who bought us—the active supremacy in conscience of our moral redemption. It is the absence of the note of authority that is the central weakness of so many of the churches; and it is the source of their failure to impress Society with their message for the practical ends of the Kingdom of God. It is useless to preach the Kingdom when we do not carry into the centre of life the control of a King. The first duty of every soul is to find not its freedom but its Master. And the first charge of every Church is to offer, nay to mediate, Him.

§

The authority of the preacher was once supreme. He bearded kings, and bent senates to his word. He determined policies, ruled fashions, and prescribed thought. And yet he has proved unable to maintain the position he was so able to take. He could not insure against the reaction which has now set in as severely as his authority once did. That reaction has long been in force; and to-day, however great may be his vogue as a personality, his opinion has so little authority that it is not only ignored but ridiculed. In that respect the pulpit resembles the press, whose circulation may be enormous, while elections, and such like events, show that the influence of its opinions is almost nil.

But between the press and the pulpit there is this mighty difference. The pulpit has a Word, the press has none. The pulpit has a common message and, on the strength of it, a claim, while the press has no claim to anything but external freedom of opinion and expression. The one has a Gospel which is the source of its liberty, the other has no Gospel but liberty, which in itself is no Gospel at all. Liberty is only opportunity for a Gospel. The true Gospels not only claim it, they create it. But, in itself, it is either the product of a Gospel, or a means thereto; it is not an end. It is no more an end than evolution is, which is only the process of working out an end that the mere process itself does not give, Liberty in itself is not an end; and it has only the worth of its end. The chief object of the liberty of the press is facts. It must be free to publish facts. But the pulpit has not merely a fact but a Word. The press is there for information, or for suggestion at most, it is not there for authority; but the pulpit is there with authority; and the news it brings is brought for the sake of the authority. The press may offer an opinion as to how the public should act, but the pulpit is there with a message as to whom the acting public must obey and trust. The press is an adviser, but the pulpit is a prophet; the press may have a thought, the pulpit must have a Gospel, nay a command. If I may use press language, the pulpit's news is there for the sake of the leader, the leader is not a mere opinion about the news. The Gospels are there for the sake of the Epistles, for the sake of the Gospel.

Therefore, the pulpit has an authority. If it have not, it is but a chair and not a pulpit. It may discourse, but it does not preach. But preach it must. It speaks with authority. Yet the authority is not that of the preacher's person ; it is not mere authoritativeness. For us that goes without saying. What does not go unsaid, what needs saying is, that the preacher's authority is not the authority even of his truth. In the region of mere truth there is no authority. Mere truth is intellectual, and authority is a moral idea bearing not upon belief but upon will and faith, decision and committal. (See Lect. VIII.) It is not statements that the preacher calls on us to believe. It is no scheme of statements. It is not views. It is not a creed or a theology. It is a religion, it is a Gospel, it is an urgent God. In the region of mere Theology we may be bold to say there is no authority ; the authority is all in the region of religion. The creed of the Church Catholic should have great prestige, but not authority in the proper sense. Belief, in the region of theology, is a matter of truth or truths ; it is science, simple or complex. And science knows no authority. But in the region of religion belief is faith. It is a personal relation. It is belief in a person by a person. It is self committal to him. With the heart man believeth unto salvation. It is a personal act towards a person. It is trust in that person, and response to the power of his act. It is soul answering soul, and act act, and choice choice. In science, knowledge is the relation of a person to a fact or law—to something inferior to a person, and therefore not his authority. But in faith knowledge (I shall show later that faith is an organ of knowledge) is the relation of a person to a person who is like us yet over us. It is a moral relation of obedience and authority.

The authority of the pulpit is thus a personal authority. Yet it is not the authority of the preacher's person, or even of his office. His office may demand much more respect than the fanatics of freedom allow, but it cannot claim authority in the strict sense. The personal authority of the pulpit is the authority of the divine person who is its burthen. It is an external authority, but it is the authority of an inward objective, living, saving God, before whose visitation the prophet fades like an ebbing voice, and the soul of the martyr cries invisible from under the altar of the Cross.

§

I know well the feelings which arise in many at the very mention of words like " authority " and " external." They are feelings of recalcitrance and resentment—often very blind. We are put upon the defence of our independence. It seems forgotten that the supreme thing in life must be uppermost, not merely in place but in dignity, not merely in position but in right, not as a stratum might be, but as a throne. It is not the soul's top storey but the soul's suzerain power. For the soul, and conscience, the words higher or lower mean authority or they mean nothing. Even in the celestial time when the Soul shall be in complete harmony with God the relation must always be worship, and therefore authority and obedience. The supreme thing is not a weight that lies on us but a crown that governs us and lifts us up for ever. Unless we frankly adopt the positivist position, where humanity is to itself not only a law but an object of worship, there must be an authority both for man and men. And as for the externality of it— surely if there be an authority it must be external. It must come to us, and not rise out of us. It must come down on man and not proceed from him. It is a word to our race, not from it. The content of our conscience descends on us, it is no projection of ours. It were less than conscience if it were ; for the law that we made we could unmake and the order we issued we could recall. Treat the autonomy of conscience as you will, but do not remove the accent from the *nomos* to the *autos*. If it be a *nomos* it is a product of more than ourselves, more than man—it is of God. Otherwise it would be but a self-imposed condition, from which at any time we might be self-released. And it could bind none, even while it remained binding, but him who had imposed it on himself. And then it would not be conscience but earnest whim.

But then, it is asked, is it not one of the greatest

and surest results of modern progress that, if there
be an authority, it must be inward, it must be in
the soul, it must be by consent ? Yes, indeed, that
is one of the greatest and best blessings of the modern
time. But do you realize what that means ?
Surely the more inward it is the more is it external.
The more we retire to our inner castle the more
we feel the pressure of the not-ourselves, and the
presence of our Overlord. The more spiritual we
are the more we are under law to another. To
internalize the authority is to subtilize it, and therefore to emphasize it ; for it is the subtler realities
that bear upon us with the most persistent, ubiquitous, and effective pressure. The more inward we
go the more external the authority becomes, just
because it becomes more of an authority, and more
unmistakably, irresistibly so.

If we were not so Philistine that the most accurate
words seem pedantic, the proper word would be
not external but objective. Because external has
come, for the man in the street, to mean outside
his own body, or his own family, or his own self-
will, his own individuality ; while what we are really
concerned with is outside our own soul, our own
personality. What we are suffering from is not
mere externality but unconquered inwardness, subjectivism, individualism, ending in egotism. It is
our subjectivism which gives externals their enslav-
ing power over us. If within us we find nothing
over us we succumb to what is around us. It is
a cure for our subjectivism that we need, a cure

for our egotism. And that is to be found in nothing physically external, nothing institutionally so, but only in an objective, moral and spiritual, congenial yet antithetic, in an objective to the ego, yea to the race, which objective alone gives morality any meaning. Our suzerain must indeed sit in the court of the Soul, but he must be objective there. What he is he must indeed be for the soul —the soul's *vis-à-vis*, which must be also soul. Soul is relative only to soul, will to will. But, while he is not anything else than soul, he is other than *my* soul. He is not *an* other, but he is *my* other. He is my objective. But objective he must be, no less than he must be mine. He is my authority, but it is not a heteronomy, it is no foreign rule. Any autonomy of mine is due to his congenial power, to the homonomy of his authority, to its kinship with my soul.

By all means then the divine authority must be inward—if we are sure what we mean, if we do not come to mean that we are our own authority—which I am afraid is the popular version with which the preacher has to contend. The authority must be inward, it is true. The modern preacher must accept that principle, and correct all its risks of perversion and debasement. His message must be more and more inward. But it must be *searchingly* inward. That is to say, it must be inward with the right of search, as an authority; and not simply as a servant, a suppliant, an influence, an impression, a sensibility. It must be above all else a moral authority,

having right and not mere influence or prestige, demanding action, obedience and sacrifice, and not merely echo, appreciation, stirrings, and thrills.[1]

Thus when we move the authority from an external church or book to the forum of the conscience, when in the face of humanity or society we claim to call our soul our own, we have not ended the strife ; we have but begun one more serious on another plane. And, in many cases, we have but opened the gates of confusion, and let loose the floods of inner tumult. The recognition of the inwardness,

---

[1] It must be a moral authority. The *grand être*, the oversoul, the totality of supreme being, call it what you will, which teaches us our place and conducts us to it, and so to our blessedness, must be moral in its nature. The law of being is a moral law. The nature of reality is not only experience, as the modern drift of thought teaches, but it is moral experience. It is a will's action. It is decision. Now religion is no exception to the universe of reality. That is not what is meant by its autonomy. Rather is it the key to that universe. It opens reality. It contains it. Religion is part of our consciousness. And consciousness is primary ; it is not deduced from any prior reality of another nature. It is part of reality. Reality has therefore the nature of consciousness. And consciousness is moral. For it is of the will in its nature. We are conscious of ourselves as will-powers. The great reality is thus a supreme will. And our recognition of it is an act of moral submission. That is, it is a relation of authority and obedience. And the preacher's word of grace to faith is thus all of a piece with the word of the universe to the Soul, with

> Der ewige Gesang,
> Der unser ganzes Lebenlang
> Uns heiser jede Stunde klingt.

in many cases, seems to destroy the authority. Perhaps it does so in most cases at first. We are too full of ourselves to desire another to rule over us. And even when we desire it there are few who are so familiar with their inner selves as to be able to distinguish with any certainty the shepherd's voice, amid the gusts or sighings of their own fitful selves.

§

The questions that arise are such as these :—

1. What is the inward authority, to which the claims of a Gospel, or its preacher, must be brought ? Is it the natural conscience, uneducated, and therefore (it is said) unsophisticated ? Is it the stalwart *Natur-kind* from the far West, whose pockets bulge with Walt Whitman ? Is it the amateur private judgment, so dear to the sturdy moralist of the street ? Is it a moral mother-wit, sitting with a hair-trigger at the centre of an individualism whose self-confidence is impregnable, and passing its prompt verdict upon everything done or devised ? There is no doubt about the popularity of this order of rationalism, especially among the more independent races, and their more unschooled strata. It is a claim, too, which a democratic Christianity does much to encourage. The pushing tradesman of a small town enters a theological discussion to say that he always wants a straight answer to a straight question ; and he is not going to be cowed by the people who understand it, or bent to a theological popery. But that the

supernatural eternal Gospel should be staked on an appeal to the healthy and untutored natural conscience is a view so far outgrown that perhaps it need not occupy us longer. Sociology teaches us that even the most self-sufficient man is not a self-made man, but he is made by centuries of heredity and ages of solidarity. And if Christianity meant healthy-mindedness, that itself would surely mean something more than the light of nature or the verdict of the decent pagan man. We may, moreover, take it that the authority of a holy Gospel cannot be proved to the natural man. The offence of the Cross has not ceased. It must first capture him and make him a supernatural man.

§

2. Then, is the adjudicating faculty which chooses our authority the natural conscience educated, when it has in some serious fashion gone to school ? Is it the natural conscience refined ? Is it the natural conscience stimulated by contact with historic and imaginative ideals, and thus developed to a nicer tact of judging the higher claims ? Well, no doubt, a moral teacher and hero like Socrates has a rich and rare power of rousing the conscience, and educating it to approve ideas it once ignored or condemned. He wins our admiration and trust. He elicits our personality. He stirs in us a mind as constant as his own. He quickens also our moral intelligence, and trains our moral discernment. And he does so by sympathy and not antagonism,

by an imperative which is congenial and not merely imperious, dialectic and not only dogmatic. He may rouse bitter hostility but he also rouses heroic friendship, insight, imitation, or obedience. Or, if he do not actually raise our self to his own height, at least he stirs in us the sense that we ought so to rise, and to become such a soul in our place and way. A moral nature is born, or he leaves us morally more than he found us.

It is here recognized, you note, that the appraising self must be educated in some due school ; it is not ready to our hand. The preacher would be then principally a formative pastor, tutor, teacher. He is educative rather than evangelical. His method is dialectic and maieutic rather than regenerative. He analyses our truth, and brings our best self to light, rather than creates a new man. But is his result, in this conception of him, always a success ? Does he lay more problems than he stirs ? Does he give us power to deal with final questions and command final answers ? Does he plant us on the rock of finality, where the problems range about a base which they cannot eat away ? Does he not rather stir new questions more urgent than the old ? Thus : " I ought to rise to that height. But how shall I ? I know I should, I do not know how I can. In this region I feel an impotence I feel nowhere else. I can master problems, but how am I to rise to tasks, and keep at their level ? I am a sinful man. My new ideal does as much to oppress me as to exalt me, and often much more. The more it teaches me to see,

the less I am able to do. The more it smiles on me
as my ideal, the less it seems as if it could ever
become mine. 'It is lovely, but it has no arms.'
It does not grasp, it does not save. O, wretched
man! How shall my ideal become my destiny,
and my vision my goal? How can my sinful
self become my true free moral self? I want a
power to give me not vision, nor truth, nor conviction alone, but myself. Yea, I want relief from
myself. I must be redeemed from myself into the
moral freedom I have now learned to crave.

> " 'O for a man to arise in me
> That the man I am may cease to be.' "

§

It is not with our moral freedom, you may mark,
as it is with our ordinary mental vision. Intellectual progress takes what it finds already to hand, and
builds on it. Thus each generation adds to the great
reef which is growing under the waves of time to a
new mental world. We take up science, discovery,
or invention, where our fathers left them. But it is
otherwise with our moral selves, and especially with
our spiritual selves. We have to start from the beginning, or very much nearer it than the intellect
does. There is little historic progress in the region
of the elemental humanities. Love, hate, jealousy,
valour, loyalty, awe, pity, or beauty, are substanti-
ally the same for us as they were for Homer and his
age. Man is very permanent in what most makes
him man. In the case of our central moral man,

for all the latent furniture of heredity, and all the long bias of evil, we can say of each soul—

> "He is the first that ever burst
> Into that silent sea."

What we have with each soul is rather a fresh case than a new development.   And so when God comes to us He brings more than a mere extension of our previous horizon, a supplement to nature, or a development of it.   It is not a mere enrichment of our previous mentality.   His is not the touch which unfolds the latent germ.   It is not merely a case of slitting our husk, or of eliciting the vitality.   It is not education.   It is revelation.   It is not giving effect to our native power, and enlarging us to the destined fulness of our hidden resource.   It is not the opulent expansion of our individuality.   That is all too romantic.   It is a fresh spontaneity of His, a new creation, a free gift.   It is a pure gift to our weakness, our need, our helplessness.   It is an absolute salvation, not an aid to our self-salvation. Our receptivity is room rather than faculty.   We receive a new life rather than gain a new facility. There is not an evolution so much as a new creation.

Between man and man it is otherwise.   What man does for man is on a basis of parity.   He tries to elicit what is latent in a common humanity. It is give and take on both sides.   The teacher may even gain more than the taught from acting upon him. But it is not so when one of the parties is God.   It is then a relation of disparity.   The Christian God at least is man's God in being his Saviour, i.e., in virtue of His difference from man rather than His identity. Christ always stood with God over against man. The object of God with man is not to elicit slumbering divinity, and kiss the sleeping beauty into life. Nor does He gain from us as the teacher does from the taught. God needs none of us as we all need Him. It is not give and take ; it is all giving on His part. In receiving anything from man He receives but what He gives, and in His life we live. Our synergist pride is quelled as we realize that. Our self-satisfaction has its saving rebuff. We are no partners with God, fellow-workers as we may be. Our best faith with all its works is purely the gift of God, because it is roused by His one gift, Christ. He receives man in no such sense as man receives Him. His work with us is much more than educative, more than maieutic. It is paternal, creative. The conscience before Him is in a state where education will not serve it. Merely develop sinful man, and in spite of all the good in him, you only have a greater sinner. The disparity of God and man is not gradual, it is not a matter of degree. And what God has to deal with is not our relative imperfection. He does not simply stoop to us as we keep doing our poor best to reach Him. He does not simply wait for us, and cheer us on with a tender remembrance of the time when He was at our stage and felt the need of a sympathetic father or even brother. The gulf between us is much more, even than the gulf between the creature and the Creator. Great as that distance might be it does not exclude communion. What ails us is not limitation but transgression, not poverty but alienation. It is the breach of communion that is the trouble—the separation, the hostility. We are not His counterparts but His antagonists. There is not only the distance. between Creator and creature, father and child in the natural sense ; but there is a vast and serious disturbance of even that relation. There is a huge dislocation. There is that in us and in our sin which is in its very essence intractable to all the processes of a reconciling idea ; something which, to the end, by its very nature, refuses to be taken up as a factor into the largest and most comprehensive procession of divine action ; something which can never be utilized, but can only be destroyed in a mortal moral war ; something which, if God cannot kill it, must be the death of God. And as a race we are not even stray sheep, or wandering prodigals merely ; we are rebels taken with weapons in our hands.

Our supreme need from God, therefore, is not the education of our conscience, nor the absorption of our sin, nor even our reconcilement alone, but our redemption. It is not cheer that we need but salvation, not help but rescue, not a stimulus but a change, not tonics but life. Our one need of God is a moral need in the strictest holiest sense. The best of nature can never meet it. It involves a new nature, a new world, a new creation. It is the moral need, not to be transfigured but to be saved. And the inner authority is the power which does that.

It not merely aids us, nor enlightens us, nor kindles us, nor presents us with an ideal, or a contagion, or a sympathy ; but it redeems us by the destruction of our guilt, the neutralizing of the evil we have done, and the hallowing against us of His own holy name. It is the authority of a Redeemer, of one who is the organ to us of a new world. It is a new world in total contrast with the old, yet interpenetrating it ; underlying it, yet not imbedded in it like a germ, but haunting it and urgent at every point, and at one point leaping to light and final effect.

§

3. This authority of the Redeemer is the final authority in Christianity. And, observe, I do not say the authority of Christ, but the authority of Christ as Redeemer, as our new Creator, the authority of Christ's person as wholly gathered up and completely expressed in the Cross, its work, and its Gospel. He is our peace not in His person alone, for that were too quiescent, exemplary, and aesthetic —but in the mediation which is the energy, act, and effect of His person for ever. I certainly do not mean the authority of Christ's teaching, supreme as that is over all other teaching on spiritual things. Nor do I mean the authority connected with the magnetism, the impressiveness of His personality—the authoritativeness of it. Still less do I mean the authority of such of His beliefs as were solid with the naïve religious consciousness of His land and age—as for

instance, His references to the Davidic authorship of a Psalm. I mean His authority in the true region where the word authority has its ultimate meaning, in the region of personal interaction, in the moral, the religious region alone, the region where grace acts and faith answers, the evangelical region and not the theological. In the theological region I have said there is, properly speaking, no authority—authority being predicable not of a truth in theology, but of a theological person whose action on my person makes my religion. This is the authority realized by the most classic types of the Christian experience —the authority, not of the conscience however enlightened, but of Christ in the conscience ; and in the conscience, not as its oracle simply, or its needle, but as its redeemer, regenerator, and new creator. The seat of authority is not the enlightened conscience but the redeemed and regenerate.

Thus alone do we do justice to moral realism. It is a moral authority that concerns us, I have said. That means, it is the authority for men not in some abstract and conceivable position, nor in some primeval perfection which never was real, but for historic man in his actual moral state ; which is a state not of imperfection only but of impotence for holiness, and not of impotence alone but of collective guilt. The more we realize the solidarity of man the more his moral condition becomes a collectivism of guilt. That is to say, the moral authority must be in relation to guilt, and to the guilt of the race ; it must be more than ethical, it must be a religious authority, a saving one, an evangelical one. It is an authority acting not merely on our moral perception but on our moral perdition—at least on our moral crisis—and acting by way of redemption, and not merely by way of injunction, nor by way of impression, nor by way of prestige. And the redemption thus demanded by our actual case is not merely eschatological, at the far consummate end of things. Nor is it merely ethical, in the way of promoting our moral development and improvement. The chief criterion of Christianity is not its ethical results and amendments. These are but the consequences of it, the fruits of its reconciliation. It is evangelical in this way—that it begins with reconciliation. It is the destruction by God in Christ of sin's guilt and sin's distrust, and sin's blocking of the sky. Such is our central case and need. Whatever, therefore, meets that is the final and sole authority of our race, from which all that claims authority must deduce. Set that right in every man by what sets right also the race, and right views and right relations will follow as the night the day. The great creed and the great millennium must be alike confessions of the living faith which is our contact with Him who sits on the throne and makes all things new and true.

§

But this is to say that the final authority in human affairs is, after all, the preacher's authority. It is on this authority alone that the preacher must rely; and the preacher's is the only function that must rely on this authority alone. He, of all men, is most dependent on his message. He is depen dent on his personality only as his Gospel makes it, and as it shows forth the Gospel. You hear it said, with a great air of religious common sense, that it is the man that the modern age demands in the pulpit, and not his doctrine. It is the man that counts, and not his creed. But this is one of those shallow and plausible half-truths which have the success that always follows when the easy, obvious underpart is blandly offered for the arduous whole. No man has any right in the pulpit in virtue of his personality or manhood in itself, but only in virtue of the sacramental value of his personality for his message. We have no business to worship the elements, which means, in this case, to idolise the preacher. (Fitly enough in Rome the deification [1] of the priest continues the transubstantiation of the elements.) To be ready to accept any kind of message from a magnetic man is to lose the Gospel in mere impressionism. It is to sacrifice the moral in religion to the aesthetic. And it is fatal to the authority either of the pulpit or the Gospel. The Church does not live by its preachers, but by its Word.

§

The last authority, then, is the evangelical.

[1] "Eritis sicut dii." Cp. Gen. iii. 5 with the *Catechism of Trent*, II. 7. 2 : " Sacerdotes non solum angeli sed dii appellantur."

For what is our authority but that to which we are not our own ? And that is what we find absolutely in our evangelical faith. Its appeal is not to the natural conscience, individual, amateur, and self-sufficient. Nor is it to the enlightened conscience of civilization, cultivated by all the moral thought and discipline of history, society, or imagination. But it is to the *actual* conscience of the race, to the conscience taken as we find it, to the conscience as sinful and redeemed, the conscience struck into self-despair, horrified with the world's moral tragedy, and plucked into salvation by God's and man's last moral crisis in the Cross, where the greatest tragedy turns the greatest triumph of all. The appeal is to a conscience in such a state that it must be saved, and re-empowered ; and saved by no mere contact with God, but only by a moral act of God at least as energetic as the universe, as real, historic, and tragic as the sin, i.e. by God's holy reaction of grace, of invading, mastering, regenerating grace. The inmost authority being moral is the most objective thing we know ; speaking to and through the conscience, and to a conscience made capable by grace of appraising and appropriating in a way impossible to the natural self. It emerges and wells up under psychological conditions, but it is not a psychological product. It may be subliminal rather than supernal, but it is not ourselves, it is objective. And nothing is so objective, so authoritative as that which at our inmost moral centre saves us from ourselves. The thing most immanent in us is a transcendent thing, nay, a descendant thing. The more immanent the forum, the more objective and invasive do we feel the redemption. But we must be redeemed, ere we realize this. To the natural man it is foolishness. He finds all salvation to be but the great recuperative effort of man's inalienable divinity, his indefectible essential identity with God, which is the only true eternal life. And the act of saving grace is nothing but our own act of faith in our profound and innate selves. Against all which I would say, in a word, we have to be redeemed into the power of appreciating redemption, and appropriating the greatest moral act man knows —the Cross.

Thus we can never settle the question of a final moral authority (which is the last authority of all) except in the region where will meets will and faith takes home God's act of grace. It is quite insoluble in the region where cosmic process takes the place of moral action, or in the region where conscience responds but to an ideal, or reason accepts truth. It is not with truth we have to do but reality. And reality is a moral thing, a matter of a person, and his will, and his act. Life in its reality is a great act and choice, and not a long process. And therefore, the authority is not a standard, as a truth, or an architecture of truths, might be. It is a living law. And a living law, not in the sense of a historic institution, acting as the custodian of truth, and the trustee of its development. It is a living, holy, historic God and Saviour witnessed, preached, and truly conveyed, by the whole Church, but dispensed

by none. It is a living and holy God in much
more than presence (which were mere mysticism).
It is God in power, in moral power, in historic
and sempiternal action. It is a God real in a
historic act, which is perpetual in its energy,
achieved at one point but throbbing at every other,
a timeless act, parallel with every human action,
and mutually involuted with it (if one may so say),
but involved in the way of struggle and conquest
rather than mere permeation—an Eternal Cross
rather than a universal Spirit. It is this act
that is prolonged as the arduous emergence through
history of that Kingdom of God, which, for all its
immanence, is much more a gift to history than
its product. The last authority is God in His
supreme, saving act of grace to mankind in Christ's
Cross, which is the power of God addressed to what
is at once the power and the weakness in us, our will,
conscience, and total moral self. Our last authority
is something we can only obey by subjugation,
reconciliation, and worship, and not by mere assent.
It is that saving act of God which makes all our best
moral action possible. It is an invasion of us, however inward, it is not an emergence from us ; nor is
it merely the stroke upon our hard shell which
releases our innate divinity. It is an invasion,
creative more than tonic, redeeming rather than
releasing, putting into the Soul a new mainspring
and not disentangling the old which had caught.

But, invasion as it is, it is yet no assault on the
sanctuary of our personal freedom. We are mastered

but not concussed. For it is the one influence, the one authority, that gives us to ourselves, and puts us in possession of our moral freedom. The true freedom of man springs from the holy sovereignty of God, which we only know in Christ, in redeeming action. There our freedom has its charter and not its doom. Even if we started psychologically free, the result of the choice of evil is to impair freedom ; and an impaired freedom goes on to a destroyed freedom. Who doeth sin is the slave of sin. But God's sovereignty is redemption. He is never so sovereign as there. He is never so absolute as in making freedom. Redemption is not a second best sovereignty, in the room of a best of all forever lost. It is a deliverance which makes us choose Supreme good. And to choose good is to be free ; while to be good without choice is neither goodness nor freedom. To choose good is not like choosing evil. It is not immaterial to our freedom what we choose so long as we are choosers. If we choose evil, our very choice enslaves us. But if it be good we choose we acquire ourselves and our freedom. And if we choose good it can only mean that we choose it, not as our ally, but as our sovereign. That is to say, it is choosing God and God's choice. And God's authoritative choice of us is a choice into life and therefore liberty. His sovereign choice of us is choosing us to choose good and enlarge our freedom. The authority of our Redeemer then does not concuss our personality—as an authority would do which was institutional, impersonal, external in that sense, like a church, or even a book.

For the authority of our Redeemer over our person is a personal authority. And the redemption itself is the greatest moral act of existence ; and therefore it is the freest act. Therefore also it is the act most creative of freedom, and therefore most authoritative for it. Our inchoate personality bows herein to something more personal than itself, and not less, something not less spiritual but more, something in which it comes to itself. The authority as redemptive is a living power, person, and act, revealing, making, giving freedom. It is the holy and complete person, creating personality. It is not a truth, nor an ideal, nor an institution, with their external and aesthetic effect, but it is a personal act, the eternal act of an eternal person, with all the moral effect due to that. As a redeeming authority it says, " Be free and obey." It does not say, " Obey and be free."

§

Thus, if the classic religion is Christianity, the classic type of Christianity is the experience of moral redemption and not merely ethical reform. Or rather it is the experience of a redeemer. Because it is not the *sense* of the experience that is the main matter, but the *source* of the experience, and its content. It is not our experience we are conscious of—that would be self-conscious piety—but it is Christ. It is not our experience we preach, but the Christ who comes in our experience. We preach not ourselves, but Christ.

§

4. Christ, I have said, is the source of our experience. Let me, in addressing preachers, dwell on that. The age in which we live shows a singular conjunction in its return to the historic Christ, on the one hand, and its devotion to a subjective type of religion, on the other. Its allegiance is distracted between the historic Christ and the Christian spirit—meaning thereby the Christian style, manner, ethic, or temper—between Christ's person and the Christian principle. At one moment it pursues its quest for a biography of Christ ; at another it says that this were but the Christ according to perishable, passing flesh ; and it devotes itself therefore to the worship and culture of a perennial principle of which Christ was but the supreme expression. And faith then becomes a devout and altruistic frame of mind, a subjectivism, instead of an act diffused through life, a life-act of self-committal into Christ's hands and Christ's Act of Grace. Attention is withdrawn from the contents of faith to the mood of faith. If we press for attention to the content of faith we are ruined by the charge of theology. For the mere temper of faith is comparatively indifferent to its theological veritable content. Let us have sweetness and charity at any cost to reality. And its machinery works whether you drop into the slot the legitimate metal or an iron disc.

Well, you can have no adequate Christ without

theology when you turn seriously to realize or explain Him. But Christ is not there simply as the theological content of faith. That would not give Him His authority. He is not there simply as the substance of our belief, nor simply as the object of faith. He is there, above all, as the standing *source*, nay, the *creator* of our faith. This is where our sense of communion with Christ differs by a world from any alleged converse with Virgin or Saint. They are at most but the helpers, and not the fountain, of our faith. If our Christian experience tell us anything, it is not about ourselves in the first place, nor about our creed, but about Christ. And it tells us of Him as the Giver of faith, the source, the creator of the experience. That is what is meant by saying that our very faith is the gift of God. It cannot be worked up by us, nor by any one working at us. It is evoked by contact with Christ, who is the gift of God. That is why we must preach Christ, and not about Christ, why we must set the actual constraining Christ before people, and not coax or bully people into decision. If we put the veritable Christ before them He will rouse the faith before they know where they are. Our faith says, then, that He is the Creator of our faith. He is not simply its datum. You do not simply explain your faith by a historic, or a psychological reference to Christ as postulate. You do not use Christ to account for your faith, in a reflective, dialectic, hypothetic way. Your faith is faith in Him as acting, rousing your faith, creating it, and not merely receiving it. In your faith you

are more conscious and sure of Him than you are of
your faith. For your faith, you well know, may
fail Him, but you know still better that He will
not fail your faith. And you are more conscious
and sure of Him, as the source and cause of your
experience, than you are of the experience itself,
which you forget to think of. The very apostles
never asked us to believe their experience, nor to
believe on the ground of it, but to believe with
them in Christ. What your experience tells you is
that both the frame of mind and its stateable contents
were produced, and are produced, by Him and His
act. He, as the creator of your faith, is more real to
you than the fabric of your faith, or the sense of it.
He is not behind your faith in the sense of being a
datum which you must assume for it, and which
one day you will verify. But he is realized in your
faith as its effective cause and permanent reality
That is in the very definition of faith. He is not only
objective there, He is initiative. He is known not
simply *in* the experience, but as the creator of the
experience. He is not simply reached by faith,
He brings it to pass. It is the very life and movement of the faith to worship Him as its creator.
That *is* faith, it does not flow from faith. Faith
does not imply Him, it answers Him. Faith is
nothing else than myself believing. And it is Himself I meet. And it is me He saves and re-creates. I
do not infer Him, therefore, from my faith. My faith
is myself, my moral self, finding Him, and finding
that He first found me. It does not simply bear

upon Him, it flows from Him. And our Christian experience is not merely an appreciation, or even an appropriation, of Christ, but the life action of Christ in us, and His action as Redeemer appropriating us. We are " potential Christs " only in this sense —not that we grow into Christs, but that by faith Christ is formed and grows in us, and we live not, but Christ lives in us. And in this capacity He is our one authority, to whom we are not our own. And the preaching of our faith is what I venture to call the prolongation of His action and His Gospel.

Our experience of Christ is thus quite different from our experience of an objective world. Our moral sense of an agent, and that agent a Redeemer, is a different thing from the inference or postulate of an objective world behind sense to account for our impressions. That may be a cause but this is a Creator. When the objective announces itself as a heart and will, which not only chooses, or influences, me, but saves me, then the response of my active will, of myself as a person, is a different thing from the commonsense that instinctively places an object behind passive sensation. The relation of a cause to a sensation is not analogous to the relation of a person to a person. And our relation to Christ is no less different from our attitude to an auxiliary presence, like Saint or Virgin, which aids but does not redeem, and which is not my master because I owe it something much less than my eternal self.

§

These are not metaphysical considerations, however trying they may be to our loose religiosity, but they are positive, practical and experienced religion taking itself in earnest, bringing itself to book, taking a census of itself. I but make explicit in the statement what is implicit in the experienced fact, and present there though all unknown. And its testimony is that Christ does not stand as the crowning, stimulating, releasing instance of the best that is immanent in man. He is not the divine virtuoso, who thoroughly understands his human orchestra, and can bring out of it what none else can. He is not the sublime divine comrade, full of endless cheer, because he has been through it all before us, and has come out on the other side. He is not the herald of God's forgiveness for sins that but hamper our development or soil the surface without tainting our core. But, for all the classic Christian experience, from the New Testament down, He is the Redeemer of our total personality from its radical recalcitrance to God's will, and from its impotence to obey it, even when it has moved to desire it. The natural man is a *nisus* against God, against a God he cannot but feel. And the world's treatment of Christ shows that the higher and better God's will for us is, the more man repudiates, rebels, and fights against it. The authority which is really in question is the will of God. It is personal. And that is why our personality resents it. We yield far more readily to a process or an idea, because it makes no such demand on our self-will as the will of a personal God does. There are many attractions for self-love, vanity, or ambition, in Monism with its vague lack of moral realism and severe imperative. Everything leaves us with a subtle sense of superiority and self-satisfaction but the Will of God, which breaks us to our true peace. And the only means of reducing us to acknowledge the place and practicability of that will is by Redemption. To assert it was useless ; to magnify it failed. It had itself to redeem us in Christ, and to bring such a remission of past guilt as should change our total attitude towards self and God, give us a confidence in self despair, bring us into loving communion for life, and confer on us the Gift of Life Eternal.

There is but one Authority therefore for human life—that life being what it is. It is its historic Redeemer, in the one critical and creative moral act of its history. All the amateur philosophandering of the hour is fumbling to escape from a historic, positive, evangelical Christianity, and to preserve before God a remnant of self-respect, self-possession, and selfwill. But the prime content both of Christian and human experience is the Saviour, triumphant, not merely after the Cross, but upon it. This cross is the message that makes the preacher. And I have tried to make good what I said at the outset of this lecture, that the preacher is the organ of the only real and final authority for mankind. As to creed in its form and detail, if all men accepted that practical and absolute authority for their moral selves there would be no lack of either an inspiration or a standard for their belief, thought, action, or affection, throughout. An authority absolute in our experienced religion will marshal to its place by an inevitable moral psychology, our theology, philosophy, and politics alike. The King alone can make the Kingdom. The Christ of our faith will organize our life. The power that makes the soul will make the Church. What makes the faith will make and remake the creed. And the Gospel that made the book will bless the book, and give us the freedom in it that it gave us through it. If the son make us free we shall be free throughout, and free indeed. To be the slave of Christ is to be the master of every fate. And this is as true for Humanity as it is for every soul.

THE PREACHER AND HIS CHURCH, OR PREACHING AS WORSHIP

III

The Preacher and His Church, or Preaching as Worship

I HAVE been complaining (in the close of my first lecture) that Christians do not know their Bible. But even if they did, the preacher would still be at a loss in another way. He has to face the modern man's neglect of the Church no less than of the Bible. He meets impatient reformers who take a tone of superior realism, and coarsely speak of Church life and the edification of believers as a mere " coddling of the Saints." He lives in an age when the Kingdom of God engrosses more Christian interest than the Church of Christ, and Christian people are more devoted to the busy effort of getting God's will done on earth than to the deep repose of communion with God's finished will in Christ. It is characteristic of much of the Christian activity of the last half-century that it aims not so much at a Christocracy, where Christ has a household and is master of it, as at a Christolatry—a mere λατρεία of Christ, where he is worshipped mainly through the service of the public. It is needless to point out to the student of the New Testament how flatly this contradicts its genius. And it is useless

75

to urge the point with those who treat the New Testament as archaeology.

Some of us who are greatly in sympathy with these churchless efforts, like the Salvation Army, may yet believe that if they became the ruling type their end would be lost. We may believe that, by the will of Christ, it is only through a real Church, truly Christianized, that Humanity can be served and saved for the Kingdom. We may feel that the love of Humanity could not survive apart from not only our love of Christ, but also from the personal communion with Christ in a Church which feeds that love. The φιλανθρωπία is only possible through the φιλαδελφία. Do good to all men, *but especially to those that are of the household of faith.* Our fellow Christians have claims on us that may precede those of our fellow men. The Communion of saints is more to God than the enthusiasm of Humanity. The neighbour, in the New Testament, is not the same as the brother.[1] The brotherhood of the New Testament is indeed meant to cover the race at last, but it is the brotherhood of Christian faith and love, not of mankind. The victory which overcomes the world is not humane love but Christian faith. It is won not by the natural heart but by the re-creating Cross. The goats in the parable were condemned not for being of the world ; for they were a part of the Church ; they were not wolves or dogs. But they were false to the love which makes

[1] This point would richly repay working out in the interests of a true Social Christianity.

the Church, the love which crowns true faith in
Christ with kindness to the needy ones of the
sacred flock. The tragedy of the race is too awful
and sordid for any salvation that is not constantly fed by the Saviour ever rising through
His community from His Cross and grave. Devoted
men and women, who go on now by the impulse
from centuries of the cross, would break down under
the horrible conditions of life where it most needs
saving, if the habit of a faith and fraternity bred in
the Church alone were to die out.

Many of us realize that. But great numbers of
people, even Christian people, do not realize it.
They call roughly upon the preacher to spend less
time and concern upon maturing the converted,
or edifying comfortable believers ; and they urge
him to go straight to the world—to Society or to the
masses, to the natural man, cultured or coarse. It
is a large question that opens here. I cannot do
much more here than place myself on the side of
the sound principle that it is the Church that is the
great missionary to Humanity, and not apostles,
prophets, and agents here and there. If a preacher
is to act on the world he must, as a rule, do it through
his Church. And his Church, if it be not built up
in its faith, will in due course cease to exist. Many
Christians are like Peter. They need several conversions (Luke xxii. 32). And a neglected Church
will lose that collective wisdom which alone forms
a sound judgment on the difficult moral issues of
Society Practical wisdom speaks only amid the

full-grown ; and our souls mature only in a living Christian community. Of course, if the preacher so preaches that his Church cultivates the snugness of pious comfort instead of the humble confidence of evangelical faith, then also the Church is in decay, and it will in due time become but a religious circle. But for all that the minister's first duty is to his Church. He must make it a Church that acts on the world—through him indeed, but also otherwise. He is to act at its head, and not in its stead.

In this matter the preacher must refuse to have his duty dictated by those without, who have little or no Church sympathy or responsibility. I have observed that the demand on the preacher to ignore his people and go straight to the world, is largely made by the world, by influences, at least, which voice the verdict of the world rather than the insight of the Church, by religious parliamentarians, eager socialists, or by people who are willing to utilize the Church but quite evade its responsibilities. Some are, like many sections of the press or of literature, voices that stand aloof from the Christian burden and speak often in severe criticism. Or they are that end of the Church which is more moulded by these influences than by Bible or Faith. They speak as if Christ's first obedience had been to human needs and not to God's will. And they are not much entitled to an opinion as to what the proper method of the Gospel is, or the consequent duty of the Church. The genius of the Gospel is after all best understood by the personal believers in the Gospel. And that genius certainly is to go to the world ; but it is to go there through the Church, and the Church's Word. It goes through the common action of believing men, who are mature enough in their educated faith to have measured both the world and the Gospel, and to be sure, beyond cavil, that their Gospel is the tragic, desperate world's one hope. They are men who have been evangelized to good ripe purpose. The Gospel of a moral salvation will never seize the world through men who are but thinly sure, or personally neutral, and have only an admiration for Christian ethic. The act of Grace can never be conveyed by men on whom it does not act. As little will it capture the world through men who are converted and no more, who are not built up by the spiritual education and insight of a living Church.

§

The one great preacher in history, I would contend, is the Church. And the first business of the individual preacher is to enable the Church to preach. Yet so that he is not its echo but its living voice, not the echo of its consciousness but the organ of its Gospel. Either he gives the Church utterance, or he gives it insight into the Gospel it utters. He is to preach to the Church from the Gospel so that with the Church he may preach the Gospel to the world. He is so to preach to the Church that he shall also preach *from* the Church. That is to say, he must be a sacrament to the Church, that with the Church he may become a missionary to the world.

You perceive what high ground I take. The preacher's place in the Church is sacramental. It is not sacerdotal, but it is sacramental. He mediates the word to the Church from faith to faith, from his faith to theirs, from one stage of their common faith to another. He does not there speak to un-faith. He is a living element in Christ's hands (broken, if need be) for the distribution and increment of Grace. He is laid on the altar of the Cross. He is not a mere reporter, nor a mere lecturer, on sacred things. He is not merely illuminative, he is augmentive. His work is not to enlighten simply, but to empower and enhance. Men as they leave him should be not only clearer but greater, not only surer but stronger, not only interested, nor only instructed, nor only affected, but fed and increased. He has not merely to show certain things but to get them home, and so home that they change life, either in direction or in scale. It is only an age like the present age of mere knowledge that tends to make preaching the statement of sound and simple truth, interesting but powerless. It is only an age which starves the idea of revelation, by its neglect of the sacramental idea, that reduces preaching to evangelizing alone. It is only an age engrossed with impressions and careless about realities that could regard the preacher's prime work as that of converting the world, to the neglect of transforming the Church. It is only such an age that could think of preaching as something *said* with more or less force, instead of something *done* with more or less power. We spend our polemic upon the Mass, and fitly enough in proper place. But the Catholic form of worship will always have a vast advantage over ours so long as people come away from its central act with the sense of something done in the spirit-world, while they leave ours with the sense only of something said to this present world. In true preaching, as in a true sacrament, more is done than said. And much is well done which is poorly said. Let the preacher but have real doings with God and even with a stammering tongue and a loose syntax he will do much for life which has never yet been done by a finished style. The preacher may go "lame but lovely", to use Charles Lamb's fine phrase. His word may lack finish if it have hands and feet. He is a man of action. He is among the men who do things. That is why I call him a sacramental man, not merely an expository, declaratory man. In a sacrament is there not something done, not merely shown, not merely recalled ? It is no mere memorial. How can you have a mere memorial of one who is always living, always present, always more potent than our act of recall is, always the mover of it ? What he once put there might be a memorial, but what he is always putting there is much more than that. It is at least his organ. It is, indeed, his act. It is something practical and not spectacular. A revelation may be but something exhibited, but in a sacrament there is something effected. And the one revelation in the strict sense is the sacrament of the cross, the cross as an effective act of redemption. A revelation of redemption is a revelation of something done ; and it is only a deed that can reveal a deed. If the preacher reveal redemption he does it by a deed, by a deed in which the Redeemer is the chief actor, by some self-reproduction by Christ, some function of the work of the Cross. He has to reproduce the word of the beginning, the word of the Cross which is really the Cross's own energy, the Cross in action. No true preaching of the Cross can be other than part of the action of the Cross. If a man preach let him preach as the Oracle of God, let him preach as Christ did, whose true pulpit was His Cross, whose Cross made disciples apostles, in whose Cross God first preached to the world, whose preaching from the Cross has done for the world what all His discourses—even His discourses—failed to do.

The preacher, in reproducing this Gospel word of God, prolongs Christ's sacramental work. The real presence of Christ crucified is what makes preaching. It is what makes of a speech a sermon, and of a sermon Gospel. This is the work of God, this continues His work in Christ, that ye should believe in Him whom He hath sent. We do not repeat or imitate that Cross, on the one hand ; and we do not merely state it, on the other. It re-enacts itself in us. God's living word reproduces itself as a living act. It is not inert truth, but quick power.

All teaching about the truth as it is in Jesus culminates in the preaching of the truth which is Jesus, the self-reproduction of the word of reconciliation in the Cross. Every true sermon, therefore, is a sacramental time and act. It is God's Gospel act reasserting itself in detail. The preacher's word, when he preaches the gospel and not only delivers a sermon, is an effective deed, charged with blessing or with judgment. We eat and drink judgment to ourselves as we hear. It is not an utterance, and not a feat, and not a treat. It is a sacramental act, done together with the community in the name and power of Christ's redeeming act and our common faith. It has the real presence of the active Word whose creation it is. If Christ set up the sacrament, His Gospel set up the sermon. And if He is real in our sacramental act still, no less is His deed real in our preached word which prolongs that deed. And it is known to be real by the insight of faith, however many counterfeits there are, with no insight but only zeal, and sometimes with nothing but stir.

Our Catholic opponents charge us with having cut ourselves off from the true Church by having lost the sacramental note. And I will confess to some fear that it may be true, though in another sense than theirs. For them the centre of gravity in the sacrament is in the elements—in the change effected on them, and, through them, on us. But for us the centre of gravity in any sacrament lies not in the material element but in the communal act. That is the

site of Christ's real presence.   It is not metaphysical
but moral and personal.   It is not corporeal but
collective.   We do not partake of Christ's body in
the form of any substance, however refined and
ethereal.   For us the body of Christ means the
person of Christ,[1] and the whole person of Christ
is gathered into His saving, atoning act.   And what
we perform is an act of communal reunion with
His person in its crucial and complete act.   His
great act of Redemption renews itself in His Church.
We re-enter by act the communion not of Christ's
substance but, as the apostle says, of His death—that
is, of His saving act.   It is in the Church's act that
the real presence behind it takes effect, the real
presence of Him who was above all things the will
and deed of God, God's eternal will and new testament.   It is the Great Act of Christ finding itself
anew in the act of the Church.

Now this is really what occurs in another aspect
in the Sacrament of the Word, in the Church's
preaching of the Gospel.   To be effective our
preaching must be sacramental.   It must be an
act prolonging the Great Act, mediating it, and
conveying it.   Its energy and authority is that of
the Great Act.   The Gospel spoken by man is the
energizing of the Gospel achieved by God.   Its
authority is not that of the preacher's personality, nor
even of his faith, nay, not even of his message alone,
but that of the divine action behind him, whereof

---

[1] "All flesh" = all persons.   "One flesh" = one dual
personality.

he himself is but as it were the sacramental element, and not the sacramental Grace. If our preaching is not more sacramental than the Catholic altar— I do not say more eloquent or more able, but more sacramental—then it is the altar that must prevail over all our No-Popery. For religion *is* sacramental. Where it is not it becomes bald. And the only question is, where the sacrament lies. We place it in the Word of Gospel. *Accedit verbum et fit sacramentum.* Nothing but the Word made Sacrament can make a Sacrament out of elements, and keep it in its proper place. But what a task for our preachers to fulfil!

It is this sacramental note that I fear our preaching often loses. It is this objective power, overruling both the temperament of the preacher and the temper of his time. We speak freely and finely about the Gospel, but does the Gospel come to its own in it all? Does it preach itself through us with power? Are our sermons deeds, 'action-sermons'? They cost much labour, and what do we take by it? They are not without some effect, but are they real causes in the religious life? If they are not, is it because they lack will-power, because they are exercises more than acts, productions more than powers, which aim at impression more than at change? Is it because they lack behind them the volume of a Church's conviction, a Church's faith, the impact of a whole Church's will? Is it because we are more eager to have in our pulpits the manly man than the new man?

86   The Preacher and his Church

§

True preaching presupposes a Church, and not
merely a public. And wherever the Church
idea fades into that of a mere religious club or
association you have a decay in preaching. Wherever the people are but a religious lecture society
the pulpit sinks. When it is idolized it always sinks.
It does not lose in interest, or in the sympathetic
note, but it loses in power, which is the first thing
in a Gospel. If the preacher but hold the mirror
up to our finer nature the people soon forget what
manner of men they are.

But you point out to me that the preaching of
the Apostles was addressed to the public, that it
was very largely of the gathering, of the missionary,
kind. Yes, but even that began and worked from
the faith it found. It began with the susceptible
among the Jews. At first it was not so much converting for Gentiles as stirring for Jews. It was always
with the local synagogue that Paul began when he
could, with the votaries of the Old Testament Word ;
and while he could he worked through them or their
proselytes. Jesus Himself began so. His relations
beyond Israel grew out of His relations with Israel.
It was His earnest dealings with Israel that provoked
the Cross, which alone universalized the Gospel. So
the preacher has his starting point in the stated and
solemn assemblies of the Church, though he does
not end there. Through these, he works also
on his public who are present, though not of the
Church. Then in the end he goes to the world

without.   But his first duty, if he is a settled pastor,
and not a preaching friar, is to his Church.   Nothing
could be more misplaced, when a young preacher
enters on a Church, than a neglect or contempt
of its corporate life and creed, or a sudden inversion
of these in order that he may get at the world.   He
has no right to stop the building that he may start
elsewhere.   He has no right to use his Church
merely to provide himself with an outside pulpit.   It
is together that they must go to the world, he and
his Church.   What Christ founded was not an
order of preachers, nor the institution of preaching,
but a community, a Church, whose first charge
His preaching should be.   It is Church and preacher
together that reach the world.

The preaching even to the Church, being in the
presence of the public, has of course due regard
to their presence.   The sermon is not a mere
homily to an inner circle.   It is gospelling.
The Church is addressed in the presence of
people who are not of the Church.   The preacher
indeed renews for believers the reality of the
Gospel ; but he does it in a large way that concerns also those who have not confessed their
faith explicitly.   He dwells for the most part on
the large and broad features of the Gospel rather
than on individual and casuistic situations.   He
declares the whole counsel of God ; that is, the counse
of God as a whole.   If he handle individual cases,
it is as illustrations of wider truth.   He leaves cases
of conscience to private intercourse.   He is not

in the pulpit a director of conscience so much as a
shepherd or a seeker of souls. And he may give expression to his own private experiences only in so far as
is seemly and useful for the more public aspects of
his Gospel. If he is ever beside himself, it must be
privately to God ; for the people's sake he is sober
and sane. Preaching is not simply pastoral visitation on a large scale. Teaching from house to house
meant for the apostles not visitation, but minister-
ing to the Church gathered in private houses, as
it had then to be.

The first *vis-à-vis* of the preacher, then, is not
the world, but the Gospel community. The word
is living only in a living community. Its spirit
can act outwards only as it grows inwardly and
animates a body duly fed and cared for. The
preacher has to do this tending. He has to declare
the Church's word, and to utter the Church's faith,
to itself, in order that he and the Church together
may declare them to the world. The Church may
use, but cannot rely upon, evangelists who are
evangelists and nothing else. When the preacher
speaks to believers it is to build them *up as* a Christian community ; when he speaks to the world
it is to build them *into* a Christian community.
And the Church is built up by taking sanctuary, by
stopping to realize its own faith, by the repetition
of its own old Gospel, by turning aside to see
its great sight, by standing still to see the salvation
of the Lord.

§

Its own old Gospel ! It is not needful that the

preacher should be original as a genius is, but only
as a true believer is.   What he brings to the Church
is not something unheard of, and imported from outside, to revolutionize it.   He has to offer the Church,
in outer form, the word which is always within it,
in order that the Church, by that presentation,
may become anew what by God's grace it already
is.   He must be original in the sense that his truth
is his own, but not in the sense that it has been
no one else's.   You must distinguish between novelty
and freshness.   The preacher is not to be original in
the sense of being absolutely *new*, but in the sense
of being *fresh*, of appropriating for his own personality, or his own age, what is the standing possession of the Church, and its perennial trust from
Christ.   He makes discovery *in* the Gospel, not *of*
the Gospel.   Some preachers spoil their work by
an incessant strain after novelty, and a morbid
dread of the commonplace.   But it was one no less
original than Goethe, who said, the great artist
is not afraid of the commonplace.   To be unable
to freshen the commonplace is to be either dull
or bizarre.   Yet to be nothing but new is like a
raw and treeless house shouting its plaster novelty
on a beautiful old brown moor.   The artist may
treat revelation as discovery. He may create
what he finds but as chaos. He finds but power,
and he issues it in grace.   But it is otherwise with
the preacher.   It is the converse.   He finds revelation in all discovery. He finds to his hand the
grace which he has to issue with power.   His

word is to send home a Word which was articulate
from the beginning, "What we have seen and heard
of the Word of life declare we to you." The
artist's grace is not the preacher's. Nor is it true
without modification that "all grace is the grace
of God." The preacher has often been compared
with the actor, and often he has succumbed to
the actor's temperament, or to his arts. But there
is a point of real analogy. The actor creates a
part, as the phrase is ; but it is only by appropriating a personality which the dramatist really
created and put into his hands. And that is what
the preacher has to do. He has to work less with
his own personality than with the personality
provided him in Christ, through Christ's work in
him. He has to interpret Christ. Moreover, the
actor's is a voice which is forgotten, while the
poet's is a voice that remains. So also the preacher's
originality is limited. By the very Spirit that
moves him he speaks not of himself. He must not
expect the actor's vogue. Self-assertion or jealousy
are more offensive in him than in the artist. It is
enough if he be a living voice ; he is not a creative
word. He is not the light ; he but bears witness to it.
   " *Je ne suis pas la rose mais j'ai vécu près d'elle.*"
   There is even less room for originality of idea
in the pulpit than elsewhere. What is needed is
rather spontaneity of power. This is quite in
keeping with the conservatism that must always
play a part so much greater in the Church than
in the State. The preacher not only appeals to the

permanent in human nature ; he is also the hierophant of a foregone revelation ; he is not the organ
of a new one. His foundation is laid for him once
for all in Christ. His power lies not in initiation,
but in appropriation. And his work is largely to
assist the Church to a fresh appropriation of its
own Gospel. It is not to dazzle us with brand-new
aspects even of the Gospel. God forbid that I
should say a word to seem to justify the dulness
that infects the pulpit. Alas ! if our sin crucify
Christ afresh, our stupidity buries Him again. But
the cure for pulpit dulness is not brilliancy, as in
literature. It is reality. It is directness and
spontaneity of the common life. The preacher
is not there to astonish people with the unheard
of ; he is there to revive in them what they have
long heard. He discovers a mine on the estate.
The Church, by the preacher's aid, has to realize
its own faith, and take home anew its own Gospel.
That which was from the beginning declare we
unto you—that fresh old human nature and that
fresh old grace of God.

What a strength we all receive from self-expression ! How we pine if it is denied ! How we die
if it is suppressed ! It is life to a genius to get
out what is in him ; it is death to be stifled or
neglected. If we can but express what is in us to
ourselves it is often sufficient. If we can put
pen to paper, paint to canvas, or the hand to
clay, it may save us, even if we do not get a market
or a vogue. Otherwise it is solitary confinement,

or death.   The flame dies for want of air.   In like
manner also our private prayer receives for ourselves
a new value when in our solitude we utter it aloud.
The aspiration gains mightily from the spoken
word.   The very effort to shape it in words adds
to its depth, precision, confidence, and effect.   It is
well to sigh our prayers, but it is better to utter them.
With the heart man believeth unto righteousness,
but with the mouth we confess unto salvation.
Righteousness is well, but it must be established
and confirmed as salvation.   Just so the preacher's
address to the Church is really the Church preaching
to the Church.   It is the Church expressing itself
to itself.   The Church is feeling its own strength,
and by the feeling it is growing in godly self-
confidence, and in power to say to the world what
the whole world resists.

The Christian preacher is no prophet sent to the
public till he is a voice of the Church to the Church.
He is but a part of the Church, yet he speaks to
the whole.   We tend our body with the hand,
which is but an organ of the body.   So the preacher
tends the Church as a part of it, moved in his act,
not by the part's life, but by its share in the life
of the whole.   He is over against the Church only
as the organ is over against the organism.   It is
the body that turns the hand upon itself.   The
Church in the preacher becomes explicitly conscious
of itself.   Its latent faith becomes patent.   It
knows how much greater it is than it thought.
It is amazed with itself.   It realizes what a mighty

matter its faith is. The flush rises to the face of
its love. The gleam shines in its eye of its hope.
And it *must* reach this self-expression. It is not
merely the better for it. The expression is part of
the reality. The form is part of the life. It is
part of the joint action of the Word which is the
Church's life, and of the faith that meets that
Word. The sermon is an essential part of the
worship.

§

The preacher, therefore, starts with a Church
of brethren that agree with him and that believe
with him ; and in its power he goes to a world
that does neither. What he has to do is not to
exhibit himself to the Church, nor to force himself
on it. He offers himself to it in the like faith, as
a part of their common offering by the Eternal
Spirit to God. And the stronger the Church is,
so much the more it needs preaching, and the more
it desires preaching, preaching not only *through*
it but *to* it ; just as genius demands self-expression
in passionate proportion to its power. Only
note that while the genius demands expression
for itself the Church demands it for its Gospel.
It demands expression for its positive, objective
faith and not its consciousness ; its message and
not merely its experience. The Eternal Word
that always makes the Church, has to speak to a
Church whose experience is largely below the level
of the faith of that Word. What makes the Church

is not Christ as its founder but Christ as its tenant
as its life, as its power, the Christ living in the
faith of its members in general, and of its
ministers in particular. But it is a Christ that
only partially comes to His own in the Church's
actual experience. The faith within the Church
has to speak to its half-faith, its bewildered faith,
its struggling, or even its decaying faith.

What is done in preaching to the Church, therefore, is not to set out its own consciousness. At
any rate, it is not the consciousness of the Church
at any one stage—even the present. It is the
Spirit speaking to the Churches. It is the past
Church speaking to the present, the whole Church
to the single Church, the ripe Church to the unripe,
the faithful Church to the faltering Church, the
ideal Church to the actual, the unseen to the seen.
It is the great, common, universal faith addressing
the faith of the local community. And, in so far
as the preacher is the voice of the Church, he is
the voice, not of his own Church, but of the Great
Church that envelopes his own. The preacher
reflects the faith of the great true Church, but
neither the faith nor the views of those around him.
He is not giving expression to the average opinion
of his congregation, or his denomination. The
preacher is the mandatory of the great Church, which
any congregation or sect but represents here and
now. And what he has to do is to nourish that
single and accidental community with the essence
of the Church universal; that the members of

the Church may rise to the level of the Church, to its true nature, its ideal holiness as the called of God.   When he addresses the Church it is the ideal Church addressing the actual, the upper Church the lower, the Church of the ages appealing to the Church of the hour, the Church universal to the Church on the spot.   The inner Church addresses the outer, that the outer may realize itself anew, and apprehend that for which Christ apprehended it.   Nothing in the service goes to the root of the Gospel (and, therefore, of the Church) like preaching.   And this makes preaching the chief part of our evangelical ritual, the part which gives the law to all worship, since the message is what stirs worship and makes it possible.   Our chief praise is thanksgiving for the Gospel.   And our prayer is Christian only in the name of the Gospel. Preaching is " the organized Hallelujah of an ordered community."

But when the preacher turns from the Church of which he is pastor to the world to which he is missionary he must speak in the name of the whole Church as a unity.   Hence the slowness of missions while the parts of the Church fight and devour each other.   Hence, too, the unifying reaction of missions on the Church.   Hence, also, the missionary must preach in chief those great things which are the objective powers of the Church, and not a subjective or merely experimental piety. Let him preach the Gospel, and leave it to make its own experience in the new races, by its own

creative power. Their form of experience may
be very different from what has grown up in the
train of our civilization, with the mentality of the
West.   No preacher (I have said) is only the
representative of the Church's consciousness ; and
the missionary preacher is so least of all. He is
the organ of the Gospel that created the Church's
consciousness at the first, and has developed it
all along.

Therefore, it is not the Church that he or
any evangelist preaches.   Wherever the Church
is preached, the Gospel comes short.   We have
then Catholicism, and we cease in due course to
have the Gospel at all.   The preacher has not
even his commission from the Church, but only a
licence at most, only his opportunity.   The Church
supplies not his authority but his pulpit.   He has
his commission from God, from the Church only his
permission.   He is an officer, not of the Church,
but of the Word that the Church has in steward-
ship.   And all the Church has to do is to discover if he has the commission, by the wisest,
and even severest, tests, by a prolonged training,
perhaps, which is also a probation.   But it is
a commission the Church cannot bestow.   It can
only discern.   It cannot convey the apostolic
spirit, it can but wait upon it.   The Church has
no rights in the matter of ordination, and can confer
none.   It has but a duty to recognize the spirit's
movement and the purity of the Word, and to
facilitate the Gospel in the most effectual way.

§

Preaching, then, is part of the cultus. That is the Protestant idea. To treat it as a gratuitous adjunct to the service is Catholic. To regard it as the mere exposition of a minister's views is neither Protestant nor Catholic. It is not even Christian. It is a rationalistic way of regarding the matter, and it causes the sermon to differ by no whit from a lecture more or less popular, or from a manifesto, more or less interesting, of the preacher's personality. The sermon has always been regarded as an integral part of the service by a Protestantism which knew what it was about. It is the Word of the Gospel returning in confession to God who gave it. It is addressed to men indeed, but in truth it is offered to God. Addressed to men but offered to God—that is the true genius of preaching. Christ sees in it joyfully the travail and the trophy of His soul. Like all the rest of the worship, it is the fruit of the Gospel. May I call it again "the organized Hallelujah" of intelligent faith.

In so viewing preaching, Protestantism has reverted to the New Testament idea, and to the first Church. There more attention (to say the least) is given to the proclamation of the Word, than to the worship. And quite as much as is given to the Sacraments—which were sometimes outside the personal concern of an apostle like Paul. He thanks God he had baptised but two in one Church. Our Lord, we are told, baptised not.

On the other hand, the apostles could not but preach. It was an essential part of their grateful, worshipful response to the Word of Grace which had found them. It was a creation of that Word. " It pleased God to reveal His Son in me that I might preach Him among the Gentiles." That is to say, the preacher's commission was given in the very nature of the revelation which made him a Christian. The revelation by its very meaning left him no choice. The self-same act of the cross which made him worship Christ, made him preach Christ as part of the worship. And by a consequence that hearing the preaching was also part of their worship to whom he spoke. Real preaching then was bound up with the worship of Christ, with a faith that could not but worship. The testimony to men was as truly an acknowledgement to God of His gracious Gospel as was any express act of confession or praise. And the men who heard had a part and a responsibility as great as the preacher's. The confession of sin, which all call a part of worship, did not mean so much as the confession of holiness in a Saviour—which is the preaching of the Church.

Further, if preaching is a main part of the Church's worship, it is a part especially of the minister's own personal worship. It is for him an act of worship, in a far more intimate and real sense than anything he may do in the serving of tables, the organizing of work, or the carrying of help. Nothing tends more to lower the quality of preaching than a loss of this sense on the preacher's part. Nothing will destroy public respect for it so fast as the preacher's own loss of respect for it. And that respect is lost when, for the preacher himself, the preaching is more speech than action, when he feels its practical value to be more in what it leads to, than in what it is. If great art is praise, true preaching is so no less. Much preaching that is not popular is still true worship.

Preaching is thus the creation of the Gospel, and not our mere tribute to the Gospel; therefore, it has one great note which should appeal to the modern mind—the note of inevitability. It was the inevitable word, so prized now by the connoisseurs of style—the authentic Word. It was the triumph of the Gospel genius, the royalty of the Gospel way. It came forth with the ease, aptness and weight wielded by full and conscious power. However verbose preachers may be, preaching is not the verbosity of a Word whose truer nature would have been reticent like a ritual sacrament. The preacher may be illogical, but preaching is there by a spiritual logic, and a psychological necessity, in the Gospel itself. It was the Church's great spontaneous confession of its faith both to itself and the world. There was something almost lyric about it—as the great creeds were at first hymns. They expressed not merely belief, but triumphant irrepressible belief. Nay, it was more. It was the belief of men more than conquerors, more than triumphant. They were the harbingers and hierophants of the world's foregone but final conquest.

They were more than victorious, they were redeemed
They were victorious only because redeemed.
They could not be parted from Christ's love by
any tribulation, anguish, peril, or sword (Rom. viii.
35–9)—not because they had overcome these things,
even in His name, but because He had, already and
in advance, put them under His feet for good and
all, for Himself and His people. They were
trophies of Christ's conquest more than victors in
their own. And it was more joy to be a trophy
and captive in the triumphal procession of Christ
than to sit with Cæsar in his car. What made them
preach was a victory gained, not by them, but in
them and over them. And they sang their joy
in preachings that captured the world for which
they were themselves also captured in Christ.

Preaching then is the Church confessing its faith.
And it is as surely a part of the service as the reciting
of a creed could be. It is another aspect of the same
response to the Word given. It is less organized,
but no less collective than the great creeds. And in
the Churches where there are no formal creeds it
takes their place. The place of the sermon in the
more democratic and non-Catholic Churches is due,
in part, to the absence in their ritual of a recited
creed. It is all that some of them, like the Congregationalists, have for a creed.

§

This fact, of course, lays a corresponding responsibility on the preacher ; though it is a responsibility

that is sometimes ignored or resented by preachers, who claim for themselves a freedom that properly belongs only to the Church. For the minister of a Church in its pulpit is not a free lance (I say in *its* pulpit, not in *his*). He is not a mere preaching friar, a vagrant Evangelist, gathering his audience in streets and lanes, hedges and highways, as he can find them. He enters on a position of trust which he did not create. He is licensed to it when he is called by its custodian, the Church. Any call to a minister is, in substance, a licence conferred on him, however much in form it may be a petition addressed to him. He stands on a platform, an institution, which is provided for him, and he owes practical regard to the Church that provides it. He bespeaks men's attention, not in virtue of his personal quality merely, but in virtue of a charge and Gospel, given both to minister and Church, which both must serve. He is not free to vend in his pulpit the extravagances of an eccentric individualism, nor the thin heresies of the amateur. He is not entitled to ask men to hear with respectful silence the freaks of mere mother-wit, or the guesses of an untutored intelligence. When a man is entrusted with the pastoral care of a Church from its pulpit he accepts, along with the normality of Scripture, the obligations, limitations and reserves of the pastoral commission. He that sweareth by the altar sweareth also by that which is upon the altar : and he abuses his position if he simply unload upon his charge certain startling views by way of relief to his own egoist conscience.

To the older members of the flock that can be upon occasion the heartlessness of intellectualism, or the cruelty of youth. A man speaking his genuine experience in the experimental region of religion is always worth listening to. But if a man takes leave to assault the great doctrines, or to raise the great questions as if they had occurred to him first, if he knows nothing of what has been done in them by experts, or where thinkers have left the question, he is out of place. No man is entitled to discuss theology in public who has not studied theology. It is like any other weighty subject. Still more is this requisite if he set to challenge and reform theology. He ought to be a trained theologian. He need not have been at college, if he show sufficient evidence of real study. To read theology is not enough. Reading may be no more than the browsing of a mental epicure at will. The subject must be studied, and studied at fountain heads. No man should ask for a public hearing on a theological question unless he has mastered his New Testament at first hand, together with one or more of the great classics which are landmarks and points of new departure for theological thought. If we had more honest work behind our theological talk we should not, for instance, have popular clap-trap like the statement that the Athanasian Creed is a jumble of Greek metaphysics, when its whole substance registers the vital effort of the Church to overcome metaphysic in the interest of a historic redemption; as it were to be wished the victims of metaphysic would do who essay to reform our creed to-day. But it takes a mastery of metaphysic to escape from metaphysic. And it takes a real knowledge of theology to lead theology on its broadening way, and at the same time preserve the depth and intimacy of its Gospel.

A man is not invited into a pulpit just to say how things strike him at his angle, any more than he is expected to lay bare to the public the private recesses of his soul. Nor is it the preacher's first duty to be up-to-date, to be in the van of tentative thought. He can do his work well without the very newest machinery. The professor should know the last thing written, but the preacher need not. If he is young, and has not been well trained in his subject, perhaps better not. He is there to declare the eternal, which is always in the van, equally present, equally real for every soul, everlasting, final, insuperable for every age. He is not in the pulpit, primarily, as the place where he can get most scope for his own individuality, and most freedom for his own idiosyncrasy. He is there, as the servant both of the Word and the Church, to do a certain work, to declare a certain message, to discharge a certain trust. He is not in the pulpit as the roomiest place he has found to enable him to be himself, and develop his genius. Some young preachers are more concerned about their own freedom than their people's service. They are prone to think they must get freedom to develop their individuality before they have any positive idea what they are to do. But you cannot develop your individuality except obliviously, in the doing of some definite objective thing. Without that you are taking yourself too seriously. You are but "pottering at the pyramid of your own existence," or modelling yourself in clay. No, you "are taken into Heaven backwards." You must grow in the doing of some definite thing, to learn which thing and the handling of it your individuality ought to go to a very severe school. Your duty is not to be yourself. "To thyself be true" is not a Christian precept. It is automatic for the Christian man, whose one concern is to be true to Christ. The first thing due even to yourself is to go to school. Learn. Find a master. Let the past and its trust make you yourself! The first duty of a man is not to assert a freedom, nor to use a private judgment, but to find an absolute master. There is put into the preacher's hands a trust, a message, which is not merely like the artist's, the subjective trust of genius with a responsibility as to how it shall be used ; but it is the objective trust of the Gospel, of a positive word which he must deliver however it may affect his self-culture. Any genius that he has can but enrich his Gospel. He is given the word of a foregone and final revelation—not its idea but its word, not its surmise but its arrival, not its conception but its visitation, not its intuition but its revelation, something which is his because of its insight into him rather than his insight into it, something wherein he is known rather than knows, something finally done which is the root of all our best doing. The King-

dom of God is among us, and has long been
among us. Such is the standing message of the
Church, and it is at once the source and the limit
of her theological liberty. It is the Gospel of the
achieved more than the call to achieve. It bids
us not to make, so much as to rest in something
we find made. It teaches us that all good we do
is but the energy in us of the best already done.
It is an *opus operatum*. That is the standing word of
Gospel. And the business of each preacher in
charge of a flock is to translate to his small Church
this message and content of the great Church, that
he may integrate the small Church into the great, and
that he and it together may swell the transmission
of the World to the world. That is the true Catholicism,
the universalizing of the universal Word. That is
the principle which makes a Church out of a sect or
conventicle, and puts a preacher in the true apostolic
succession. The true succession is the true inheritance of the eternal Word, and not the due concatena-
tion of its agents. The great apostolate is one, not
in the heredity of a historic line but in the solidarity
of a historic Gospel, not in a continuous stream but
in an organic Word.

§

We have thus some guide to answering the question
whether a minister's first duty is to his Church or
to the world. If we must choose, in what is perhaps
a false dilemma, it is to his Church. The duty to the
world is a joint duty of preacher and Church.
Churches are always forgetting this, and reducing

preachers to priests in spite of themselves by making everything turn on the preacher. It is part of the price that we pay for popular preachers that we fall into a way of thinking as if, when a gifted speaker appears, the main duty of the Church is to give him his platform, or even his pedestal, and then stand out of his way. Hence manifold mischief to preacher, Church, and Gospel ; the cossetting of the preacher's selfwill, the elimination of the communal will, the deflection of the will of God. The task of the great preacher is at bottom the task of the smaller preacher who can but be faithful. It is to act upon the world through his Church and not merely *from* his Church. His Church is not the arena for his individualism (far less the pedestal of his vanity) but its school. A man who is truly, through the Word, the agent of the great Church will never become the mere exploiter of his own Church. The captive of the Gospel will never lord it in the Lord's house, nor simply use the flock he is there to feed.

§

There are some consequences that follow, if we grasp the great principle that the sermon is an essential part of the worship.

1. The minister (as I have said) may not use the pulpit merely for the exposition of his own views. Any views of his must be given as such, and be used, directly or indirectly, for the ruling purpose of the message from God. In proportion as he puts in the front views and opinions of his he may expect

public abstension, or contradiction, from those who have differing views. Farther, the minister may not sacrifice the pulpit to mere instruction, mere lectures, or intellectual or aesthetic treats. Let the lecture room or the Bible Class be used for that. Of course I speak of such habitual use of the pulpit, not of exceptional occasions.

2. As a corollary of this it is the preacher's duty, in most cases, to touch questions of Bible criticism only in so far as they clear the ground for a real and positive Gospel. The structure of the Bible may be discussed in the pulpit only in so far as it affects the history of revelation, and not merely of religion. The popular religion of Israel is one thing, and the divine revelation that gradually emerged through it and subdued it is another. And though it is no part of the preacher's work to treat of the religion of Israel for its own sake, yet it is his to disentangle those parts of the Old Testament where the revelation of God is forcing its way through the popular religion, in ways which even the writers themselves but dimly understood. Still the preacher is not an academic ; he is an evangelist. The minister's conscience is not scientific but pastoral. For this purpose he must often exercise a discreet reserve as to scientific truth in the interest of higher truth, or truth on the whole.

> Although we hold the doctrine sound
> For life outliving hearts of youth,
> Yet who would preach it as a truth
> To those that eddy round and round ?

The thinker and the scholar have a freedom, and even a duty, which do not belong to the pastor who has a cure of souls. The savant may owe to the public, or the lecturer to his class, what the preacher does not owe to his charge. To rend a Church on a point of speculative theology mostly argues some tactlessness on the preacher's part, or a misconception of his office, or an egoistic sense of duty. There may be many points on which he should keep silence, partly because he or his people are not ready, partly because these are points which do not directly concern his Gospel. He should not allow his hand to be forced, especially by outsiders. No outsider has his responsibility, nor, indeed, any insider either. He should be the best judge about his own reserves as pastor. And he should not force the convictions of his people. Of course if the first charge on him were the integrity of pure doctrine (as was once thought), if he were one of the theologians he derides, then perhaps he ought to treat his Church as a class and at once indicate his departure from tradition. But his charge is to educate those people not in a correct theology, old or new, but in a mighty Gospel. He is a minister of the Gospel, not a professor of scientific theology. " There are truths we must say to all, and truths we should say to some ; and there are truths we can only tell to those who ask." It is not the preacher's duty to tell everything he knows about the Bible ; but it is his duty to tell everything he knows about the Gospel, and, in this reduced yet enlarged sense, in this plenary but not exhaustive sense, to declare the whole counsel of God. He has to give the Gospel its divine place in knowledge, and not knowledge a supreme place in the Gospel. The whole counsel of God, not the whole results of scholarship, is the preacher's burthen—these last only when they remove obstacles from the Gospel, or enrich its message. It is no business of the preacher, at the stated occasions of worship, to enlarge on the stratification of the Pentateuch, or the postexilian origin of the Psalms ; unless he is engaged in opening larger sweeps of God's method of revelation, or expounding Christ's true relation to the Old Testament, as its fulfilment, and not its professor.

3. We discourage the position of those who are impatient of the sermon, who walk out when it comes on, or who paralyse preachers by a demand for brevity before everything else. I speak of those who do so on the ground that they go to Church to worship God. I should like to say here that in my humble judgment the demand for short sermons on the part of Christian people is one of the most fatal influences at work to destroy preaching in the true sense of the word. How can a man preach if he feel throughout that the people set a watch upon his lips. Brevity may be the soul of wit, but the preacher is not a wit. And those who say they want little sermon because they are there to worship God and not hear man, have not grasped the rudiments of the first idea of Christian worship. They but represent the indifference of the natural man, his Catholicism,

They but swell that Protestant Catholicism which is preparing so rich a harvest in due course for Rome. For remember that Catholicism is the Christianity of the natural man. It is easy with human nature. You cannot quench the preacher without kindling the priest. If the preachers are not satisfactory, let the Church take steps to make them so. If they bore the people, let the people not be too patient. But let us not go wrong as to what preaching is for the Gospel, or for any Church that is in earnest with the Gospel. A Christianity of short sermons is a Christianity of short fibre.

THE PREACHER AND THE AGE

IV

The Preacher and the Age

THE question raised in the last lecture as to the preacher's attitude to the world is worth closer definition. Is his mental attitude to the world, to all that passes as civilization, or culture, to be one of isolation or accommodation ? I am not asking now whether he should know the results of contemporary culture, nor how far, if he knows them, he ought to press them on his own people. I am asking whether he should do much or little in construing his own conception of his message in the mental vernacular of his time ? It is not here a question of pedagogy with his charge, but of his theology and his truth. It is a larger question than concerns his procedure or style with the public. It concerns his Gospel and its intellectual content. Shall he become here all things to all men ; shall he use here the opportunism that he may freely use in practical affairs, where he has to work *with* other men rather than *upon* them ? Or shall he, at the other extreme, deliver a message manifestly, and almost aggressively, independent of the fashions of thought, with small concern whether men hear or forbear ?

Shall he use the old categories and terms of the Gospel like redemption (always, of course, in a living way, and not as a dead orthodoxy) ? Or shall he be eager to discard such terms as being "the language of Canaan"; and shall he seize on the latest thing in thought or action, and force his message into wholly modern terms ? Shall he discard redemption and take up with evolution ? Shall he reject atonement and speak only of sacrifice ? Shall he cease to think evangelically if only he think ethically ? Shall he give up speaking of faith, and talk of spirituality ? Shall he forswear revelation for the God-consciousness, and drop from his vocabulary a word like incarnation to make room for immanence ? Shall he be silent about the Church in order to speak of the Kingdom of God, or say little even about that, that he may not repel those who will only hear about the brotherhood of man ? Should he give up alluding to the bond of the Spirit, and dilate upon sympathies and affinities ? That is to say, are the intelligible terms of his message to be given it chiefly by current thought ? Is its substance so poor, its matter so impotent, that it has been unable to frame a permanent terminology for its own spiritual experiences, and is forced to borrow and adapt the current language of the cultured natural man ? Is the preacher's terminology to have regard only to men's business and their bosoms, to the vocabulary of commerce and affection ? And must he cast off the specific language created and con-

secrated by classic Christian experience because it
is theological and non-natural ? If he keep any
theology, is it to be adjusted entirely to modern
thought without any call made on modern thought
to adjust itself to a theology given in the Gospel and
peculiar or inevitable to it ? Is his mind, for all its
heavenly birth and lineage, to be entirely naturalized
in the better quarters of the world ? Or is he to be
palpably less at home in the world's ways of thinking
and writing, a stranger and a sojourner as all his
fathers were ?

An acute form of the difficulty occurs when a
preacher is faced by the question, Shall I preach to
the modern age, whether by my theology or my
methods, at the cost of rending my Church ? Well,
with a man of real culture, sympathy, and good
sense, (I have said) probably the dilemma need not
occur. In very many cases where such crises arise
they arise from the preacher's lack of sympathy and
judgment. Either that, or he lacks a sense of responsibility for anything but what I have called the unload-
ing of his own egoistic conscience. But if the crisis do
come, if a headlong policy of vigour and rigour call for
a decisive answer, it would be this, in my humble
judgment. A man whose action on public affairs
promises to rend his Church should resign his Church,
and seek one that will go solidly with him. I know
it is a very difficult question. But the Church is
not there with political or social reform for its
prime object. And when a Free Church minister
has to fight his people for his position it is

time to leave it. Victory is mostly sterile for
him ; and defeat may be heartbreaking, without
the dignity of the Cross. His Church is not there,
as I have said, to be his platform merely, but
the body of which he is the head ; he must animate
it with his principles and not dissolve it. The brain
must not quarrel with the nerves. He is the Church's
organ rather than the Church his. His first duty
is to the Church. His whole manhood goes primarily
to the Church. If his duty to the public threatens
to destroy his Church, then he should release himself
and his Church likewise. The order of obligation for
a preacher is first to the Gospel (in its nature, not its
particular applications), second to his Church, third
to the great Church, and then to the public. He
is not first a prophet of social righteousness but an
apostle of the Gospel. He is not merely an agent of
the ethical kingdom. Every Christian is that. But
when he adopts the ministry as a life work, he adopts
what is an office of the Church. He becomes something else than a prophet, and something more.
He represents the Spirit which abides like a dove and
does not swoop like an eagle. He accepts the conditions of a stable society, its position, its aid, and,
along with these, responsibility to it. His place is
not a prerogative of his own. It is not a right that
belongs to him by his mere subjective sense of a
Charisma. He is not a wandering seer.

§

In all such cases the line a man may take will be

much affected by his idiosyncrasy. And I do not
say that it ought not, so long as we understand that
idiosyncrasy is not the decisive thing. It is a
question here of the principles that prescribe the
general attitude of the Church to the world, not of a
man to his circle. For these large principles prescribe
the preacher's attitude, in so far as he is more than
the victim of his temperament and becomes the
servant of the Gospel in a Church. And from this
point of view there are two things to be said in
answer to the question with which I set out.

1. First, in the great and crucial ages of the
Church she saved herself and her word by taking
the attitude of detachment—not to say intolerance—
rather than accommodation. She faced the world
with a boon but also a demand. Is there no intolerance in the Johannine writings ? She served a world
she would not obey, in the name of a mastery it
could neither confer nor withstand. She did not
lead the world, nor echo it ; she confronted it. If
she borrowed the thought, the organization, the
methods of the world, she did so voluntarily. And
she only used them as a calculus. She was but
requisitioning the ladders by which she escaped from
the world, and rose to its command. She used the
alloy not to debase the metal, but to make it work-
able, to make it a currency.

The mention of the Johannine writings reminds us
that the first and greatest of these crises was the
conflict with paganism, and especially with gnosticism
in the early centuries. And what was it that then

saved the Church for the future and for the Gospel ? It was not the apologists nor the line they took in presenting Christianity as the noblest of all the cultures, the most comprehensive of all the philosophies, the most efficient of all the ethics, the consummation of prophecies immanent in pagan humanity, and the apotheosis of all its latent powers. That was a line that developed the gnostic tendency, as it is the leading line in the gnosticism of to-day. But the situation was saved by the other line, by Athanasius, who developed everything that distinguished his position out of the principle of the experienced redemption of a ruined world. To express this unutterable reality he had to do as Paul did, to capture and transform the speculation of the day ; and he had even to coin a new metaphysic. He converted the past more than he developed it. He descended on the world, like the true preacher he was, rather than arose from it. He defied it rather than deified it (if the quip may pass). He made the Church victorious by making it unpopular. He compelled the world to accommodate itself to him by preserving an evangelical isolation from it. He overcame the religious liberalism of his day by thought too profound to be welcome to the lazy public, and too positive to be welcome to the amateur discursive schools.

And perhaps the Church has never, since that time, been in a position with the world so crucial as it is at the present day. The old gnosis has never since risen in such critical and yet plausible antagonism to the Gospel till its recrudescence in our own time. The paganism of the Renaissance and its humanism was threatening enough ; but it rested more on the classic scholarship and taste of a few than on the vague and romantic intuitions which, in the religious experiments of to-day, appeal to the general public, borrow the mantle of Christianity, and simulate the voice of the authentic Word.   So that even apostles of that Word are found speaking rather as adventurers of the soul.   They are more drawn to the gnosis of speculation, the occultism of science, the romance of the heart, the mysticism of imagination, than to the historic and ethical spirituality of the evangelical Christ the crucified.   Now there will be no doubt of your popularity if you take that gnostic course with due eloquence, taste, and confidence.   For it expresses the formless longings and dim cravings of the subjectivity of the day. But it has not the future, because it misses the genuine note of the Gospel, and the objective Word and deed in the true moral crisis of the Soul. You will add religion to the vivid interests of the public ; but you will not come with that authority which men at once resent and crave.

The capture of the Western Church by classical philosophy in the shape of medieval scholasticism was very complete ; but it was not comparable to what would have happened had gnosticism got the upper hand in the first crisis.   For Aristotle did not represent the religious element in paganism which gnosticism exploited, the spiritual, imaginative, kindling, popular element. Gnosticism was romantic, it was classicism turned romantic. Its roots are dim because they are outside the literature by which classicism has become known to us for the most part. It represented that element in paganism which was not contributed by cultured Greece so much as held by Hellenism in common with other paganisms, held by it outside the literary class, and chiefly developed in the dreamy East. It stood for the deep human passion to be redeemed; though it did not realize, as historic Christianity alone did, the moral depth of the need, or the holy passion in God to redeem. The redemption which was the passion of Asia was a much more intense though a much less positive and effectual thing than that demanded by the more free and ethical West. It moved among spiritual processes rather than moral and historic acts. And it steamed up, like slow and spectral vapours, from the cauldron of the prisoned, seething world, rather than issued in the effectual shape of a hero and a deed.

Now, had this early gnosticism had its way it would have stifled the young Church in its cradle; whereas medieval Aristotelianism only infected a Church whose evangelical constitution was shown by the Reformation to be now too mature to succumb. In the early period the very affinities of gnosticism with the redemptive idea in Christianity increased the danger by their plausible advances to the burdened soul's demand; and they gave the gnostics a huge advantage over the whiggish apologists and their liberal Christianity, which ignored that idea. But the Gospel triumphed, and, thanks to Athanasius, by the middle ages the evangelical idea had become so imbedded in the constitution of the Church that Aristotle could not smother it, and it leaped to life in the Reformation. Doubtless the Reformation issue was one of life and death. But not so profoundly as in the gnostic strife. It was between two sections of the Church; it was not between the Church and the world, the Church and civilization, the Church and humanity, God and man. Everybody in civilization then belonged to the Church. And even after the Reformation it was only a question of which Church a man belonged to; it was not whether he belonged to Church or world, whether he was Christian or pagan.

But to-day it is the latter question that we ask. The bulk of the civilized public of Europe, practically, either belong to no Church, or they are indifferent to which Church they belong. And most culture is rather with the world than with the Gospel. We are thus in the most critical time since the first centuries. And, if history teach us rightly, does it not teach us that the main policy of the Church must be the same now as then? It must be self-sufficient, autonomous, independent. I say the main policy, for the accommodations to modern knowledge and modern criticism must be many. But amid all these adjustments to the world of natural and rational culture, the Church must in principle be detached. With all her liberalism she must be positive. She must insist on the autonomy of faith in the matter of knowledge and certainty. She must descend on the world out of heaven from God. Her note is the supernatural note which distinguishes incarnation from immanence, redemption from evolution, the Kingdom of God from mere spiritual progress, and the Holy Spirit from mere spiritual process. She must never be opportunist at the cost of being evangelical, liberal at the cost of being positive, too broad for the Cross's narrow way. And she must produce that impression on the whole, that impression of detachment from the world and of descent on it. The minister may be licensed by the Church, but the Church, as Christ's great minister for the kingdom on earth, depends on no licence either from the schools, the world, or the state. The Saviour of the world was not made or moulded by the world; and the world knew, and still knows in Him a presence that must be either obeyed or destroyed. He always looked down on the world He had to save. He always viewed it from God's side, and in God's interest. He always stood for God against the men he would save. It was indeed with divine pity he looked down, and not contempt ; but it *was* with pity, it was not with co-equal love. It was not the love of give and take, but the mercy which gives all and claims all.

And this must be the note of the pulpit. It must of course be liberal. That is to say, it must not be obscurantist. It must give knowledge its place and modify accordingly. It must leave to the region of knowledge much that used to be held part of saving faith. If you are not humane, as civilization understands it, you do not speak the language of the time. You must wear the intelligible forms of living faith, the fair humanities of kind religion. But still more must you be divine and positive, else you do not declare the Word of God which is Humanity's one hope. We do not approach men in order to interpret them to themselves, as a genius might do, but to interpret to them God in Christ. Christ is ours not because He represents our best but because He redeems our worst, not because He set a seal to our manhood but because He saves it, not because He elicits it but because He gives it. You must not tell men that the way to understand God is to understand the human heart, nor that the way to be true to men is to be true to their own selves. We are not true to men till we are in Christian relation to them; and that comes from being true to Christ and to the Word of His grace. As angels of the Churches you must descend on men. That must always be the ruling note of your word and work. If you wash His disciples' feet it must be not merely as a poor serving brother but with the kind dignity of the agent and apostle of Christ. And you must always so speak as the oracles of God, as the ambassadors of Christ, and king's messengers. You must always tell men that they can never be right with each other except as they are right with God in Christ and in the atoning Cross of Christ.

§

2. So the second thing to be said is this. If we accommodate ourselves to the world in one way we must be exigent in another. Our demands must never be submerged by our sympathies. The more kind we are, the more lofty we must be with our kindness. The goodness of God must never minish the severity of God. His gifts of love must never obscure the prior claim of holiness. His grace must never abolish His judgment. Fatherhood is not the fatherhood of Christ's God if it erase from our faith the necessity of an Atonement offered not to man alone but to God. The love by which God's offspring are called sons of God is not His kindness to His creatures, but it is a special manner of love bestowed upon us with the gift of Christ and not with the gift of existence, by a Redeemer and not a Creator (1 John i. 3).

But the particular bearing of the principle in my mind at the moment is this.—If we so accommodate ourselves to the world as to reduce the bulk of our *creed* we must insist on more serious attention, more concentration, by the world upon the quality of our *faith*. Reduction of belief on our part must be balanced by concentration of faith on the part of the public.

Reduce the burden of belief we must. The old orthodoxy laid on men's believing power more than it could carry. That orthodoxy, that Protestant scholasticism, was in its way thorough. It went in its way as Ibsen's Brand did in his—it was all or nothing. It moved altogether if it moved at all. It attracted the all-or-nothing spirits, whose tendency was to move like a prairie fire, covering the whole area but spreading only in one plane. It was comprehensive and acute rather than profound and subtle. It threatened to organize the faith clean out of belief. It seemed to sacrifice colour to drawing, and life to form. It had no atmosphere, no flexibility. And, great as it could be, it came at last to be more vast than great. It brought to men more to carry than power to carry it. And like its predecessor, the medieval scholasticism, it was disintegrated by its own subtlety; it crumbled through its own acuteness; it died of its own insatiable dialectic; and fell of its own thin and ambitious imperialism.

This appeared conspicuously in regard to the claims made for the Bible as replacing the Church. ' The whole Bible or none,' it was said. ' Take but a stone away and the edifice subsides.' This came of the Bible having been reduced to a fabric instead of an organism. And how many sceptics that course has made! How many Pharisees! How many spiritual tragedies! If I were a Secularist I would not touch by assault the doctrine of plenary verbal inspiration and inerrancy. I should let it work freely as one of my best adjutants. But this all-or-nothingness applied also to the whole system of Protestant scholasticism. Dislodge but a pillar of the porch and the house fell in. Lop a bough and the tree died. Train a branch another way and it pined.

The habit of mind, I say, was in its way thorough. And, indeed, I often wish we had the like thoroughness of design and excellence of building on the foundations of the present. But we now build with a sense that systems do not last, and so we do not build well. We build but to house a generation or a couple. The systems we frame are all revisable, all on lease ; and the framers naturally leave much to the tenants and inspectors of the future. It was otherwise with our fathers. *In aeternum pinxerunt.* The systems they built aimed at finality. Every part was of the same steel. The nuts and screws were of the eternal. *Nuance*, evolution was an unheard-of thing. So that when the end came it came for many as it has been immortally symbolized for us by the American spirit of comedy in Lowell's *The One Hoss Shay*. That must be the end of every system which aims at being universal and final.

But in such systems we have ceased to believe. Finality is but in God and His act. With a final system we should have no God. The finality would then not be a living soul but a scheme. We believe, on the one hand, that scientific theology lives the growing life of every other science, in respect of its element of knowledge or statement. And we believe, on the other hand, that salvation is not a matter of scientific theology, but of personal relation to the Gospel. And the truth of the Gospel is portable in proportion to its power. "Few things are needful—or one." The one principle of holy grace carries in it all Christ and Christianity. A few

mighty cohesive truths which capture, fire, and mould
the whole soul are worth much more than a correct
conspectus of the total area of divine knowledge—
and especially for the preacher. A minimal creed,
an ample science, a maximal faith—that is our aim.

§

There is one misunderstanding I should like to
avert. When I speak of a reduction of belief I do
not mean an attenuation of belief. I do not mean to
discredit an ample theology. I do not think of
consigning the greater part of faith's area to the
region of Agnosticism, and compelling the mind to be
satisfied with a few general principles. By the
reduction of belief I mean reducing the amount of our
claim upon the belief of the public, shortening the
articles of association, so to say. I do not mean that
every truth of theology should be capable of verification by experience—the pre-existence of Christ is
not. Theological truth is far wider than experience.
But I do mean that we should not base the Church's
appeal to the public upon truths which are outside
experience—meaning Christian experience. In asking people to concentrate more upon what we offer
we cease asking them to attend to what they have
not means of understanding. We ask them to go in
upon their moral experience with more earnestness
and resolution. We would remove their interest
from things they are incompetent to solve, and
kindle it on matters that appeal to their own soul,
conscience, and destiny. So that what we offer is not

so much a new system of theology as a new pronun-
ciation of theology. It is theology uttered with a
change of accent. The stress is differently distribu-
ted. The emphasis falls on other parts of the
great Word. We certainly would escape from the
monotone of a whole system of equal value and obligation in all parts. And we would dwell with but
minor force upon some truths which are not so much
saving truths as their corollaries. If I took an example of what I mean, I would say that we ought to
restore to Christ's Atoning Cross much of the popular
interest so easily arrested by His birth and its manner.
We should lean but lightly on the Virgin Birth, which
does not make a moral appeal to us, but too often
appeals to a ready interest either in a baby or a miracle;
and we should bear far more heavily on the centre
of all moral action and regeneration in the Cross,
which the popular mind so readily shuns because
there the world is crucified into us and we unto the
world. And a like transfer of emphasis should take
place from the truth of Christ's pre-existence, which
is outside the range of our experience, to that of His
risen and royal life, wherein we ourselves are made
partakers of His resurrection and vouchers of His
real presence. So that in the order of importance
we should go to the world first of all with the Atoning
Cross which is the Alpha and Omega of grace;
second, with the resurrection of Christ which is the
emergence into experience of the new life won for us
on the Cross; third with the life, character, teaching, and miracles of Christ; fourth with the pre-

existence of Christ, which is a corollary of His Eternal
Life, and only after such things with the Virgin
Birth, which may or may not be demanded by
the rest.   It is not a case of denying any of these
points or even challenging them.   They may all be
accepted, but let it be in their true perspective, the
perspective of faith.   And they are offered to the
public, and belief is claimed, in the degree of their
relevancy to a vital Christian experience of the one
Christian doctrine of grace.   For when we carry
reduction to its length we condense upon that one
principle and power of grace which has in it the
promise of the potency of all the soul's life and all
Christian truth.

§

We must therefore practise a reduction of belief
and with it a redistribution of emphasis.   We
must call in our main army from lining the
long ramparts.   We must rally at the great strate-
gic forts ; and from them command with our new
weapons, firing quick and carrying far, the whole
region we have to defend.   To do this will give us
fresh impetus.   The change from walls to guns means
the change from defence to attack, from form to
life, from system to power.   It is a change which
brings immense gain.   How much moral force we
have squandered !   We have to admit frankly, if
sadly, that a great deal of what lives were once lost
for, and hearts broken, and torture endured, is not
worth the while.   What an awful course history has

had to take, to teach us things that seem so simple now. What an irony it all is ! Does He that sits in Heaven laugh ? At least we cannot be surprised that some should think He does. Heine spoke of the great Aristophanes of heaven. Arnold asks, Was Heine one of those enigmatic similes ? Is the irony of Christ in the Gospels still in the face and grace of God over human history ? Truly, our great simplicities are most costly and elaborate things. The reason why they seem so simple now is because they were so hard and bitter then. We do now almost automatically what meant once labour and sorrow. We enter into the labours and deaths of others ; and we see clearly only from the shoulders of greater men than ourselves, who had to keep their eyes on the paths for our sakes, and did not see the land.

§

But now if we do thus narrow the demand on the world for belief, are we not entitled to require that this retraction of claim on our part shall be met by a corresponding concentration on the part of the public ? If we bring intellectual relief we must plead for moral attention, the narrowness of intensity. What marks the modern man is the mobility and dispersion of his interest. And what does that mean but weakness of will, the lack of power to attend, to decide, to choose ? Such irresolution is the chief of all reasons for the lack of response to Christ, or even to Christianity. That is why such large sections of culture have no part or lot in Christ ; why they have no more than an interest about Him. For culture in many cases not only does not exercise the will, it dissipates it, it narcotises it. Men are stupefied morally by all the thousand impressions of the hour. They are quick to feel, and keen to know ; but they are not only slow, they are averse, to decide. Yet it is for decision that Christianity calls, nay, it is for decision that the energetic universe calls, far more than for a mere impression in response. We are not set in such a world as this simply to return its note as artists or esthetes, but to act. And Christ asked for faith, which is an energy of the will, far oftener than for love, which is a movement of the heart.

And in this respect Christianity can endure, not by surrendering itself to the modern mind and modern culture, but rather by a break with it : the condition of a long future both for culture and the soul is the Christianity which antagonizes culture without denying its place. Culture asks but a half Gospel ; and a half Gospel is no Gospel. We must, of course, go some way to meet the world, but when we do meet we must do more than greet. A crisis has from time to time to be forced, a crisis of the will. And the world, which is not unready to profess itself enchanted with Christ, must be converted to Him, and subdued, and made not merely a better world, but another world reconciled and redeemed. A new departure is not enough ; there must be a new creation. Refinement is not reform ; and amelioration is not regeneration.

We are not being fairly met if the public bestows upon the few things we now hold crucial no more attention or effort than if they were merely a sample handful scooped at random from a mass of loose or languid truths.

It is very singular that on the most grave concern of life a serious man so often makes up his mind in an offhand way. His religious views are of the most casual kind. He seldom really takes pains with the matter. He does not attend to it. His opinions are a sort of spontaneous deposit on the surface of his mind. If it were a business matter he would go into it. If it were a scientific question he would train his mind, and then examine. He takes business and science seriously. But his religion he does not. Scientific people who begin to desire some acquaintance with theology will betake themselves, not to the masters of that discipline as they would with any other science, but to popular sciolists who happen to have a vogue. It is not a matter worth study, as history, literature, philosophy, economy, or the markets are. I do not say a man's religion must be the result of professional or technical study, like these subjects. But it should receive no less earnest attention, and engage him no less seriously and personally, and not be taken at haphazard. That casualness is the source of most of the confusion of the time. Every important topic of human discussion seems a pathless thicket to the person who gives it no attention. It is only after you have taken it seriously for a year or two that it opens into clear-

ness and order. Religion is confused and pathless
chiefly to those who treat the greatest concerns with
most levity. And it is clear and great not from
without the Church, but from within. To look at
a building like the Albert Hall, or even St. Paul's,
from the outside, you would have no such impression of its vastness or grandeur as you receive
from its interior. And so with Christian truth. It
is really and mightily true only from within.

Now in reducing the bulk of belief we do far more
than scoop up a chance handful from a heap.
That is not how we arrive at the few mighty beliefs
we select. That is not the proper principle, or the
proper method, of treating the ponderous systems.
We must proceed by a serious and laborious process.
A coherent system which has grown obese cannot
be reduced, like a statue, by chipping, or paring,
as the ignorant critic of vigour and rigour thinks.
A criticism which is mere surgery is out of place when
we are dealing with great organic systems of belief.
The methods must be more medical, more psychical,
more sympathetic, more in the nature of moral
regimen, and less in the way of amputation. We
must not cut down, but work down. This reduction exercised on the old creeds is a moral act or
process. It is not merely eclectic. Reduction is
the right word. It is working the huge tissue of
orthodoxy down to its normal bulk and place. It
means acting on it naturally through its organic
centres. To throw beliefs overboard, like superfluous cargo, is only too easy. Any ship's boy can

jettison the past like that, or as much of it as he can lift.   Thousands of thin rebels against orthodoxy stand to prove how cheap that is, and how sterile. Your pert witling, destitute of historic reverence or scientific competency, can entertain a whole company by stripping belief to the nude, and whipping it through the town in the wake of his lean team.   But you cannot dismember at will systems whose parts are neither packed together, nor nailed together, but developed from a centre with some concinnity of thought.   And such these orthodoxies were—both the medieval scholasticism and the Protestant.   The development may have proceeded under a mistaken idea, but it was done with great intellectual power, with rare acumen, and wonderful sequence.   And it cannot be undone simply by smashing the machine and throwing it on the scrap heap.   The idea of a total collapse of the old systems is all very well for poetic effect, humorous point, or popular purposes. Rather, however, if we speak mechanically let us speak (with a friend of my own) of reversing gear.

But it is still better not to speak of an organic system which proceeded from a living Church as a machine. Let us treat it at once more sympathetically, and more scientifically.   Let us treat it as an organism —as an overgrown organism, if you will, and too inert, but as being earnest in its intention and serious in its answer to problems which are real.   If we cease to feel these problems we lose far more than we do by cherishing an inadequate answer. So long as the problems are real an inadequate

answer such as the systems gave is better than
the agnosticism of none.   It took much grave
and able toil of spiritual men to rear those fabrics
we so lightly crush.   They did not do it to amuse
their leisure, or to occupy an idle life.   Had they been
less serious there would have been less temper about
it ; and, after all, the *odium theologicum* is better than
the spiritual *insouciance* of many who cultivate the
modern mind and a sentimental charity more than
they pursue reality and truth.   These systems grew in
the hands of the mental elite of their day.   In labour
they were born, and they should not die in contempt.
If they were worked up they must be worked down.
At least, they should be worked at.   They should
not be the target of the man in the street, as if they
were in the public pillory.   In their decay they are
decayed gentlefolk, somewhat heartless, perhaps,
like the French aristocrats of the Revolution, but
not ignoble, and too distinguished for the missiles
of the mob.   They should not be disintegrated in
their hour of eclipse by tearing their seamless robe
and gambling their vesture away.   If their form
must be reduced, I repeat, it must be worked down.
It was competent moral effort that put them there,
and it must be moral and competent effort that re-
moves them.   It was the science of the day that reared
them ; and it is competent science in their own kind
that should deal with them.   They should be tried
by their peers.   They should not be broken down but
trained down—if I may use the phrase.   If it was
development as they rose, it must be by development

that they subside.   They should be shed and not shot.   In evolution a living thing sheds its superfluous parts ; it is only disease that demands amputation. And it is only the raw procacity of the hour that speaks of theological science as a disease of the Church.   But quackery is the worst heresy.

§

The word I should prefer to use for the process would be distillation.   As the revelation is distilled from the Bible rather than dissected, so we should treat the theologies of the past, and so we should reduce their aged bulk.   The creed is to be distilled from the confessions.   The treatment must be honestly applied, and with insight.   We must divine the creed within the creeds.   It is not simply imbedded in them, as if the débris could be dug away by any youth with a pickaxe, or yokel with a spade.   It rather pervades them as an organic principle.   We must unsphere the spirit of Calvin and Edwards rather than disentomb their remains.   We must first know them, then " appreciate " them.   A modern theology must be an appreciation of the old, done lovingly and sympathetically, and with scientific continuity.   If we need positivity in the present we need also to reach it by the interpretation of the past.   And to interpret we must know both languages equally well.   We must interpret with an informed sympathy.   The great authors of these systems loved and trusted God at least as deeply as we do who never have the word love off our lips—at least *as* deeply, and, on the whole, perhaps, *more* deeply. They had among them some of the spiritual giants of the race. They thought in an atmosphere of Christian experience. Their theology was like the wounds of Christ, graven on their heart and on the palms of their hands. To denounce and ridicule here is sheer heartlessness. The call is for interpretation. The need of the hour in respect of past theologians (if we would escape vulgarity) is informed and sympathetic re-interpretation. We must ask what their profound and solemn minds aimed at, and what they strove by their system to guarantee ; though we may modify their way of securing it.

§

Let me take an illustration. You would not venture to preach at this time of day a sermon on predestination. You say the idea is either exploded or it is left behind. Where it is not entirely discarded it is so out of date as to be too far in the rear of the religious mind for your purpose.

Well, but it may be your duty on occasion to rescue some great beliefs from their oblivion by an age which freely casts God, heaven, and hell into the rear of its concern. You are there not simply to speak what people care to hear but also to make them care for what you must speak. And as to this matter of predestination, is there no way of preaching it so that even to-day some will listen, some will listen gladly, and some few even with a rising soul and a swelling heart ?

Men will still hear of the soul if it be a true soul that speaks—no smatterer, and no self-seeker. They will still hear of the great value of the soul. They will even hear of its absolute value, its pearl of price for whose sake all other pearls are but a currency, and all other ends but means. Tell them that this is the Christian, the New Testament faith. Say, also, that in New Testament times, when it was desired to emphasize the absolute value of anything, they spoke of its pre-existence. The Jews with their beliefs spoke thus of their Law, and of their Temple even. If your audience follow you so far, one at least will want to interject that to speak thus of the absolute value of the soul would lead to speech about its pre-existence. To which you would reply that it did so lead. Even Plato, and many since, took and followed that lead. But that was because, instead of thinking of the soul as a moral subject, they thought of it as a finely vitalized substance, finished in its kind, with an immortal existence innate in itself. The Hebrew idea was different. The Jews thought of the soul as immortal not in itself but in a destiny conferred on it. They thought of its immortality and perfection as given by God. Its destiny was there as the result of the will and choice of God. That destiny was due to the divine purpose, and it existed there, not in the soul's fibre, so to say. It was written not in the soul's creation but in its Creator, not in its germ but in its Maker.[1] Accordingly what was said to pre-

[1] You see how near this comes to our modern idea

exist was not the soul in its independent nature, as a sort of fiery particle forming an exception from the great universe of inert existence, but the will of God for the soul, its destiny as a purpose and choice of God. And as the purpose is that of God, to whom all things future are present, therefore in Him our destiny is an ever-present and ever-living reality. Thus the soul's absolute and final value was found in Christ, in the pre-existent Christ, eternally chosen, God's personal purpose, eternal and unbegotten, in whom we were and are created.

You will not of course preach in exactly those terms, but by such thoughts you may satisfy and clear and stablish your own minds, so that you can put the matter freely in a more popular way. People will listen to that—often indeed too readily, deeming sometimes of the Humanity eternal in God almost as if it were an independent entity in God which God existed to serve and magnify ; so that they speak and think as if God loved Christ for the sake of the humanity He embodied so perfectly, instead of loving humanity for the sake of Christ, who redeemed it so perfectly in God's saving purpose.

about moral personality being the nature and meaning of Soul, and about personality arriving as a growth out of experience and providence by the moral discipline of our faith. I have already pointed out how sonship is not a natural feature of the Soul but is conferred on it, though from its beginning, as a destiny, a gift from God's hand, an adoption from before the foundation of the world by God's calling and purpose.

I am not going further into that. I only want to
point out that the pre-existence of the soul in
Plato became, for a Christian thought based on
positive revelation, the pre-existence of Christ, who
was the personal embodiment of God's personal
purpose and choice with persons, the Captain of the
elect, the eternal object of God's choice, and God's
own perfect and perpetual answer to His own will.
I only want to say that, if you put it to people in
the appropriate way, and not exactly as I put it to
you who are trained men, they will listen with at
least an imaginative interest. For these realities
are great poetry, and when well handled they
satisfy and pacify. And people who rise above a
material, selfish, impatient and over-practical Christianity will listen to preaching about the soul's
destiny, about its being so absolute and precious
that it was predestiny, bound up with God's
timeless thought, will, and purpose—a purpose
pre-intelligent and pre-active and pre-redeeming
(Rom. viii. 28 ff.)—a purpose in which God fore-
knew what He was about, fore-ordained the soul,
the race, unto salvation, and fore-saved and justified it before our day, and indeed before the day of
Time. People can be made to rise above the vulgar
contempt for such interests. They can be made to
respond to efforts of this kind to translate a material
and temporal valuation of life into a spiritual and
eternal, to deliver them from polemical dogmas
about the number and specification of the elect
to the presence and sober joy of thoughts beyond

time concerning the fundamental gift and absolute reality of a redeeming salvation. It is in our forgiveness that we find our soul and its destiny. Faith in an eternally slain Christ is the foundation for the Church of all certainty of salvation, all divine destiny for the soul. From the beginning, from the heart of God, from Christ, we were destined for God's will and redemption. We were forever in His purpose in Christ our Saviour. We were from the first where Christ, by God's eternal will, ever is. And so we arrive at the great world-conquering and world-reconciling conviction which lifts the soul to a heavenly rock above the flux and storm of Time. It is the conviction that Christ in us is the hope of glory, that any hope we have of a glorious and transcendent future rests upon the finished reality of a glorious and transcendent past, not only in Calvary but in the very bosom and will of a Holy Father Almighty to save and Eternal to seal.

§

If we catch no echo in these considerations of mighty happenings beyond the light of common day, if we hear no hint or music of them from behind the veil, if, while we prepare (as you are here doing) to play our part upon this stage of time, we hear nothing of the murmur of that eternal cloud of witnesses expectant on the other side of the curtain, and if we do not rise to their interests or their thoughts, then we cannot quit ourselves well (as they would count well) when the time comes. And if people will not hear of such things, because they are stale lumber well banished to the attics of the Church when it was refurnished in modern taste, then their revolt is not from orthodoxy, dogma, or polemic but from the serious, the Christian, the spiritual, the eternal world of life and reality.

It is easy for any soft humanist or hard witling to hold up to horror or ridicule our fathers' doctrine of predestination, or reprobation.   It is easy because we believe in man (if we do) where they believed in God. We are supremely concerned about human happiness where they were engrossed with the glory of God. We are preoccupied with human freedom, and are not interested (as they were above all) in the freedom of God. We are greatly interested in freedom of thought, and little in the freedom of grace ; much troubled about freedom of thought or action, and little about freedom of soul.   But we are not just to those great spirits till we have the same prime concern, the same perspective of interest, the same sense of final values.   We are not just to them till we realize that what moved everything in them was concern for that glory and freedom of God which is the supreme object of existence, and which pre-scribes the final interests of humanity.   Nothing can make man free which does not secure in advance the freedom of God.   The old theologians saw that as I wish we could see it.   And that was what led them to positions which can seem absurd and in-human only to people who care but for the glorious freedom of man, and who use a God but as its minis-

ter. It is easy for any litterateur to sweep Calvin
out of doors of a morning, and take in a suite of
theological furniture in completely modern style.[1]
But it is not easy, it is a great moral effort, to
think our way out of Calvinism into truth more
modest and no less mighty. It is not easy, it is
laborious moral effort, as well as mental energy,
which enables us to keep in the front of our interest
that issue of God's freedom, and yet to secure it by
other doctrines than those which have now become
untenable. They have become so partly by the
growth of the humane idea, but still more by the
growth upon us of the revelation latent in a historic
Christ and His Gospel.

§

I should like to point out farther that the labour
of this reduction cannot be avoided by attempts,
like Tolstoi's or other naïve spirits, at what we may
call mere repristination—a violent return to revive
Christianity in its earliest and most primitive form.
We cannot do with our Christian ideas and institutions what we can do with our personal faith. We
cannot go back to the fountain head and simply ignore
the 2,000 years of Christian evolution. We cannot
do that now in the matter of polity. We cannot restore the exact conditions of the New Testament

[1] I was amused, while delivering these lectures, to see
over an American shop the sign of the 'Hegel Furniture
Company.'

Church. Nor can we in the matter of creed, of mental construction either of man or the world. It seems easy to the uninstructed person who has the Bible put into his hand to say, ' Why not return, in mode of life and form of thought, to what is so normative there.' He omits to note that the normative in the New Testament is not a pattern. It is there in a historic context, not on a desert island. We cannot even go back the shorter journey to the Reformation in this sense. It would be destructive to man's spiritual life, even if it were psychologically possible, which it is not. Nor is it historically possible. We have not sufficient data about that very early state of affairs. Those who suggest such a thing are devoid of the historical sense. They have no idea of the dimensions of the problem— which is a sure sign of incompetency. And it is therefore as difficult to convince them of the impossibility as it would be to perform the feat. To couple up directly with the Church order of the first century, with its literal precepts, with its mental concepts, would be in truth to break with the past in its more inward reality. We may re-interpret and re-organize, but we cannot restore it. We know what the result of Church restoration is in art, in architecture. And it is no less unhappy and impossible in the inner fabric of our faith. It is impossible for Churches to turn this mental somersault, even if individuals tried it, or sects arose upon the effort. All such attempts have been failures, and, more or less, waste. The future must grow out of all the past.

Neither Church history nor Church piety is a continuous fall from the first century, where each age feels itself at the bottom, and must start scrambling up. Rather the whole of history converges and ascends through the present. And we must interpret the originality and normality of Christ and the New Testament consistently with that. We have to solve our own problems as the whole past presents them. We have to draw from an eternity which is brought to our door by the whole course of history up to now. We have to ignore the growing bulk of the question, to fix on its spiritual core. We have to interrogate eternity through the unity of history, past and present. We must practise divination, and especially at the point where that unity is condensed and narrowed in the Cross of Christ.

Well, if such be the spirit and method of our theological reduction, are we not entitled to call on the public (for whom we are really acting) to meet us in the like earnest spirit. The work done by theologians is not done for a small group of people with an interest in that hobby. It is not sectional work at all. It is first done for the preachers and their preaching, and through them for the public, on the question of most universal moment. And we are entitled, especially we preachers who stand between the theologians and the public (as the theologians stand between the critics and the preachers), to expect from it some effort to correspond. We may ask it to make moral effort, and to treat more seriously that more portable and potent creed which we

distill from the creeds rather than pick from the
poets, or from the poetry even of Scripture. A
generous theology should not be associated with
mere mobility of sympathy and shortness of spiritual
fibre. Let our public put aside the habit of discursive attention and sustained distraction which
marks the restless, casual age. Let it deliberately
call in its vagrant thoughts, and give itself and its
mind to those prime matters of the soul. If they
deserve any attention they deserve our best. Let it
give to this high business of eternity at least some of
the same effort as it gives to the grave business of
time. Let it give to life some of the intense and
capable energy it gives to living. Let its religion
cease to be merely a refuge and a balm for men so
jaded with the pursuit of the world as to be fit on
Sundays for no more than a warm bath or a sacred
concert.

Moreover, let the religious public at least have
some consideration for its ministry, which it irritates
and debases by trivial ethics, and the impatient demand for short sermons and long "socials." Let it
respect the dignity of the ministry. Let it cease to
degrade the ministry into a competitor for public
notice, a caterer for public comfort, and a mere waiter
upon social convenience or religious decency. Let it
make greater demands on the pulpit for power, and
grasp, and range, and penetration, and reality. Let
it encourage the ministry to do more justice to the
mighty *matter* of the Bible and its burthen, and
not only to its beauty, its charm, its sentiment, or

its precepts. Let it come in aid to protect the pulpit from that curse of petty sentiment which grows upon the Church, which rolls up from the pew into the pulpit, and from the pulpit rolls down upon the pew in a warm and soaking mist. There is an element in the preacher's eloquence which only the audience can give. Let it do so by being, not less exalting but more—only, exacting on the great right things. Let it realize that for true eloquence there must be great matter, both in him who speaks and in those who hear. The greatest eloquence is not that of the man but of the theme. There is no such supporter of a minister as the man who, he knows, studies the Bible with as much earnestness as himself, if with fewer facilities. Such supporters add immeasurably to the staying power of a Church. If our people are experts of the Bible we shall have none of the rude remarks of philanthropy about the time the minister wastes on theology. I say that, in the present state of the Church, and certainly for the sake of its pulpit, its ministers, and its future, theology is a greater need than philanthropy. Because men do not know where they are. They are only steering by dead reckoning —when anything may happen. But theology is "taking the sun." And it is wonderful—it is dangerous—how few of our officers can use the sextant for themselves. Yet what is the use of captains who are more at home entertaining the passengers than navigating the ship. The theology of the Bible is but the moral adequacy and virility of the word

of the Cross, and the thews of a powerful Gospel.
A theology chiefly curious, or speculative, a secondary theology, may be left to the leisure of the schools;
but a theology of experienced Grace, primary theology, is of the essence of the Gospel. And it is not
merely of the *bene esse,* it is of the *esse* of the Church.

The Church, then, may adjust itself to the world
in reducing its demand to those experimental but
rational limits which the New Testament prescribes.
But within those limits it must descend on the world
from the side of God and the glory of his throne,
whether it come, like the Spirit, as a rushing mighty
wind, or, like the New Jerusalem, sailing down
beautiful as a bride. In the last matters of the
soul it is the Church that gives the law to the
world ; it is not the world that gives the law to the
Church. But it is the Church as prophet, not as King.
It is not the imperial Church but the serving Church,
the Church not as judge but as witness. It is the
Church not as an organization, far less as a monarchy,
but as the company of the faithful, the communion
of saints and the fellow heirs of the Gospel ; the
Church as the trustee of the Word of saving Grace,
not as the nuncio of an imperious prerogative ; as
the meek, mighty apostle of the Redeemer, not as
the gorgeous vicar of Christ.

§

Meantime let us welcome and use any signs that
the age presents of the frame of mind we desire to
see. Let us be quick to read and interpret not only

its unrest, not even its compunction, but its deep, though hidden, sense of guilt, and its keen, though stifled, sense of despair. Let us recognize that men are brooding on their moral condition much more than they own. Let us realize how they are being forced, by mightier influences than ours, upon the moral problems that set up the real crisis of the soul. Let us not be the victims of the conventional phases of sin, penitence, and prayer; of those forms of them which religious speakers work to death and rob of solemn meaning. Let us learn to discover the thing itself where the traditional expressions of it do not appear, and the ecclesiastical symptoms are wanting. If we get deep enough with the public mind—at any rate in the Old World —we shall find that men are less satisfied with success than would appear from the plaudits of the day, less the victims of things as they are than the press would indicate, and more preoccupied with their inward moral failure than their bravado will admit.

It is true, when the conscience begins to act we often find no more than a vague sense of imperfection before the Christian standard, or a dim disquiet. But that is not all. We find also an inner schism and a real sense of retribution, however vague, when conscience does bite. The curse comes home. But it is not the fear of hell, scarcely of God. It is the fear of judgment, indeed, but the judgment of exposure to man, not of inquisition by God. It is the judgment of being found out, whether by self or society. And the torment of being found out by yourself, and carrying about in yourself a living fraud, a moral corpse, can become to some as great as the exposure to the world. What comes home is the nemesis of guilt in the course of life, not in the judgment outside life. It comes home either in visible tragedy or in inward desiccation and calm despair. The sense of guilt is still there, it is often more active than we are allowed to know. And it cannot be escaped. It is very actual. Read Ibsen, for instance. You will find the dramatists much more to your purpose than most of the novelists. They get closer to life's moral realities. Read him again. Mark and learn his unsparing ethical realism. Could that remorseless insight of his through the shams and clothes of ordinary society miss the grim dull ache of guilt ? For him, as for all the rest of the tragic poets, guilt is the centre of the tragedy. " Guilt remains guilt," he says. " You cannot bully God into any such blessing as turns guilt to merit, or penalty to reward." No, God can be neither bullied nor blandished into that. Yet the blessing is there. The one thing needful is there—not the merit but the mercy. The forgiveness is there, and there from God, there of His own free gift, at His proper cost. And to realize how awful that cost is use such as Ibsen. To save your soul from sunny or silly piety, to realize the deadly inveteracy of evil, its dereliction by God, its sordid paralysis of all redeeming, self-recuperative power in man, its incurable fatal effect upon the moral order of society, read Ibsen. Yea,

to realize how it thereby imports the element of
death even into the moral order of the universe
read Ibsen. It inflicts death on whatever power
you call God. Unless, indeed, that power have the
secret (unknown to this great prophet) of transforming the death which it cannot evade. Within the
moral order there may reside, (Christ says there does
reside,) a moral power to make itself effective, not
only in spite of the wound to it, but by means of
that wound. A holy God has power to make good
the moral law by a personal resource which both
honoured its affronted but infrangible majesty,
and surmounted it in saving love. Such searching,
fundamental things a man like Ibsen enables us to
realize, and compels us to face. Our thought of
evil is too shallow till these keen, hard plough-
shares tear to the depths. Our attention is too
slight and volatile, our hearts too happy, light, and
credulous. These pessimists are a gift of God to
us. Their bitter is a tonic to our time. They are
the protest of a self-respecting conscience against an
idyllic, juvenile, sanguine, and domestic tyranny
of life. It is the great dramatists that are the great
questioners, the great challengers, the great and
serviceable accusers of current, easy, and fungous
sainthood. It is not the learned critics that present
the great challenge which draws out the last resources
of a Gospel. They are too intellectualist. It is the
great moral critics like Ibsen, Carlyle, and their kind.
They lay bare not our errors but our shams. It is
true they have no answer to the question they raise,

no covering for the shame they expose. Ibsen
does not believe that God can be bullied—that He
can be mocked, as the Bible puts it. I wish more
of us shared his belief there. But he also does not
believe in a God that cannot be foiled, in a holiness
that must establish itself upon everything, in a God
of grace, in grace with all the creative power of
God turned to redeem, in God as Lord of the moral
order also, and able to deal with it and its mockery.
A creed that can cope with such sceptics is the final
creed of the world. Why does Ibsen not so believe ?
Because, while he reads one book with uncanny
penetration, the book of Man, Church, and Society,
he has never turned the same piercing eye on the
other book, the New Testament, and never taken
Christ as seriously as he takes man. He is grimly,
ghastly interpretive but not redemptive—like
his analytic age. It is the fault, the bane, of almost
all the great critics and accusers. But consent still
to learn from them what they have to teach you—
you who are already taught by Christ, and sure of
your Gospel—perhaps too slightly sure, and too
lightly persuaded you are, or are making, Christians.
Preach to Ibsen's world, and there are few that you
will miss. Only do not preach his word. Christ's
Gospel has the same radical, unsparing, moral realism,
tearing to the roots, and tearing them up with
relentless moral veracity. It has the note of *thorough*.
You find it chiefly in the exactions, the irony, and the
wrath of Christ's love. And next to them in the
Apostle of love, in the Epistles of John. " If any

man love God and hate his brother he is a liar."
Learn, then, to shun every hymn that has the word
'sweet' in it, to find other sources of "greatness"
than the "gentleness" of God, and to look for
something else than lightness in the burden of
Christ. Let your song be of mercy, but the mercy
of judgment. And learn not to say so much
to your people of a day of Judgment sure though
far. The farness destroys the sureness. Ethicize
the reality of judgment. Moralize the eschatology. Couple it up to the hour. Drop, if need
be, the drapery of the remote assize. The
judge is at the door. Everything comes home.
It comes home in calamity if you do not take it
home in repentance. Everything comes home.
Life needs far more for most people, for all people
when you get as deep as that, far more than filling
out. It needs more than the deep breathing of tonic
oxygen. It needs remaking. It needs divine,
decisive action, forgiveness, atonement, the cancelling
of guilt, salvation in that sense, rescue from the
moral nemesis, the breaking of the guilty entail.
It needs more even than redemption, if by redemption you mean but Buddhist rescue from the tragic
ills and clogs of life. It needs, before all redemption,
reconciliation, the reopening of communication, the
dissipation of guilt's cloud which darkens for us
the face of God. It is unfortunate that so many
who preach reconciliation lose sight of redemption,
while the preachers of redemption are apt to lose
the note of reconciliation.

§

Beware, of course, of censoriousness, which is a frequent trap for the young moralist. But do preach a gospel where salvation is in real rapport with deep guilt, and redemption with holy judgment. For God's sake do not tell poor prodigals and black scoundrels they are better than they think, that they have more of Christ in them than they know, and so on. The conscience which is really in hell is the first to be angered at ingenuities and futilities like these, the more exasperating because of the poetic quarter-truth they contain.

This is where we suffer from the word of a pseudo-liberalism and humanism. It seeks to be modern by the way of extenuation rather than realism, by palliation rather than penetration, by moral tenderness rather than by moral probing, by poetry rather than prophesying, by nursing where surgery is required. So much of our modern liberalism, even when ethical, is more kindly in tone than positive in power. And, therefore, it fails to grasp much beyond the milder sins and the milder sex. It is shy of the only thing relevant—a divine atonement, or it empties it of virile force and mordant meaning. Those who so speak seem never themselves to have resisted unto blood striving against sin, nor to have been snatched from self-contempt and despair. But I venture to think John Newton's "I asked the Lord that I might grow" one of the greatest and most realistic utterances of Christian experience. And it represents the course our sunny liberalism must take as it passes from a trout stream of the morning to the river of God which is full of deep water. Our young lions suffer hunger.

Do you realize that it was the severity of Christ that made the agony of Christ, His love of God's holy law more even than of His brother men ? Do you realize how, first to last, He stood on God's side against men ? There was in existence in the Judaism of Christ's day a mild, humane, and attractive school of the law, in contrast with those teachers who pressed it into unsparing detail. And has it occurred to you to ask why Christ did not ally Himself with that kind and genial school, and work from its midst ? Nay, how was it that He stood as opposed to it as He did to the other extreme ? Because His freedom in relation to the law lay not in getting rid of it, not in easing it. He preached no mere emancipation. He was not antinomian. What He brought was not a general dispensation. The imperative note was always in the front of His preaching. He always recognized the law as the will of God. His complaint was that both extremes tampered with it ; not that the Pharisees were legalist, but that they were inconsistent with their own legal version of it. " What they bid you do do, but do not as they do." In his own relation to the law He was not so much under it, or against it, as above it. He handled it as God would. His obedience to the law was not free like the Sadducees by reducing its claim, nor slavish like the Pharisees

by not rising above its claim. It was the obedience of
the Son in His Father's house. He pressed the law's
validity by expanding its scope. His modifications
were to increase its obligations. Love was more searching, and therefore more imperative, than precept.
Law for him (as for Paul) was always exigent, never
outworn. The Sabbath was made for man. The
greater man grows the more imperative is a Sabbath,
the more serious the penalty of its neglect. Traffic
in the Temple was what roused Him, not its priests
nor its ritual. Commercialist piety was far more
unholy than sacerdotal. As Christ's love to God
was greater than His love to man, so His love for
God's law was more intense than His sympathy with
man's weakness. True His love to men was part
of God's love to men. But that shows that a divine
love of man is only possible if divine holiness is
loved as God loves it. Always the obedience to holy
God was precedent with Christ to the service of needy
men. He served men chiefly out of obedience to
God ; and His love to them was because of His love
to God. His teeming pity flowed from His love,
and His love was fixed upon the Holy One. The
hallowing of God's name always came first. And
for Christ the law was no piece of Judaism to
be overthrown with Pharisaism, but it was the
expression of God's holy will to be honoured in His
Son. The original thing in Jesus was His peculiar way
of honouring the law, and not His discarding of it.
The claim of God's holy will was never ended till
it was met. He was not, as I have said, among the

liberals of the Jewish Church. He pressed the
claim of holy law, only in a new construction. He
was neither orthodox nor liberal. It is even bad
taste to apply to Him such terms. He had the
word of living grace and searching power. That
note is what we call positive to-day. And, therefore, He was adjudged by both dull parties to
be unintelligible or a traitor. And it was only
when Christ had honoured in full the holiness of
God's claim upon the Cross that Paul could take
the attitude to the law he did, and speak of Him as
its end.

The guilt, the Pharisaism, that saturates the
Europe or America spread out before men like
Ibsen, can never be dealt with by pressing a social
ethic, or a moral order, or an enfolding sympathy for
man, while pooh-poohing the holy demand of God.
It can only be dealt with by a conception of God's
action in Christ, which shall do more justice to God's
inexorable holiness than the Judaisms of orthodoxy, or the genialities of humanism. It can only
be dealt with by making room for the judgment
grace of God in Christ's cross—applying it as judi-
ciously as you will, and remembering always the
strength of reserve and the reverence of the holy
name hallowed in silent action there.

But to this subject I shall be compelled to return
by the pressure of that idea which underlies, sub-
dues, and goes on to absorb all I say in this series
of discourse.

THE PREACHER AND RELIGIOUS
REALITY

V

The Preacher and Religious Reality

THERE are two ways of treating the Reformation—
one is to complete it, and one is to escape from it.
And there are two ways of escaping from it.
One is the way of deploring it with shame as
the grand defection of modern history, renouncing it as the grand schism, and returning
to the medievalism it abjured. That is the
Catholic way. And the other is the way of
deploring and renouncing it with regret as a
lapse into theology and violence, when all that
was needed might have been done by culture and
reform. That is the way of Erasmus, and Goethe,
the way of the Illumination. Goethe expresses
the mind of many refined Protestants when he
says that Luther's Reformation threw back the
progress of culture by centuries.

I would express the conviction, against both of
these ways, that the proper treatment of the Reformation is to finish it—to reform and complete it.
And, still further, it is not to correct it by an
extraneous principle like culture, but to reform it
by its own intrinsic principle of faith. We are

but half way through the Reformation. So mighty
was that conversion of Christianity, that second
birth of the Gospel.   Remember, it was in its nature
the Church's reforming of itself.   So it goes on still
as the self-reformation of the reformed Church.
It was evolved from the Church, it was not thrust
on it.   It was the reward to the Church for the
evangelical fidelity that had long been struggling
in it.   It began at the Church's self-reformation
by the Spirit.   That is its genius.   Therefore, it
goes on so.   That is to say, the modernizing of our
theology, as of our evangelical methods, is something demanded by the reformed faith itself.   A
new theology is to express the growth of faith and
give room for more.

I have mentioned and applied several of the
modern ideas to which we have to adjust our
message—the idea of authority, the idea of morality,
the idea of immanence.   There is another modern
passion which we must go out to satisfy, one inherent
in faith itself—the passion for reality—and
especially moral reality.   By which I need hardly
say I mean much more than ordinary sincerity.

The history of the passion for reality would be the
history of the whole modern mind since medievalism
was outgrown.   And that indeed is not so very long
ago.   The medieval period did not really expire till,
in the eighteenth century, the Illumination killed
its legatee in scholastic Protestantism.   But the
history of the movement on its moral side began
with the Reformation.   That was a vast assertion

of ethical realism.   It pursued the actual moral
condition of the soul into the recesses of the conscience, and dealt unsparingly, effectually, with it
there in the shape of sin.   It is true that almost
immediately that mighty wave began to ebb—just
as Judaism surged swiftly back on Pauline Christianity, and submerged it in Catholicism till the
Reformation.   The great moral *vis* of the Reformation subsided into the renewed intellectualism of
the seventeenth century dogmatists, so able, so
acute, so elaborate, and so irrelevant to life.   Correction then became inevitable ; and it came from
the Illumination, the rationalist, humanist movement of the 18th century, with its science and its
romance, its enlargement both of interest and of
heart, its sense of the world and of humanity, its
concrete realism.   As Luther had faced the reality of
the moral situation, the Illumination faced the reality
of the intellectual situation.   And the result now
is that we are driven back to the early moral genius
of the Reformation, to its evangelical prime, to rescue us from a mere eager intellectualism.   We are
forced back, beyond all eagerness or even earnestness,
on the thorough-going moral realism which is the
first interest of the Gospel.   We are driven there
for a refuge from the Illumination ; both from the
intellectualism which overdoes its rationality, and
from the sentiment which overdoes its romance.
At the present hour romantic religion has submerged evangelical, the religion of affection and
temperament has obscured the religion of will and

conscience, the religion of love or lovelessness the religion of holiness or sin. Romantic religion lives in the sentiments and sympathies, but evangelical religion—faith—lives in repentance, forgiveness, trust, and self-committal to the Redeemer. When Paul was in his seventh heaven, and heard things not to be spoken, it was a romantic, mystic moment in his life. But he did not boast of that, but of Jesus Christ, and the Cross, and the faith of the Cross, where was now no condemnation but peace— by which he meant not calm but the life-confidence of reconciliation and co-operation with God. His Christianity lay not in his romantic experiences but in his evangelical. We need a more searching evangelical realism to protect us from orthodoxism, rationalism, and the temperamental litterateurs. And we find it in the old faith (when we take the word faith quite seriously) with its realist demand for a new theology.

§

If we are to preach with Gospel effect to our time we must give up the idea of dragging men back to the dogmas of scholastic Protestantism. It is no more wise than the attempt to drag them back to the dogmas and institutions of the medieval Church. The worship of orthodoxy is Protestant Catholicism, Protestant Romanism. And it is what none of the great men did who have chiefly made Christianity what it is. Christianity did arise on Jewish soil ; but the fathers did not try to force the world back into Judaism, or to any oriental creed. They poured the wine of Christianity into the bottles of the Greek and Roman spirit. They met with their Gospel the real intellectual problems of their time. The misfortune was that their successors did not know when that time was by. And so it was also with the great Reformers. Luther met with the Gospel his time's moral need, Calvin its social and political. That touch their successors lost. But in completing this work we can only do it by facing the situation around us as really as the heroes did theirs.

For instance, we must meet criticism of the Bible with a hospitable face. We have learned much from it, and we have much to learn. We preachers, especially, must realize how it has rediscovered the Bible, as Luther rediscovered the Gospel. We must use all wise and tender means to give our people the results of that rediscovery, and to make the Bible for them the real historic and living book which it has so widely ceased to be. We must avoid irritating them with discoveries of what it is not, and statements of what is upset ; and we must kindle them with the positive exposition of what it is now found to be for heart, history, faith and grace. We must get rid, as we wisely can, of the amateur and fantastic habit of laying out the Bible in diagrams and schemes, which treat it like a public park, and which ignore historic and critical study. We must give up the allegorical interpretations by which some attempt to save its verbal inspiration, now hopelessly gone. And we must restrain ourselves

in the fanciful use of texts at the cost of the historic
revelation which the whole context gives. These
practices have a show of honouring the Bible, but
they really treat it with the disrespect that is always
there when we presume people to mean another
thing than they say. If you treat a text mystically
make it clear that you take a liberty in doing so.
Preach more expository sermons. Take long passages for texts. Perhaps you have no idea how
eager people are to have the Bible expounded, and
how much they prefer you to unriddle what the
Bible says, with its large utterance, than to confuse
them with what you can make it say by some
ingenuity. It is thus you will get real preaching
in the sense of preaching from the real situation
of the Bible to the real situation of the time. It
is thus you make history preach to history, the past
to the present, and not merely a text to a soul.

§

Again we must cultivate reality by preaching to
the social situation, to social sin. It is impossible to
preach with reality to an age like this and ignore the
social crisis and demand. We must face the questions
put to the Gospel by a time which is passing from
one social epoch to another. It is to the Gospel these
questions are put, though they are addressed to the
care of the Church. I hope the Church will see that
they reach their destination. We are at the junction
of two ages—the Capitalist and the Socialist. And
we who live in the supreme society of the Church,

and who possess the word of moral power for every age, must not be unprepared with a relevant word, even if we have not yet the final word. It is a work to be done with the greatest judgment. And it is not honestly done without due knowledge. We must know the ethic of the Gospel on the one hand, and the economics of the age on the other. You will not be so ill-advised as to make this the staple of your pulpit. Some should not touch it there at all. It is not for every preacher, and it is not for the preacher alone, but for the preacher co-operating with men of affairs who will add his knowledge to their own. Neither the preacher alone nor the laymen alone makes the Church, but both do. But the Church, as the great collective preacher, should have some social word that deserves public attention and respect, even if it cannot secure immediate belief. The realism of the Gospel and of the age alike require that. But the subject is so large I will not embark on it. It is one I have not ignored elsewhere. I but use it to illustrate my wider plea, and to enforce the demand for reality in our preaching.

§

I would, however, go on to press upon you at more length the demand for spiritual reality, a spiritual reality which is no more mere sincerity than spiritual veracity is mere plain truth-telling. I mean the practical recognition of the fact that the actual predicament of the human soul is its moral case, that its moral case is need and not strength, that its need is a moral more than a sympathetic need, that it is

a matter of conscience and holiness more than of
heart and affection, of sin more than wrong—though,
of course, it is both.

And here I will venture to confess that the condition of the Church may well cause to realist faith
something less than high satisfaction. Let me not
be accused of being dull to love and pity if I say
that these have been developed by the Churches
we know best at the cost of the spiritual life, of the
moral soul, and of a Gospel of holiness. I assure you I
have the affections of other men, and a passion mostly
too keen to be safely loosed and let go. I have a
sense of wrong in things that would fill many of
these lectures with violent, and perhaps some bitter,
denunciation. It is a grief to me to walk the streets,
and to see, with eyes too dim to see, the needy
waifs, the dear, poor women, the lean, weary, great-
eyed children. O, these sheep, what have they done !
Love and pity are to me a daily pain. And yet it
was not the sorrow of the world that broke the heart
of Christ, but its wickedness. He was equal to its
sorrow, and His power was never below His pity. He
began by being the world's healer. But what broke
him was its sin. That mighty heart, so capacious to
receive, and so swift to pity, had to end as the
moral Saviour. His witness of the loving God had to
become His work for the Holy. And the greatest
thing He could do in His love and pity was to redeem
us. He lived benignly among the poignant realities
of human sorrow, but what killed Him was His
realization of human sin and guilt. The healer of

our pain had to practise a more radical realism than pain stirs, and become the destroyer of·our wickedness. Only so could the love and pity prevail at last. The brotherhood of man could only come by the communion of Saints in the household of faith, of men who by the awful Cross were scarcely saved. Yet to-day this Cross, with its moral realism dredging the very bottom of the conscience, and descending even into hell, is the centre of much more sentiment than repentance, and of far more celebration than surrender.

We suffer from three things, I will say. The Church, of course, has always suffered from whatever was the great world-power of the age, and suffered either by oppression from it, or, worse, by infection. It suffered so from pagan Rome. It has suffered from the dynasties of modern Europe. And as the world-power of to-day is the money power the Church to-day suffers from the plutocracy. I do not say from the plutocrats. Many of them mean well, and do well. But it suffers from the plutocracy. But this, again, is a matter too large ; and I want to come nearer home to the matter of our spiritual realism. I will say then the Church suffers from three things.

1. From triviality (with externality).

2. From uncertainty of its foundation.

3. From satisfaction with itself.

And to cure these the Gospel we have to preach prescribes—

1. For our *triviality*, a new note of greatness in

our creed, the note that sounds in a theology more than in a sentiment.

2. For our *uncertainty*, a new note of wrestling and reality in our prayer.

3. For our *complacency*, a new note of judgment in our salvation.

And these three remedies cannot be taken by way of mere outward enterprise, (which will, indeed, collapse for want of them). They can only be taken inwardly, by means of more religion, more positive religion, and more personal religion. I believe that a Church really sanctified would develop more power, light, and machinery for dealing with the tremendous realities of the world than is possible while we are groping in the dark, picking our timid path in economics, or flogging up the energies of a flagging faith.

§

1. As to the triviality from which we suffer.

I am afraid that, for the general public, religion has become associated with the small and negligible side of the soul. Nowhere has mediocrity its chance as it has it in religion. Nowhere has the gossipy side of life such scope. Nowhere has quackery of every kind such a field and such a harvest. I know very well that this is a perversion of the tenderness of religion for the weak things of the world and for the individual case. But a perversion it is. The weak things are not only considered, they take command. They claim to give the law. They make a majority. They trade upon Christian love, and

belittle it. Eternity and its issues go out of faith
as love comes in. Churches and preachers are
choked with a crowd of paltry things kept in place
by no sure authority, and dignified by no governing
power. Both ministers and Churches have as much
of a struggle to get time for spiritual culture as if
it were none of their business. Christian ethic
suffers from what I may call inversion. I mean
this. When Paul, the persecutor, goes the length
he does in considering the weak brother it is a
very great trophy of the moral victory of Christ,
and it prescribes a principle of Christian ethic. But
it is a total inversion of that ethic when the weakling
sets up a claim, and demands as a right what the
apostle gave but as a grace. That is overweening
in the weak, and it is fatal for the Church. It turns
consideration to pampering, and makes Christian
pity the factory of moral paupers with the paupers'
audacity. Or, on the other hand, the Church's
worship, which should gather and greaten its soul,
is sacrificed to its work. You have bustle all the
week and baldness all the Sunday. You have
energy everywhere except in the Spirit. The
religious material is tugged and stretched to cover
so much that it grows too thin for anything and
parts into rents and rags. We are more anxious to
cover ground than to secure it, to evangelize the
world than to convert it. It is faithless impatience,
of the youngest thinnest kind. A bustling institution may cover spiritual destitution, just as Christian
work may be taken up as a narcotic to spiritual

doubt and emptiness. The minister's study becomes more of an office than an oratory. Committees suck away the breath of power. Socialities become the only welcome sacraments. The tea-meeting draws people together as the communion table does not. The minister may talk the silliest platitudes without resentment, but he may not smoke a cigar in some places without causing an explosion. And religion becomes an ambulance, not a pioneer.

But why need I go on with a diagnosis which is only too apt to describe tendencies as if they were results, and treat extreme cases as if they were the rule. Let us turn from observation to experience. Let us look within. Do our hungry souls not tell us faithfully that much of our vivid and ingenious talk about statistics of Church attendance, about advanced and popular methods is well, is eloquent— but 'tis not true. It regards the Church as a going concern rather than a communion of saints. It has the tone of the press rather than of the Gospel. It has not the accent of the Holy Ghost, not his solemn rushing wind, nor the piercing of his discerning sword. It is not the truth, the kind of truth, that goes to the reality of the spiritual case. It treats symptoms rather than diagnoses the disease. Suppose Christ had read no deeper than that the predicament of man and Israel! Suppose He had pierced no closer to moral reality than that ! Suppose He had measured His success by His supporters. Suppose His great and first object had been conversions.

§

For that state of things, that πολυπραγμοσύνη both in the Church and the world, there is no outward remedy. What we need most is not the re-organization of society. That is a topic so actual that the press will discuss it freely. But the actual is one thing, the real is another. The actual is the present hour, the real is the eternal power. And the reality of the situation it is hard to make people face. A business man learns the habit of facing fully his financial position, and noting it almost daily. But we have not learned the habit of facing fully and courageously the moral situation. When we do, we find that the re-organization of society is a small matter compared with the re-organization of the soul. And no new methods will do that. No reformation of our *modus operandi* will do that. You cannot do that by institutionalizing our religious agencies. The re-organizing of the soul is Redeemer's work. We have to secure our foundations anew. We Protestants have always to be securing the foundation anew. It is our genius to plant every man on the Rock, and to plant the whole man there. He has continually to refer himself to Christ, and to appropriate Christ's salvation anew. We have constantly to acquire what we inherit. The branch must ever draw from the trunk vine. We must keep in close contact at one end with spiritual reality. If we do not we are cut off and withered. That is, we become sectional and shrunk, sectarian and trivial.   And churches may become hives of little bees, with the due proportion of drones and stings, instead of fraternities of godly, great, wise, and worthy souls.

We must regain our sense of *soul* greatness, and our sense of its eternal price.   If we measure things by the Cross, which is the price of salvation, and the touchstone of spiritual reality, God cares more that we should be great than that we should be happy. He cares more that we should trust and help than that we should enjoy.   Christ's love(which was God's) was all help and no enjoyment.   Whereas for most people, Christian people, it is the other way.   A religion that makes men right and real seems to have no chance with one that makes them feel safe and " good."   But the Churches can do nothing permanent and nothing final for human welfare till the soul gets its own.   The Church is not " first of all a working Church."   It is a communion of saints and lovers, a company of believers, a fellowship of spiritual realists.   It is there first to feed the soul with eternal reality, to stablish, strengthen, and settle the soul upon the Rock of Ages.   You cannot expect ill fed people to devise much wisdom, or do much good.   And many in our active churches are very hungry as to the soul.   They are anæmic in the Spirit.   They are fed upon sentiment and not on faith.   They have hectic energy—and leanness of soul.

§

If the soul is to realize its greatness, and its union

with God's eternity in the world, it must be nourished with more congenial food. What shall that be? The philosophies, the humanities, the mysticisms? Can the soul be settled on reality by philosophies of its own cosmic place? Can it be stayed on psychologies of its mystic structure and volcanic subliminal depths? Do we come into tune with the infinite by mystic immersion in the sea of Being? Does our reconciliation consist in recovering a forgotten sense that human nature is always in unbroken continuity with the divine? Can we cultivate moral reality by a mere transcendent ethic? Many a gross Pharisee is a mighty moralist; and he believes himself sincere with it. The deadliest Pharisaism is not hypocrisy; it is the unconscious Pharisaism of unreality. Can we escape that by mere moral vigour and rigour? Can we greaten the soul for good by literary contact with epic heroisms, or æsthetic spectacles of its dramatic fate? Can we even dilate and confirm the soul into eternity by loftiest speculation upon the nature of Godhead and the psychology of Trinity?

No. However these things move us they do not make us. They may alter us but they do not change us. They refit us but they do not reform us. The greatness of the soul, the greatness of faith, cannot be sustained upon any scrutiny of the soul, whether created or increate, human or divine, not by any psychology of man or of God; but only upon the experience of the soul redeemed. The mere contemplation

of Christ will not save you.   You must appropriate
Him.   You must know the fellowship of His death.
But that means that it is moral action that is reality.   God Himself is an ἐνεργεία.   And it is by
the fellowship of the supreme moral action of the
spiritual world in Christ's Cross that our soul
comes to reality, to its true self, its real depths,
and its eternal destiny.   And most of all we
share the last realism of life by the sense, so gone
from our practical creed, *quanti ponderis sit peccatum*, what it cost the Redeemer to redeem.   No
estimate of the soul which may be reached by
itself is so true and great as His estimate, who
counted and paid the whole cost of the great war for
its recovery.   That estimate of sin is expressed in
the Cross.   And if the preachers do not feel this
(as they often do not) the Church must, and must
force the preachers' hand.   But to learn the Cross so
is no mere matter of Bible class or of theology.   We
must give it time and scope to act upon us, as we do
not now do, before we can presume to act with it
upon the world.   And then perhaps we may cease
to hear so much of that talk which paralyses the
preacher about short sermons, incessant visits, or religious bustle.   Justification is far more than visitation.

§

It is impossible to banish sentiment from religion
without impoverishing it, but it is quite necessary
to teach it its true place ; and never so necessary
as to-day.   It cannot be allowed to lead, as in

so many cases it does. What imagination did in medieval Catholicism, that sentiment does in contemporary
Protestantism. And the one is a guide no safer than
the other. Both tend to the unreal. But there is this
difference, that the Bible, which is full of imagination, has no sentiment. Such an episode as that of
the alabaster box is not sentiment but passion.
It is certain that sentiment occupies a place with
us which is quite out of the perspective of New
Testament faith. It makes the language of that faith
unintelligible. It can be for the hour, and for our
democratic Churches, a foe as dangerous to reality
as dishonesty is. It creates a demand for emotions
which become too facile in the supply, and, therefore,
thoughtless and unreal. Unreality is worse than dishonesty. And we even have in our religion what has
been called the pharisaism of the publican. One has
often to note in history the total lack of sound judgment that goes with extreme pietism, or the absence
of reality, and even veracity, that *may* go with the
saintly type. We have, moreover, the modern
and most insidious type of Pharisaism—the unconscious hypocrite, the man or woman not of fraud
but of pose, not of deep and dark design but of
subtle egoism, prompt certainty, and facile religiosity. The mischief lies in the unreality of
their faith and character rather than in a calculated
hypocrisy. The victims are fair and fickle, rather
than hollow and hard.

I would trace the undue place which modern
religion gives to sentiment to the undue subjectivity

of the whole modern type of faith, and its loss of
hold upon the mind. And, definitely, I would trace
it to the loss of a real positive authority, the loss
of an objective grasp of the world's moral crisis
in the Christian centre of the Cross. So long as
the chief value of the Cross is its value for man,
so long as its first effect is upon man and not
upon God, so long as its prime action is not upon
reality but upon our feeling about reality, then
so long shall we be led away from direct contact with reality at our religious centre ; and we
shall be induced to dwell more upon our experience of reconciliation than on the God by
whose self-reconciliation we are reconciled. There
is something fatal to a real and thorough religion
in a view which makes the finished work of
God to depend for its fate upon human experience. It makes God a mere offerer, proposer,
or promiser, until we have become receivers. It
might even descend to present God in a light little
different from that of a candidate for the suffrage
of our faith. " It generates a religion of words,
and not of purposes and facts, having its reality
in the creature and only its proposal of reality in
God " (Ed. Irving). To regain our spiritual reality
and its moral tone we must go back from our subjective experience, not only to the objectivity of
a historic Cross, but to the objectivity and the
cruciality of God's spiritual action behind that historic
Cross, to a central action within His own nature.
Our spiritual reality and its ethical results, both

for private and public righteousness, mean a fresh grasp by the Church of the work of Christ upon the holiness of God and upon the principle of evil. That is the spiritual condition on which alone we can restore the note of moral realism that has died from our sympathetic piety. I allude often to that frequent combination of rationalism with sentiment which marks both a hard orthodoxy and a hard heresy. The sentiment then represents the effort on the part of intellectualism to make up by feeling, cultivated if not forced, for the great and real emotion that flows of itself from contact with the supernatural issues involved, and from a share in the central moral drama of existence.

§

2. Besides the triviality and externality I have named, we suffer from uncertainty. For the hour perhaps the Church has more need to cultivate certainty than sanctity. It is only the certainty we lack that can give us the sanctity we desire. If we are duly certain about God's holiness our own will follow. It is only the certainty of the Cross that can give us the sanctity of the Spirit. For the fountain head of the Spirit is the Cross. An established or a Catholic Church can flourish upon mere assent ; but for our purposes we need certainty as a personal experience, certainty at first hand from God in Christ. One has truly said, " The grand remedy for the present epidemic of doubt is a personal interest in the struggle against

evil." We do not get the full force of these words
till we interpret them of Christ's decisive battle with
evil in the Cross, and our part and lot there. The
certainty which criticism is sapping can never be
regained by more positive criticism. The whole
situation is being changed by the new movement;
and we are being forced on a new basis of certainty—
or rather forced anew on the old, on the evangelical
basis of personal salvation, personal forgiveness,
experienced from the Cross of Christ as the redemption of the whole moral world.

For holiness of the evangelical type we surely
need this certainty—for the true holiness, which
grows upon our faith and we know it not. The
forms of sanctity in vogue are a little too self-
conscious, and too directly cultivated. It is always
dangerous to make religion one of the professions.
And to work at holiness can be fatal. Yet some
forms of sanctity much admired seem to me to be
pursued as a spiritual luxury rather than worn
upon faith like a spiritual halo as unfelt as our hair.
When Moses came down from the Mount he wist
not that his face shone. We languish after " peace,
perfect peace " when we should be at godly war.
The sinlessness we admire may be no more than
poverty of blood. And we sing mawkishly about
" Angels of Jesus, angels of light " when we should
be wrestling with them for the new name. It is
so easy to do Christian work, and so hard to pray.
*Magna res est, magnum omnino bonum, cum Jesu
conversari.* It is not hard to be devotional, but

it is hard to pray. *Orare est laborare.* What is
called a gift in prayer is not uncommon. What
is harder to come at is the gift from prayer, the
prayer that prevails. Men may even take up Christian work to evade the arduous toil of spiritual
concentration. And outward work often does
cost us our spiritual insight, certainty, and reality.
But without soul-certainty neither our work nor
our principle has any meaning. It is soul-certainty
that the world needs, even more than sound principles—not soul-facility but soul-certainty, not
ready religion but sure. And it is soul-certainty
that the ordinary able preacher, of busy effort,
good cricket, vivid interests, actual topics, recent reading, and ingenious prayers cannot give
you. Knowledge may give you convictions, and
thought ideas ; conscience will give you principles,
and the heart sentiments ; but that soul-certainty,
that saved certainty, which is Eternal Life, can
only arise from something very objective and
positive, which turns the truths of the preacher
to the word of authority, sets him in the Evangelic
succession, and clothes him with the apostolic
power. Our preaching has lost the note of authority—though not the air of authority, the note of
authoritativeness. That note, indeed, may be a phase
of our Pharisaism. But it has lost the stamp and
effect of authority. The minister is more strongly
induced to be the friend and comrade of his people
than their moral authority and guide. And he is
tempted to care more (as the public care more)

for the happy touch in his preaching than the great Word.

What we need is not so much something pious as something positive which makes piety. We need fewer homilies upon " Fret not " or " Study to be Quiet," fewer essays on " the Beauty of Holiness," or other aspects of pensive piety. And we need more sermons on " Through Him the world is crucified to me, and I to the world," or " Him who was made sin for us." There is the real incarnation, the emergence of God's reality, the reality of God as an energy. There is the incarnation which puts us at once at the moral heart of reality—the Son made sin rather than the Word made flesh. The incarnation has no religious value but as the background of the atonement. And here is the real righteousness of God. It is our practical, experiential incorporation into the holy Christ. It is not our success in doing God's will in a Christian spirit. That is a Gospel of whose ineptitude I confess I am tired. It is at the root of much of our present impotence. Christ's Gospel is the gift (through the gift of Christ) of a totally new righteousness, which is identical with faith, rises in forgiveness, emerges in repentance, acts in love, spreads in society, and proceeds in Eternal Life. What is sanctity if it do not bring a deepening repentance ? It was when Christ came to closer quarters with God's holiness that man's sin roused that in Him which is repentance in us, and crushed Him to death. And the repentance of the young convert is the merest regret compared

with that of the aged disciple. What is our sanctification but a perpetual conversion, the realization
of pardon in detail. That way alone lies the reality
on which man's moral soul rests, and with his moral
soul his social future and his eternal destiny.

§

The soul of the age asks us to help it to footing.
And we try—when we can steady our own feet for
a moment. And how do we often proceed ? Why,
we are so ill-found in the autonomy and supremacy
of faith, that, instead of a fresh recourse to
Christ, we cry to the men of science in the other
boat to help us. We are so incredulous of the
knowledge contained in faith, we are so sure that
real knowledge cannot come by the moral way
of faith, but only by intellectual science of some
kind, that we look with nervous anxiety for
corroboration—nay, more, for verification— from
the savants. We are actually relieved at the
prospect of ghosts, to vouch, on the authority of
the Psychical Society, for a sure immortality that
we have ceased to find in Christ. And we are
grateful to the original and delightful Professor
William James and Sir Oliver Lodge for the
way in which their fresh results make good
the sad defects of our Christian faith as to the
spiritual nature of the world, or the spiritual depths
of the soul. They tell us the old materialism is
dead, and we breathe again. They suggest that
the old agnosticism is dying, and we are cheered.

We look to them and our faces are lightened. For a time at least they are lightened, till some ingenious fellow suggests new misgivings. Then we become less certain that the new idealism will sustain the soul's life, and we grow anxious again. Or we find ourselves after a delightful evening with the subliminal self, at deadly grips with a ferocious and ignoble passion.

But we reflect, perhaps, that though we personally are weak and contrary, yet a new presentiment of the unseen has laid hold of the modern mind, and we think there may be hope for Christianity still. So when that modern mind asks us for help to a footing we still turn to men of science, to men often who evidently never in their lives read a theological classic or an authority on moral philosophy, who indeed might scout the idea, and we ask them to assure the inquirer, with a certainty beyond ours, that things promise well for a soul. We do this, instead of descending upon science or its imagination with a sureness which has nothing to gain in the way of certainty but everything to give, when it is a question of the certainty above and beneath all. Is it not a nervous and pusillanimous Christianity, devoid of self-respect? How can we hope to regain the influence the pulpit has lost until we come with the surest Word in all the world to the guesses of science, the maxims of ethic, and the instincts of art.

Meantime, all kinds of occultism exploit this groping hunger of the age in the interests of their hobby. They believe not Moses and the prophets, but they would believe if one returned from the dead. They have lost the sense of moral evidence, which is faith, and they are devoted to phantasmal, which is sight. The rubbish that is grotesquely called Christian science is the scoriae of a volcano. It means, being interpreted, that the upheaval of the hour is not due to the need for truth, formal and stateable, but for power. It is soul certainty and moral reality that we crave for more than any ology or any doxy. We demand the unseen not in the form of a doctrine, or even an idea, far less a system, but as an energy, a life principle of rescue, power, authority. Men ask us, not, "What do you believe? but "What helps you, really?" What does it matter about our belief if it do not help? And there is but one way to that reality. The reality that matters, and that helps the race is redemption. Our puny individualism is always asking, "What helps me?" But we shall get no satisfactory answer even to that question upon the lines of mere subjective feeling —as we might say of a meal "it does me good, I feel fed "—but only upon those ethical lines which include the whole race, though they may for our individual selves sometimes bring us rather to heroic confidence than to happy peace.

The note of the higher age is moral realism. It is the quest for unfailing love, in the spirit of unsparing ethical realism, the quest, in a word, for holy love. It is the quest which is met in prophet, Christ,

and apostle. And the focus of the whole answer
is still the Cross, where the holy love of the Eternal
spared not His own Son in face of the ghastly
realism of guilt. We can *trust* love only as it is holy.

§

But I can still hear the pertinacious citizen of
his own age, who is a Chauvinist or Jingo of his
own century as some are of their own country,
who is totally disqualified for reading either his
time or his land because he knows no other—I
can hear him say, " Are not Abana and Pharpar
at our own doors better than that provincial old
Jordan ? Are not art, science, ethic, sentiment,
and philanthropy, however defective, better than
these Hebrew old clothes ?   Is the answer to the
soul still in the worn old past and not in the modern
spirit ? "   Yes, that is so. The answer is in the
old past, in the historic cross of Christ or nowhere.
" But even Paul was only a Judaist of genius who
disfigured Christ by rabbinic notions. And we
are so weary of the old theologies." But I was
not thinking of theologies. I had in my mind a
deeper weariness than yours, and I was thinking of
principalities and powers. When shall we learn
that Paul, for instance, was not a dogmatist but
the apostle of an act of grace which condensed in
itself the moral energy of Eternal Reality ? He was
the vehicle of a passionate soul-experience, soul-
certainty, and moral reality. He was saturated
with theology, as you are with (let us say) psychical

science, but he was not a dogmatician. He was afire with the faith which is a life, with an experience which made his mere ideas possibly inconsistent but still incandescent. I have already pointed out how, to find expression for these experiences from the Cross, he seized every likely idea, and pressed it into service, whenever he met it—in Judaism, Gnosticism, Roman law or elsewhere. I was thinking of the weariness which the theologies were very earnest efforts to heal. It is the old perennial curse that lies on us—and it is the old eternal cure. If you feel the curse (and it is moral dullness not to feel it), where do you find so deep a treatment of it, and so many cases of cure, as in the theologies of the Cross ? That which makes the Church is still the key of the world. The act of the Cross is still the soul's centre, the centre of human destiny, and the centre of the real presence of God ; it is not the centre of our worship alone. It is the centre of that evil conscience which is the pivot of the world's tragedy, and therefore, the world's destiny. You cannot sound the great literature of the world, the great transcripts of man's moral soul, without realizing that the Pauline issues are the marrow of the great literature of the world. What moral realism finds at the dregs of life is guilt. And as yet the only effectual secret of guilt's treatment is the Cross. The reality of life is Christ—and not Christ's beauty, pity, or self-sacrifice, but His love as God's holy grace, His moral mercy, moral judgment, moral atone-

ment, and moral victory of redemption. To that
we must return, if all the world go on and leave
us. And not only so, but we preachers must steep
our soul in that, till we become charged with
the one power to which men bow at last,
Christ's conquest of the whole crisis of man's
moral situation, His power to redeem, and His
authority to forgive. The pulpit has lost authority
because it has lost intimacy with the Cross, immersion in the Cross. It has robbed Christ of Paul.
But that Church will be the ruling Church which
most frees man's conscience,—not his thought,
or his theology, but his conscience—and which
carries in it most of the power to forgive and absolve.
Only with this Gospel, authoritative because evangelical, can we make the spiritual life a world power,
take it out of corners and coteries, give it control of
the world and its resources, and save it from convent,
conventicle, and college alike, to be ecumenical, practical, and final. Our lack of authority is mainly due
to our lack of piercing moral realism, the radicalism
of the Cross. It is a power which goes not out and
comes not home except by prayer, laborious prayer
as the concentration of mind and will. " The truth
is not with the right, nor with the left, nor in the
middle, but in the heights." The secret of spiritual
realism is personal judgment, personal pardon,
and personal prayer—prayer as conflict and wrestling
with God, not simply as sunning one's self in God.
There is no reality without wrestling, as without
shedding of blood there is no remission. If you

are not called to wrestle it is only because the
wrestling is being done for you.   Somewhere it must
be done, and we must do more than watch it.   And
for the preacher it is only serious searching prayer,
not prayer as sweet and seemly devotion at the
day's dawn or close, but prayer as an ingredient
of the day's work, pastoral and theological prayer,
priest's prayer—it is only such prayer that can save
the preacher from histrionics and sentiment, flat
fluency, and that familiarity with things holy which
is the very Satan to so many forward apostles.

I speak to and of the ministry, which is at once
our despair and our hope.   If the preachers have
brought preaching down it is the preachers that
must save it.   The Church will be what its ministers
make it.   A Church of faith like Protestantism
must always be what its chief believers make it.
And these foremost and formative believers are
the ministers.   The real archbishops are the arch-
believers.   If a Church has not its chief believers
in the pulpit it is unfortunate.   And if a whole
denomination of Churches fail in this matter there
is something fatally wrong.   The ministers are in idea
the experts in faith.   They are the elite of prayer.   If
the Church is to be saved from the world it is the
ministers that must do it.   And how can they do it
but as men pre-eminently saved from the world.   And
no man has the seal of that salvation on him except
by action—by thought and prayer which become

moral action. A man has the stamp of supernatural
reality upon him only by such prayer. If another
than the minister carry that stamp in any Church
he is its true minister. The true minister, in the
pulpit or out, does all his business in the spirit
of this prayer. The man of commerce may say
he cannot. I will not argue that now. I will
only say that the minister has this advantage—
he not only can but he must, if he know his business,
and is to keep it going. And no man ought to take
up this business unless he know it. A preacher
whose chief power is not in studious prayer is, to that
extent, a man who does not know his business. A
stringent ethic would say he was in danger of
becoming a quack. That of prayer *is* the minister's business. He cannot be a sound preacher
unless he is a priest. Prayer of the serious, evangelical, unceasing sort is to faith what original
research is for science—it is the grand means of
contact with reality. It is the soul's fruitful contact
with that which for the soul is Nature—God in
Christ. It founds us there upon the rock, and with-
stands the gates of hell. The religious life, the
life which has religion for a profession, is the
most dangerous of all. There are so many temptations to unreality in it—especially in connexion
with what is sometimes called the deepening of the
spiritual life. The bane of much sanctity is its
unreality. I do not mean its insincerity, so much as its
lack of contact with world-reality, moral, historic
reality. Our great peril is not the coarse hypocrisy,

which the common critic can see and scourge amid
cheers. It is the subtler, deadlier unreality which
may settle upon the executioner of hypocrisy, which
is hidden even from ourselves, hidden by our very
peace of mind, or hidden by the cheers, hidden, it
may be, by our very well-doing. It is not the
amusing hypocrisy of Mr. Pecksniff but the alarming hypocrisy of Mr. Bulstrode, so much more
terrible because more true to actual life, because
it waits for us at our own door. The preacher feels
the full force of these temptations. At least he
receives their full force, whether he always feel it
or not, from his exposed position. He is a dealer in
words ; and it is very hard to keep them full of the
Spirit, and yet to keep himself their master. He is
a popular leader ; and it is hard to lead the people
without being led by the people to yield to them.
The winning of souls, or the leading of souls, often
costs the soul. A man can be popular and real
both, especially as a preacher. I do not know of any
line of life in which the combination is more possible. But to continue to be popular and also to be
real depends on much. And then the preacher
has the sophistries of his own egoism, the egoism
even of his own conscience, the seductions of his
own vanity, and the insincerities of his own heart,
which are always most dangerous in the guise of
piety. Some preachers appear to have no humiliation, confession, penance, or absolution in their
soul's habit or history. Ephraim is a heifer unbroken
to the yoke. Many a fervent prayer in the pulpit,

and many a thrilling sermon, has but deepened the
perdition of the unreal soul that uttered it—heartfelt
though it was for the hour. Against such things
private searching prayer, prayer much alone with
the Judge of the Pharisees, is the corrective—prayer
whose *keynote* is the Bible, however its *motives* may
be the experiences of the soul. It is better and
safer to pray over the Bible than to brood over self.
And the prayer which is stirred by the Cross is
holier even then that which arises from the guilt
that drives us to the Cross. What really searches
us is neither our own introspection, nor God's law,
but it is God's Gospel, as it pierces us from the merci-
less mercy of the Cross and the Son unspared for us.

§

3. The third vice of the Christian hour is spiritual
self-satisfaction, well-to-do-ness, comfort. The voice
of the turtle is heard in the land.

This is the religious counterpart of that intellectual
self-sufficiency in many sections of science, where
men are quite sure they have, in the experience that
deals so successfully with parts, a key to the infinite
whole. Their science gives them a closed scheme
of all existence, which only needs filling in with
discovery or filling out with invention. They do
not realize that the knowledge of a world, a whole,
is a knowledge by faith and not by science. None
has ever seen or realized a whole world by any
scientific experience, only by an act of faith. The
more we know things or men the less we under-

stand them till faith explains them by their goal.
We see not yet all things, but we see Jesus.

Such also, in its way, is the self-satisfaction
of so much naïve religion, denominationalism, or
Churchmanship, the religion of the plain man who is
always saying he is Davus and not Edipus, who
hates riddles, and who talks to you of his sectional
interests or idols as if they must be of equal
interest and volume to all the world.

> " Who takes the murmur of his little burg
> For all the mighty music of the world."

We live too happily on the middle register. It
is all so interesting—the day's doings, the vivid world,
the Church, the Bible, the meetings, the movements,
the singing, the preaching, the books, the reviews, the
music, the marrying, the giving in marriage. We
enjoy the long picnic, by the still waters, in com-
panies upon the green grass. The flood, indeed, is
already in the hills, and trained and gifted ears hear
it, and give the alarm. And yet we sit down easily
and agreeably beside the modern man, with his
mixture of refined materialism and scrappy culture,
to whom religion is but a phase of his general
interests, or the key-stone of the social arch.
Religion is to-day debased to a mere means of
human happiness, to a social utility, as it never
was before. It was once a political pawn, it is
now a social facility. And the result is unfaith,
or, worse, an affectation of faith. We are so
healthy, so poetical, so kindly, so optimistic.

P.P.

13

God's love and patience and mercy are all so much in line with life's innocent charm, all so much a matter of course and of congratulation. And we are so strange to heart-hunger, or soul-despair, or passionate gratitude, or heavenly home-sickness. Whole tracts of our religion are bare of spiritual passion, or spiritual depth. Christianity speaks the language of our humane civilization ; it does not speak the language of Christ. The age, and much of the Church, believes in civilization and is interested in the Gospel, instead of believing in the Gospel and being interested in civilization. And we treat as fanatics those who tell us that there is no reconciliation possible between the Cross and culture, when each knows its own mind, except as culture itself submits to be redeemed. As if Christ did not come to redeem us not from sin only, nor from worldliness, but from the world.

I once addressed a meeting of ministers on the necessity of the evangelical consciousness, by which I meant the central or even daily life of forgiveness, repentance, humiliation, and their fruits, in contrast with what is vaguely known as the Christian spirit. And I created a good deal of bewilderment. For one of them came to me afterwards, and asked me if he had understood me right, as, to his knowledge, the experience was one that few ministers possessed. If that was so I need not say another word to account for the loss of pulpit power and authority. It is not more religion we need so much as a better order of religion, and a more serious idea of the soul, its sin and its salvation.

For an ill like this there is but one cure. It is a deeper, daily, though perhaps reserved sense, not only of our unworthiness, but of our perdition except for the Grace of Christ, the mercy of the Cross. And this deepened sense will not come. It must be sought, courted, entreated. The deepening of personal religion ! It is something much more that we need. We need the humiliation in which we forget about religion, the faith in which we forget about either faith or works, the sanctity that has no knowledge of its own holiness. We need an experience of Christ in which we think everything about the Christ and not about the experience. We need that preachers shall not keep demanding either a faith or love that we cannot rise to, but shall preach a Christ that produces and compels both. And we need that the Christ we preach shall not be our brother, ideal, or King only, but also our judge. Nay we read that He is chiefly our judge, because He took our judgment on Him for our redemption. Every great revival in the Church has gone with a new sense of Christ's vicarious redemption, and not merely with a new wave of pity. Our great need is not ardour to save man but courage to face God—courage to face God with our soul as it is, and with our Saviour as He is ; to face God always thus, and so to win the power which saves and serves man more than any other power can. We can never fully say " My brother ! " till we have heartily said " My God ; " and we can never heartily say " My God " till we have humbly said " My Guilt ! " That is the root of moral reality, of personal religion, and social security. It is only thus that we really meet the passion for reality, which is so hopeful a feature of modern time, because it is the ruling passion of a Holy God.

PREACHING POSITIVE AND
LIBERAL

VI

Preaching Positive and Liberal

THE first requisite for a Christian man is faith. That is what makes a soul a member of Christ and of the true Church—the faith that works and blossoms out into love. Being faith in Christ, how could it but work and flower out into love? The fact that so often it does not must mean that in so many cases it is not really faith, or not faith in Christ. It is not personal contact and commerce with Him. This faith it is that is the greatest thing in the world, having in it all the promise and potency of love, godliness, peace, and joy in the Holy Ghost. It is such living faith that makes a man a Christian.

But among Christians the preacher stands out in a special place and work. And the first requisite for the ministry of a Church is a theology, a faith which knows what it is about, a positive faith, faith with not only an experience but a content, not glow only but grasp, and mass, and measure. The preacher who is but feeling his way to a theology is but preparing to be a preacher, however eloquent he may have become. He may be no more than " the hierophant of an unapprehended inspiration." And that kind of inspiration may be mantic or romantic, but it is neither prophetic nor apostolic. The faith which makes a man a Christian must go on in the preacher to be a theology. He cannot afford to live on in a *fides non formata*. A viscous unreflecting faith is for the preacher a faith without footing and therefore without authority. In special cases it may have a certain infection about it, but it has not authority. Yet it is authority that the world chiefly needs and the preaching of the hour lacks—an authoritative Gospel in a humble personality. And for authority, for weight, we need experience indeed, but, still more, positive faith.

It is but a little way that experience will carry the herald of the Gospel. He has to expound a message which, because it is eternal, far transcends his experience. He has to do more than set to his own personal seal. Every Christian has to do that. The preacher has to be sure of a knowledge that creates experience, and does not rise out of it. His burthen is something given, something that reports a world beyond experience, a world that is not of experience, though always in its shape. Experience is but in part, yet he has to dogmatize about the whole. He has to be sure of what ever is, and evermore shall be. Experience is in time, and he has to be positive about eternity. His experience covers but his own soul, or at most a few besides that he touches ; yet he has to declare a certainty about the eternal destiny of the whole world, and the eternal will of the whole God. That is a knowledge far beyond experience. It is not realizable except in experience, but experience could not reach it, could not assure it. It is a knowledge that comes by faith. Wherever you have a universe you have something beyond experience, and accessible only to faith. Experience is not the only organ of knowledge, however it may be a condition. Experience deals with but the one, or the several; faith deals with a whole; for it deals with God, eternity and the world; it deals with a reality of the whole, which we experience but in a measure. There is a knowledge by faith as sound of its kind as the knowledge by experience, by science; and its kind is much higher, deeper, more momentous. It is the knowledge of a person in his purpose, not of a thing and its features, not of a force and its laws. It is not simply faith as a personal experience that is the burthen of the preacher, but faith as a knowledge, the inner objective content of faith, the thing in faith which always creates the experience of it; in a word, the person, will, and action of God in Christ. It is there, in the objective personal content of faith, and not in the subjective personal experience, that the authority of the preacher lies. His experience may make him impressive at times, but it is his faith that gives him permanent power. That power really lies not in the preacher but in his Gospel, in his theology. For the preacher it is most true that his theology is an essential, perhaps the essential, part of his religion. He may be quite unfit to lecture in theology as a science, but he is the less of a preacher, however fine a speaker, if he have not a theology at the root of his preaching and its sap circulating in it. And if he is a pastor, producing his effect not by a few addresses but by a cumulative ministry, all this is still more true.

§

The first requirement of the ministry, then, is a positive theology. But by that I do not mean a highly systematic theology, nor an orthodox theology. For a systematic theology easily becomes doctrinaire, and an orthodoxy soon becomes obsolete. It were, well to banish antiquated words like orthodoxy and heterodoxy as anything but historical terms. They belong to an out-grown age, when a formal theology had a direct saving value for the individual soul ; when there was but one true theology instead of many, as there was but one true Church ; when there was an external authority, to make a standard, in an inerrant Bible, a final confession, or an infallible Pope. The one orthodox Church, the Greek Church is the deadest of all the Churches. And we should have been as dead if orthodoxy had had its way with the West as it had with the East. For at its worst it is mere conformity ; and at its best it is the régime of intellectualism. It reduces religion to an intellectualism with a divine charter. And its reaction in heterodoxy is natural, equal, and opposite. Both are intellectualist and theosophic. Let us consider the words, therefore, as

archaic and defunct for faith. And instead of
speaking or thinking about an orthodox theology,
which is canned theology gone stale, let us think
of a positive theology which is theology alive, alert,
and in power.

§

Again, by a positive theology I mean naturally
the opposite of a negative. But when is a theology
negative ? Negative of what ? Negative of a
tradition ? No, of a power. Negative of the
Gospel. A positive theology is an evangelical
theology. Positivity in this connexion has a
chief reference to what I have often to describe as the
primacy of the will. It is moral ; but moral in a far
higher sense than a mere imperative—moral as being
not diffused in an idea or organized in thought, but
concentrated in a personal act, in redemption. The
love manifested by Christ in His life was positive
in the sense that it was not merely affectional but
rational and moral. That is to say its great features
were first that it understood the total situation—
so far it was rational—and second that it condensed
into one definite practical purpose—it was saving
and moral. It understood God uniquely ; no man
knoweth the Father but the Son. It understood
man to his moral centre, and needed that no man
should tell it what was in man. And it was concentrated into crucial action both on God and on man.
It was decisive and redemptive. Positive means
moral in the great evangelical sense. That is to say,

in the first place, it means that the supreme form
of God's love was a real act, central in history and
critical for eternity. It was a holy life not simply
in the sense of being spotless but in the sense of
being one vast moral deed, one absolute achievement
of conscience, affecting the being both of God and
man and the whole spiritual world. It was not
merely impressionist. It was not an influence but
an act, not a fresh stimulus but a new creation,
not a career opened for the race but a finished
thing. Holiness has no meaning apart from an act
into which is put a whole moral person ; and if there
be an eternal person it is an eternal act, and not
merely a past event, or the attribute of an eternal
being, or an infinite presence, as the mystics dream.
Accordingly, in the second place, God's gift was an
eternal life, something beyond natural goodness,
however good, and however refined. For what is
morality, when we are at the height to which we have
now come ? It is not a mere obedience. That were
in the end but some kind of Pharisaism, of which indeed Protestantism has been greatly the victim. No
compliance with a mere law or creed, however good
or fine makes a moral action. Morality is the expression of our personality ; and to grow moral means to
grow in personality, and not merely in a certain exercise of personality. It is our creative action. It is
the soul co-operating with the holy energy of God
and fulfilling its redeemed destiny. To live in the
Spirit is not simply to walk in the light. The Spirit
is creative energy ; and to live in the Spirit is to

exercise this energy. It is eternal life in its countless concrete forms of actuality, experience, and
history—in worship, art, science, politics, in Church,
State, or family. Positive Christianity then is
Christianity which recognizes the primacy of the
moral in the shape of life, and of holy life. It is
Christianity which first adjusts man to the holy and
then creates the holy in man, and does both through
the Cross with its atoning gift of eternal life. It is
evangelical Christianity—Christianity not as a creed
nor as a process but as a Holy Spirit's energy and
act, issuing always from the central act and achievement of God and of history in the Cross of Christ.

But the name of evangelical theology has often
been monopolized by a theology which has not
really escaped from the idea of orthodoxy, a theology
not only elaborate but final, irrevisable, and therefore obscurantist, and therefore robbed of public
power. By an evangelical theology I mean any
theology which does full justice to the one creative
principle of grace. Any theology is evangelical which
does that. A theology is not evangelical by its
conclusions but by its principles, not by its clauses
and statements, not by its spirit or temper, but by
the Holy Spirit of grace and power. It is the statement of a Gospel of Grace, it is not the scientific
explication of that Gospel's corollaries and implicates.

§

Some forms of evangelical theology are too fond
of describing a critical theology as negative. I do

not like the word negative. There is a certain
unpleasant suggestion in it which we should avoid.
I would rather use the more correct and current
antithesis of positive, and say liberal. Here again,
however, we are in difficulties. For in the first place
if what we oppose is liberal, are we not illiberal in
opposing it ? And is there not an unpleasant suggestion in that ? And in the next place, if we follow
current use and say liberal as the antithesis of positive, do we mean that a positive theology is only
conservative and incapable of modification with
time to meet the progress of thought and knowledge ? The answer to that, of course, is that a
confession of faith not only can be, but must be
modified in this way. The creed must take the
expression which gives the best effect at the time to
the grace which creates it. In this regard it reflects
the almighty power of God which (if Christ be His
revelation) is chiefly shown in His capacity for any
self-limitation needful to give effect to His holy
will of grace and love at a particular juncture.
Theological form must be adjustable. The old faith
demands a new theology. For, in the first place, its
nature does, and in the second, its history.

First, its nature does. Christ, as the standing
object of our faith, is the meeting-point of changeless
eternity, and changing history. In Him the eternal
emerges at a fleeting point. But, if He is the same
yesterday, to-day, and for ever, this final utterance
must be expressible at every other such point.
His eternal revelation is vocal and relevant for

every age. The changeless Gospel must speak
with equal facility the language of each new time,
as well as of each far land. If it be missionary
to every soul it is also missionary to the whole soul
of history. There is an ironic, socratic docility in the
everlasting Gospel. It must be flexible if it is to
search and permeate. It must be tractable and
reasonable because it is so supreme and sure. It
must have the power to vary, and to meet the
forms of thought and life which it does so much
to produce. We could never preach to the time if
our Gospel had but a lapidary and monumental
eternity. Remember Lot's wife.

There must be such a thing as a history of Christianity, not merely a history of the effects of Christian doctrine in the world. That doctrine is not a
rock in a stream. The religion itself must have an
elasticity of its own, a variableness and adaptability
which do not alter its substance. It is not like a
philosophic system which cannot reappear in a
modified form, but can only be replaced by another
system. Christianity must modify, for it is not a
fixed quantity cut and dried. It has no existence
outside of the life and the will of moving man.
Therefore while it has a continuity it has also a
history and not a mere persistence. No otherwise is
it a living potent religion. Only the lowest religions,
like the lowest races and creatures, are without
a history. And Christianity has a history because
it is under the constant renewing of the Holy Ghost.
It is a new and independent power of life within the

stream of time. It is not a mere section of civilization. And its history has a unity quite different from the development of religion in general. It is not simply a limb in the organism of spiritual evolution.

In the second place, the history of the old faith demands a re-interpretation of theology, even if we may not say a revision. For I have already noted how the greatest Apostles and fathers of the Church translated the Gospel into the current mind. And I note farther that in history fixed and final dogma constantly tends to produce a type of life quite other than that produced by the old faith. Where you fix a creed you flatten faith. Where dogma is idolized, life is sterilized. Where you canonise a system you demoralize men. But the effect of the faith of the Gospel is entirely the other way. It rouses, exalts, kindles men. A fixed and final system is therefore incompatible with the genius of the Gospel. That is the principle of the Reformation. Living faith means growing form. Orthodoxy, Catholicism, in different degrees tend to petrify life. Therefore they lose the power of the Gospel, no matter what the amount of zeal may be. Dogma is not an end in itself. And even doctrine is but the expression of life, it is not the life indeed.

The old faith of the Gospel, therefore, is not merely patient of new form, a new theology, but it demands it. It produces it. It fits itself in a masterly way to the shape and pressure of the time, unless we prevent it. The very power of its eternity, its supernatural power, shows itself in this, that it uses time and is not left behind. What is eternity but the soul's command of time ?

§

But, if a positive Gospel thus asserts its positivity by irrepressible adjustment, why should we set in opposition positive and liberal. Well, as a matter of fact, theological liberalism has tended to destroy positive belief, distinctive experience, and aggressive Christianity. But perhaps the terms are not happy. Still there they are in use. They are part of the accepted language of the discussion. And the word which is employed to express the adjustments native to a positive Gospel is not "liberal" but "modern." A modern theology is one thing, theological liberalism is another. Ritschl represents one Gospel, Pfleiderer another. And they are disparate and incompatible. Paul and Luther cannot dwell with Hegel. The one is a function of faith, the other is a school of thought. I am not pleading for the terms. I am simply accepting them. They cover distinct things. It is the things I wish to distinguish. And I do so in the course of an attempt to make good my case that a positive and modern theology is a first requisite for a preacher of the Gospel. Of the Gospel, note. For the first requisite for a mere preacher is a temperament. And a temperament without a Gospel is more of a bane than a blessing to a public man. The more of a temperament a preacher has the more he needs a positive Gospel to carry it, and save it from shipwreck. Of course, I imply by my words that what is called liberal theology, as distinct from theology modern and positive, works on the whole against the preaching of the Gospel, and becomes little more than an enlightened Judaism.

I may here anticipate what I go on to say later by explaining in brief that by liberalism I mean the theology that begins with some rational canon of life or nature to which Christianity has to be cut down or enlarged (as the case may be) ; while by a modern positivity I mean a theology that begins with God's gift of a super-logical revelation in Christ's historic person and cross, whose object was not to adjust a contradiction but to resolve a crisis and save a situation of the human soul. For positive theology Christ is the object of faith ; for liberal He is but its first and greatest subject, the agent of a faith directed elsewhere than on Him. It is really an infinite difference. For only one side can be true.

§

We need, for our pulpit efficiency, a theology that is new when compared with catechismal orthodoxy, a restatement of doctrine which may be either "modern" or " liberal." Now which does the Gospel demand ? What is the difference between a modernized positivity and liberalism, as I have defined the terms ?

Let me name some vital distinctions.

1. I begin with the most essential. *The posi-*

tivity of the Gospel means the effectual primacy of the given. And this primacy of the given means two things. I have said that we can think modern and end positive. We can keep abreast of both thought and knowledge and yet emerge with the results of positive faith. We can still believe in the primacy of the given in these two aspects—first in respect of history or the origin of our religion, second in respect of theology or the nature of our religion.

First, in respect of the *origin* of our religion, when we say it is positive we mean that it is historical. The revelation is not primarily in my soul but in a fact which is in the chain of history. It is in Christ and His Cross. Positivity means therefore in the first place historicity. It opposes a religion whose genius is thought or idea instead of historic event. Christianity is founded *in* the historic Jesus, it was not merely founded *by* Him. In Him we have the revelation and not merely the first believer in the revelation. And in Him, in that historic figure, is the final and absolute revelation; He is not a mere stage in the history of revelation. His religion is not simply one among others and the best of them all. It is religion in the final sense of the word. And it is the religion that believes and worships Him; it is not simply religion that believes with Him, and with Him worships God.

Second, in respect of the *nature* of our religion, or its theology, positivity as the primacy of the given means that we take it seriously as the religion of grace. The Gospel descends on man, it does not rise from him. It is not a projection of his innate spirituality. It is revealed, not discovered, not invented. It is of grace, not works. It is conferred, not attained. It is a gift to our poverty, not a triumph of our resource. It is something which holds us, it is not something that we hold. It is something that saves us, and nothing that we have to save. Its Christ is a Christ sent to us and not developed from us, bestowed on our need and not produced from our strength, and He is given for our sin more than for our weakness.

That is to say, the first feature of a positive Gospel is that it is a Gospel of pure, free grace to human sin. (And you will find that liberalism either begins or ends with ignoring sin or minimising it.) The initiative rests entirely with God, and with a holy and injured God. On this article of grace the whole of Christianity turns. "Christianity," says an unfriendly critic, "stands or falls with its doctrine of forgiveness." A positive theology means the doctrines of grace—brought up to date by all means, but only so as to give larger scope to the Gospel of grace than to the claim of religious culture.

A liberal theology has most to say of God's love, a positive of God's mercy. The one views God's love chiefly in relation to human love, the other chiefly in relation to human sin. In relation to sin chiefly—because a positive Gospel is a revelation of *holy* love, and our answer to it is not merely affectional, but holy, obedient, and

worshipful. If the great revelation of God is in the
Cross, and the great gift of the Cross is the Holy
Spirit, then the revelation is holiness, holiness working outward as love. It is not simply sacred love,
as it comes, for most people, to mean ; but it is
holiness working out into love on God's side, as our
faith does on our side. God's love is the outgoing
of his holiness, not as exigent law, but as redeeming
grace, bent on reclaiming us, all bankrupt and
defiant, to his full, rich, harmonious, eternal life.
The holiness of God is His self-sufficient perfection,
whose passion is to establish itself in the unholy by
gracious love. Holiness is love morally perfect ; love
is holiness brimming and overflowing. The perfection
speaks in the overflow. It is in redemption. Love is
perfect, not in amount but in kind, not as intense but
as holy. And holiness is perfect, not as being remote,
nor as being merely pure, but as it asserts itself in
redeeming grace. Love, as holy, must react against
sin in Atonement. Holiness, as grace, must establish
itself by redemption in Satan's Seat. It is not the
obstacle of redemption but its source and impulse.

The primacy of the given, then, is only another
way of expressing the final authority of grace. The
question of the hour, for all life, and not only for the
religious, is that of authority—the true effective
authority. Where is it ? At the last it is here. It
is in God's eternal, perpetual act and gift of grace, met
by the absolute obedience of our faith. Faith is absolute obedience to grace as absolute authority. Personal faith in the holy, gracious God of Christ's

Cross is the one creative, authoritative, life-making, life-giving, life-shaping power of the moral soul.

Now a modernized theology is not only compatible with this old faith, it is inevitable to it. But the liberal theology, as I am describing it, is fatal to the old faith. For all its varieties have this in common. They are indifferent to a doctrine of the Holy Ghost. It is this doctrine that prevents us from describing the progress of Christianity as a mere spiritual process, or the spread of a movement. Any theology that places us in a spiritual *process*, or native movement between the finite and the infinite, depreciates the value of spiritual *act*, and thus makes us independent of the grace of God. Its movement is processional spectacular, aesthestic, it is not historic, dramatic, tragic or ethical. If it speak of the grace of God it does not take it with moral seriousness. It understands by God's grace no more than the Idea moving to transcend our error, or love acting in generosity, or in pity. It reduces mercy to a form of pity by abolishing the claim of holiness, the gravity of sin, and the action of an Atonement. It does not take either the measure of holiness or the weight of sin. It makes the Cross not necessary but valuable ; not central but supplemental ; not creative but exhibitive ; a demonstration, but not a revelation ; a reconciliation but not a redemption. It makes the Church a company of workers and not believers, the brethren of Christ rather than His flock and His property, a genial body rather than a regenerate, a band of lovers rather than of penitents. It attenuates the Fatherhood which it softens. It interprets it as His creating love. Now God the Father is indeed Creator, but it is not as Creator that He is Father. We are all destined to be sons of God ; but the sonship is in our destiny rather than in our origin or state. A distinguished president of the British Association for Science recently described the child as " a candidate for humanity." And we are all but personalities in the making. We are sons by an election rather than a creation. We are sons not by heredity but by adoption; not by right but by redemption. In the Old Testament as in the New Testament the son is no created being, but a chosen. Israel in the Old Testament, and Christ in the New, are the Sons of God by His election and not by His creation. Christ is increate. The whole Bible use of the word Father refers it to an act of choice and a purpose of redemption. God is Father by His choosing will and not by His creative power, by gracious adoption and not by natural generation. Of His will begat He us, and by no instinctive process. We are sons " begotten in the Gospel." God is, directly, the Father of Christ alone. He is our Father only in Christ. God has but one Son ; the many sons are sons in Him ; and He is Son in none.

A positive Gospel, therefore, is given as a power to our Christian experience, while a liberal theology may bear little trace of Christian experience, and it may exist but as a truth in Christian reason. A positive theology is at bottom the theology of converted men, and not of academic intelligence brought to bear on the soul,

the world, or history. It is faith giving a reasonable
account of itself ; it is not reason shaping, amending,
or licensing faith. It carries in its body the marks of
the Lord Jesus. Its datum is in history, not in
thought. It has the stigmata of the Cross on its heart.
The positive theology is more devout (I am not speaking of the theologians), the liberal is more doctrinaire. The one is more concerned with life, the other
with truth. The one is pneumatic, the other dogmatic. The one is evangelical and moral, the other
intellectualist. The one is part of the religion, the
other is a view of the religion. Thus the liberal
theology is the more theological, in the opprobrious
sense of the term ; for it is more engrossed with
views and truths than experiences of faith.

2. *For liberalism the modern mind constitutes
itself the supreme court,* and claims that nothing
should survive in Christianity but what is congenial
to it. Christianity, in so far as it is true, is simply
" the passion which is highest reason in a soul
divine." It is, as the old Apologists said, the
practicable and effective completion of the revelation
that was labouring for outlet in Paganism. It is a
new branch of culture. It is an immense, not to
say infinite, extension of our old horizon. We
are, on Christ's shoulders, lifted but not saved,
not as lost sheep rejoicing in a new life, but as eager
disciples rejoicing in a wider, deeper prospect of
things. The way to God is thus really the world and
not the word. His seat is the heart at its best, and
not the conscience at its worst.

A positive theology starts with the experienced grace of God to sin as a historic gift in Christ and His Cross. It is a gift which is at once our source and our standard, a gift whose divinity is approved by faith's obedience on the principle that he who willeth to do God's will shall know congenially the moral quality of the doctrine. But the liberal theology starts from certain rational, metaphysical, or ethical principles existing in human thought, which determines by science, and not by obedience, whether any revelation, even Christ's, is divine. The one is theology, the other is theosophy. The one starts from the primacy of the ethos, the other from the primacy of the cosmos. The one is voluntarist, the other is intellectualist. The one is teleological, finding the world's destiny in the historic Christ as the source and surety of that destiny ("We see not yet all things, but we see Jesus"); the other is cosmological, engrossed with the world's structure or with its movement in reason. For positivity God's decisive revelation is in his action in Christ, and its effect is active in a Church; for liberalism it is in reason, and its effect is contemplative or theosophic in a school. The one acts historically, subjugating the world to Christ: the other aesthetically subduing it to thought. The one modifies from age to age according to the intrinsic requirements of growing faith; the external *Zeitgeist* being but the occasion which releases the latent genius of belief. The other modifies wholly in the interest of scientific thought, whether physical, psychical,

metaphysical, or critical, as if Christianity were a
phase of civilization. The one regards the revelation of grace as autonomous, the other will have
it licensed by the schools, or countersigned by the
humane " heart." The positive starts with the
holy and saving Christ, the liberal with Humanity,
rational or affectional. The one handles sin, grace,
and salvation according to the world's moral mutiny :
the other deals but with weakness, ignorance, and
their evolutionary conquest, confirming the world
in its pride of power. A modern theology, in a
word, is demanded by an autonomous evangelical
faith : the liberal is prescribed by an aggressive, cosmological science. But we must start with that faith ;
its synthesis with any kind of science is a hope for
which we wait and patiently work. The theologian,
that is, can wait ; but you preachers cannot.

Now, when we preach on this liberalistic basis it
is not Christ preaching to an age so much as one age,
or one part of an age, preaching to another. It is
not a message from God to man, it is a message of
the *élite* to the mass, a summons from the super-
man. It is man trying to lift himself by his own
collar. Positivity, on the contrary, has its source and
its standard in one, in the historic origin of Christianity, the pure word and deed of God in Christ
and His finished grace. We preach a historic message
from God to humanity, and not a message of
historic humanity to itself ; a real rescue by a hand
from heaven at our utmost moral need, and not a
scaling of heaven by our intrinsic moral strength.

It ought to be said in justice that the rationalism of the liberal position takes two forms, a Christian and an anti-Christian. And it would not be fair to charge those who press the normality of the Christian consciousness with the sterilities of scientific rationalism. It ought, however, also to be said, that if the Christian consciousness of each age is the supreme court, the end is Catholicism—the supremacy of the Church's voice, of faith's latest stage, over the Gospel. Of course a modern positivity admits the reason as a critic of the Bible, of the mere sacred history, but not of the holy Gospel. The Gospel which recreates our moral experience in the end criticises us. We cannot judge our judge.

§

3. *Positive theology is creational, liberal is evolutionary.* For the positive theologian the course of religious history has been chiefly determined by the due intervention of supernatural and incomparable factors. The spirit of man was invaded by the spirit of God, as the whole Rhone shoots into Leman. Every doctrine of God's immanence must be compatible with that supreme moral experience, and licensed by it. Liberal theology on the contrary views the course of religion as an immanent evolution accounting even for experience. The action of God is not to recreate our spiritual power so much as to release and forward it. It is not a raising from the dead, but only a loosing and letting go. Religious experiences are inevitable products of the spiritual

nature of man and the world as created and constituted by God. Whereas, according to a positive
theology, they are produced, in the crucial cases at
least, by a special action of God. What is uppermost is a person and not a process. The Church
represents not simply the influence of Christ but
His Holy Spirit. Christian experience, through
that Spirit, must always be more than spiritual
evolution. It comes from contact or communion
with a living Lord ; and faith is only explicable as
His gift by the Spirit. In faith, we do not feel ourselves initiative or creative except as we feel ourselves
a new creation. Now as preachers we must choose
between these two versions of Christianity. In the
preaching of a Gospel it is the one theology rather
than the other that serves us. For the Gospel of
liberalism whatever it may be in theory, is in effect
but man calling to men ; while a positive Gospel
is man called by God. You will observe that I am
not trying to exhibit the extent to which Christianity
may find room for evolution. That would occupy
another inquiry. It is more needful in the interest
of preaching to set out the antithesis. And here,
the interest of preaching, is the interest of the soul.

§

4. *As the most recent phase of evolutionary
religion we have the historic-religious movement,
challenging the absoluteness of Christianity.* Liberalism here rises from the study of the religions that
abut upon the age of Christ with this question,

" Did they not make Him and the faith of Him ?
If they did not entirely create the historic figure of
Jesus, did they not supply the ideas that Christianity
thought were revealed in Christ ? Did they not
create the supernatural Christ, the pre-existent Christ,
the propitiatory Christ, the Christ that should
judge the world ? If so, how can we speak of the
finality of Christ, the absoluteness of Christianity ?
Is it not all relative to what went before, all a creation
of history, all just the past writ larger ? Is it not
relative to the future ? May it not be superseded
in its turn ? How can anything historical be more
than relative ? How can it do more than serve its
place and time, and then, when it has advanced these,
retire to make room for something greater ? How
can we speak of the absolute and final value of Christ ?
How can we speak of Him as veritable God ? "

To which a first answer is, that historical study
certainly does compel us to include Christ in His time
and world, and to alter in some points the fashion of
His claim on us. In doing so it makes a real historic
figure of Him, a real man, and not a magical prodigy.
He shared the life of limited man, the life of His
age, the life of His land. In the region of mere
knowledge He was not infallible. He thought much
in Jewish categories, He felt human finitude, He
confessed to some human ignorance. We modify
the impossible and Byzantine Christ into a national
figure real and mighty, and only by doing so do we
find His true universality. And a second answer
would be this, that if the ideas that have been most

active in Christianity were drawn from Judaism (which itself was largely shaped by the farther East) then the best Pharisees of Christ's day were more responsible for the foundation of historic Christianity than Christ Himself, which seems a *reductio ad absurdum* that I need not, perhaps, for my present purpose pursue.

But we go farther. We say that this limitation in Christ was the result, the expression of His absolute power. It was an exercise of His will. It was self-limitation, an effect of His self-emptying. It was the very power of God under conditions imposed not simply by human nature but by holy love, grace divine, and saving purpose. And therefore it was an expression of His absoluteness. By His own eternal self-determined will He became lower than the angels. He exerted power over both the natural and the moral world. For He overrode natural law, and broke the entail and Nemesis of guilt. His very obedience to nature was a voluntary and masterly obedience. And His " becoming sin " for us was a voluntary act, a moral achievement of a kind possible only to Godhead. He parted with a physical omnipotence but never with a moral, never with the omnipotence of love, which is the Christian meaning of the Cross. The limitation of His consciousness was no limitation of His moral power, but its exercise. His ignorance of many things we know at school was part of His divine renunciation. His subjection to nature, to death, to dereliction, was the act of His free grace.

" 'Tis but in limits that the master shows." And
the absolute mastery of Christ was made perfect in
the relativity He assumed. It was an absolute relativity as being self-determined. Otherwise I do not
understand what Troeltsch means by "a relative
absoluteness." The absolute is less than absolute
if it has not the power of the relative. If the
infinite could not be finite, it is less than infinite.
For there is then a region outside its range. He
had power to do anything perfectly that was due
to love and to the will of God. The absoluteness
of His obedience to that was the absoluteness of
His moral power, which is the only absoluteness we
have to do with at last.

No doubt the preacher of a Christ merely relative
brings Him nearer to our *conditions*, but it is the
preacher of the absolute Christ that brings Him nearest
to our *need*. To be near our conditions makes a man
interesting, but to be near to our moral need makes
him a power. To humanize Christ is to popularize
Him, no doubt. But it is His Deity that makes Him
outstay popularity, surmount the desertion of the
Cross, and become universal. What we need is a power
to enter and save us which is possible only to the
God we wronged; we do not need simply the most
interesting of historic figures. Our trouble is not
our ennui and not our ignorance, it is our sin. It
is our Holy One that spoils our feasts and troubles
our dreams. Is it not clear which of these two
views belongs to a preached Gospel, and to our
moral case? Our moral predicament, the actua

need of the race, demands chiefly, not a more human Jesus, but a more divine Christ.

§

5. *A positive theology finds the essence of Christianity in the core of the New Testament Gospel,* cleansed of those temporary hulls that clung to it in the first century. You may seek this core in the heart of Christ's teaching alone, or you may find it in the Cross as the heart of the whole New Testament Christ. That is a controversy which, for the moment, we may pass by. The point is that the source and norm is in the New Testament. The simplification of faith is effected by going to its centre and origin. That is to say it comes from a deepening of faith, and not merely from an easing of it. The maxim of textual criticism has a higher sense—*lectio difficilior potius.* Distrust the simple solutions of old problems. A simplification of Christianity which is not also a deepening of it is fatal to it. Its real simplicity lies at the centre not on the surface. To simplify faith we must be taken to its heart. The simplicity *of* the heart may be very shallow, but the simplicity *at* the heart is deep. And history has driven Christianity to more simplicity chiefly by forcing it in on its centre, and not by thrusting it to the surface. The Bible has done much for history, but also history has done much for the Bible. It has driven us in on it. It has simplified not by lucidity but by concentration. It has clarified the issue by staking all on the centre, and by compel-

ling us to feel in that deep core our infinite power. It has removed our first concern from the Bible to the Gospel within the Bible. It has forced us from the simplicity of clearness, obviousness, and ease to the simplicity of centrality, depth, and power.

I speak about Christ and the centre of Christ, which is to be found at the head of Christianity, in the Cross, as the Epistles exist to say in a very positive fashion. But the liberal theology finds the essence of Christianity to consist of the spine, so to speak, or marrow, or continuity, or, as Hegel would say, the " truth," of the whole development of Christianity which Christ but initiated. You must, (it says,) include the whole Christian history in your field of induction. The spinal cord has the same value as the brain it prolongs. The Church (viewed historically and not dogmatically) is essential for our definition of Christianity. You cannot read the Gospel aright except along with its results in a Church.

One objection to this is that, if that be so, the first Christians, like Paul, had next to no data to go on ; and therefore they were less in a position than we are to say what Christianity really is. They had not the Gospel's results before them, but only the Gospel itself. This is also an objection which tells with equal force against the common and thoughtless saying that the real evidence of Christianity is the lives of Christians. God help us if that were so ! It was not Christianity that made Paul a Christian, it was no church. It was not even the story of Jesus ; it

was the personal contact with Christ. It was his
invasion by Christ. Paul had nothing to speak of
before him in the shape of evidential Christendom.
From the Church he had at most but testimony.
He had to proceed entirely on Christ's evidence
for Himself.

Another difficulty is that, on the liberal view, the
field of induction has no limit. We cannot make the
books up. The history of Christendom still goes on.
The record of results is not yet done. In some ways
it is not well begun. The region before us is in-
definite. The half has not been told How do we
know that the weightier part of the evidence is not
yet to come? As with an iceberg, the larger part
of the mass is as yet under water. It is future and
unseen. And there might be something preparing
there which would change the centre of gravity and
upset the whole fabric. Has God conquered sin,
death, and the world in Christ? Or is it still an
open question whether these will not foil, conquer,
and mock God?

Were Christianity but an evolutionary spiritual
process then it were right to look for the key at the
close, and not at the origin. That is the principle
of evolution. Man explains the monkey, not the
monkey man. It is age that explains youth, and
eternity time—" the last of life for which the first was
made." Were Christianity mere evolution we should
have no key to it, since we have not yet its goal.
But it is not a case of evolution; it is a case of
positive revelation. Our destiny is given us in

our new creation. Paul's apostolic commission, I
have reminded you, was given him in his call to be
a Christian. "It pleased God to reveal His son in
me that I might preach Him among the Gentiles."
So the whole genius of Christianity is given us,
not by an induction from its history (which would be
sight) but by a deduction from its head (which is
faith). We do not see eternity but we realize it in
Jesus, who is the substance of what we hope, and
the reality of the unseen. In all the more spiritual
products it is so. On the dawn of poetry we have
Homer, the Eddas, the Kalevala, the Mahabarata.
We have extraordinary precocity most abundant
in the most spiritual of all the arts—music. In
life we take the most momentous and formative
decisions, as to a profession, or a wife, at the thresh-
old of life. And conversion, on which Christianity
itself essentially rests in one shape or another, belongs to the first part of life rather than the last.

It is not in the genius of Christianity that its
essence should be distilled for us out of its whole
history. The key is given in its source. Were it
otherwise we concede the whole principle of an
evolutionary Catholicism, as represented in the
modern Romanism of Newman and Möhler, with its
deep scepticism and lack of personal certainty.

§

6. All this is to say that positive Christianity has a
historic standard in the New Testament. We have
there the norm for every form. Liberalism has

none, beyond a thing of fleeting hues, like the modern man, the modern mind, the modern conscience. But is it not hard to fix what the modern mind is ? Shall Goethe represent it or Nietsche, Wordsworth or Byron, Hegel or Haeckel, the metaphysicians or the psychologists, the optimists, the pessimists, or the naturalists ? One says, follow impulse, man is essentially divine. Another says yes—man is essentially divine, and mainly so in his power to quell impulse. One says with Morris " Love is enough—enjoy.' Another says with Goethe " Die to live—renounce." One again says " Follow to the bitter end your individual conscience and its responsibility. Go, with Brand, for all or nothing." Another says with Comte, " No, the social conscience is lord with its hereditary and racial responsibility." And a third translates this social conscience into Christianity as the Church, which relieves you of your conscience altogether and takes charge of it for you. Which of these represents the modern mind ? Do we find it in life-vigour or life-weariness ? In Bismarck or Amiel ? in Roosevelt or Tolstoi ? America or Europe ?

Not everything new is modern, in the good sense of that word. That alone is worthily modern which really adds to the spiritual power of the race, and continues to develop from the old the real spiritual life of the world. " Oddities do not last." But still there is the question, What is spiritual life ? and what is soundly progressive ? What makes us sure in each case that we have more than a mere variant ? How to tell a development from a sport, a purpose from a freak, a destiny from a whim ? In the middle ages every-thing was modern which was outside the logic of the period, just as to many to-day everything is modern outside eighteenth century orthodoxy. There is much modernity in antiquity. How shall we dis-cover and disentangle it ? What is so modern, so fresh, so mighty in every age as eternity ? How discern it ? Where is the favoured haunt of the eternal voice, the region of its choice, where the soul owns its entire control ? Do we not feel that amid our unexampled wealth of broad interests, new departure, swift change, teeming variation, and external mobility life is flattening and starving to-day for want of the eternal stay of Christ, as a gorgeous tent slowly sub-sides to the dust as the pole decays ? All our escape from tradition and from bondage, all the fires, feats, or freaks of freedom, the roses and raptures of romance, or even the heroisms of the great, do not permanently lift the tone or dignity of life. Where are we to take our bearings and find our north ? Where shall we rest our lever ? Where does the eternal well up through time to flood history ? To such questions a positive Christianity has an answer in the Gospel of the Cross, taken seriously and object-ively, the Cross where eternity springs up anew in every soul. But what is known as liberalism has none. It believes in the logic of the idea, or in human nature, divine human nature, man failing often but unfallen still, man as God made him. Human nature—where Iago succeeds and Brutus

fails, indeed! Which wins at history's close?
The only answer we have to that is in the absolute
finality of the Gospel of the Cross. Human nature!
It is indeed wonderful. But, alas!

> "Unless above himself he can
> Erect himself, how mean a thing is man."

§

7. *A liberal theology*, a belief in the unbroken
unity of man with God, a creed of man's essential
divinity superseding the need of redeeming grace,
needing but benignant grace—such a theology *may
suit those who are constitutionally ready to believe
in goodness* from simplicity of nature, or through
lack of imaginative lucidity, moral shrewdness,
or knowledge of the world. It may satisfy those
who can turn easily to life's varied interests and
energies for relief from the bleeding wounds of the
soul, or those who feel indeed the tragedy *in* the
world, but have no power to realize the tragedy *of*
the world. It may meet those whose reason serves
them so well that revelation is not called for, who
are young enough to rely on their own self-respect,
and to trust to their own self-help. But the modern
man is inwardly more of a pessimist than that, in
the old countries at least, where they have outgrown
youth's happy knack of hope, and have long borne
the white man's burden. The modern man represents
the bankruptcy of natural optimism, and more and
more craves for deliverance. He tastes life's tragedy
and guilt, and pines for a Saviour, even when he

disowns ours. "O, had I lived," says one of them,
"when Jesus of Nazareth walked in Galilee I would
have followed Him, and lost all my pride in the love
of Him." Now, a positive theology comes to this
jaded, impotent life with the note of a real, foregone
redemption. It comes to modern Europe, the Europe
of the Renaissance, and the Illumination, and the
Revolution, and it comes to a Europe disillusioned
of them all, as it came to the *débâcle* of classical
antiquity. And man's extremity elicits the central
resource of God the Saviour. As the time grows
short God grows swift and keen. "As, the shorter
time Satan hath, the more is his rage, so, the shorter
time Christ hath, the more is His zeal for His saints
and indignation against His enemies. His heart
is set on it, and therefore it is we see in this latter
age He hath made such changes in the world. We
have seen Him do that in a few years that He hath
not done in a hundred years before. For, being
King of nations, He presses His interests ; and being
more near His kingdom He takes it with violence.
We are now within the whirl of it and so His motions
are rapt." Thus even Goodwin the Puritan.

It is true a fresh young people, like America,
has a somewhat different note. But it is useless
to refer the weary Titan of Europe merely to the
young Hercules of the West. The young men too
shall grow weary, and their strength shall utterly
fail. Nature has its due course to senility, and a
natural optimism has its dying fall. It is the waiters
on God that renew their strength. Christianity comes

to-day as it came in the first centuries, to a paganism
which is disillusioned about itself and is sinking into
pessimism. In those first days Christianity took the
world at its own estimate, and brought the message
that the situation required. Even Stoicism then
despaired of the mass of mankind in spite of its
high conception of Humanity. It could not make
a religion of that idea. It had the dream but not
the power. It had not the Redemption, the secret
of a new creation. This was the one thing the age
craved, and it was the one thing Christianity brought.
And it was to this outworn world Christianity came.
It was not to the northern world of the fresh Teutonic
races. Its method was not to save an old civilization
by the infusion of a new and hopeful race. Or do
you think that what saved antiquity was not the
Christian redemption but the incursion of the Northern peoples ? Well, Europe to-day is rapidly
moving to where antiquity had come, to moral
exhaustion, and to the pessimism into which natural
optimism swings when the stress and burden are
extreme. Do you think that that situation is to be
saved by the spontaneous resources of human nature,
or the entrance upon the *Weltpolitik* of a mighty
young people like America ? Is there no paganism
threatening America ? What is to save America
from her own colossal power, energy, self-confidence
and preoccupation with the world ? Her Christianity no doubt. But a Christianity which places
in the centre not merely Christ but the Cross and
its Redemption, in a far more ethical way than

America is doing ; a Christianity which is not only
set in the presence of Christ's person but caught
into the motion of Christ's work, which is not only
with Christ but in Him by a total moral and social
salvation.

For the time, however, your young optimism
hardly realizes the tragic need for an absolute salvation. You are too Pelagian. I feel that Christianity
comes with a less redemptive word, perhaps, to a
fresh and dawning race ; as to the vigorous Teutons
of the fourth century in the north of Europe it
came with a more Arian creed than was extorted
from the Gospel by the desperate case of dying
Rome. To youth the harmony of Christianity with
the nobler natural man may appeal more strongly
than does its blow to nature from the Cross.
Your energy insists on synergy with God. Your
lack of tradition discredits a great theology. The
transfiguration of humanity may be more attractive
to you than its death and resurrection in Christ,
because it is less deep. Hegel with his calm
process of reconciliation may seem more Christian
than the pessimists with their cry for redemption,
and the iron quivering in their soul. It is easy to
believe in man when the world is young, when
every woman is a queen, and every goose a swan.
It is easy to speak in pantheistic philosophemes of
the essential divinity of human nature, and man's
homogeneity with God. What has Christianity to
do with that ? That is for the philosophers. What
brought Christ, and brought Him to the Cross, was

man's alienation from God and his hate. To harp on continuity when we need communion, and for communion redemption, betrays that the moral eye has still its scales ; that sin has not yet bitten ; that there is not yet resistance unto blood ; that the holy has not yet outgrown the homely ; that grace is untasted still, however the heart takes its fill of love ; and that the holy has not become the one reality. It indicates the ethical amateur brisk in his studies, though at times abashed ; but not the broken man, the broken and contrite spirit, shamed, desperate, and delivered, lost and found. In such a Gospel as that of man's natural and indelible sonship we not only have no need that God be reconciled to us; we hardly seem to need to be reconciled to God. All we seem to need is to be reconciled to our inner truer selves. Be true to yourself, is the note of this youthful Gospel, and stir up one another to love. Cultivate the Spirit of Jesus. Believe and work for spiritual progress. Meet with a shining face the dawn of God who loves to see His children happy. Yes, but meantime, where is the anguish of the new birth ? And where the stricken confession " God be merciful to me a sinner " ?

In a positive Gospel, on the contrary, everything turns on a real supernatural revelation, on a fundamental perdition, a radical evil, and a rescue from without as the one thing that makes a Christian humanity. Our salvation is not the mere contagion spread by powerful religious personalities. Nor is it the progress of a gradual spiritualization. It is a unique and finished work of God in Christ, to be taken, not made. It is not a piece of impressionism; it is a real redemption in the heart of things, in creative deed and not in stirring word alone. You cannot deeply preach without the note of a tragic and total redemption. To harp upon this as a truth is easy, I know, and it can be tedious; and the world has been well bored by it often. But to preach it, to saturate with the power and principle of it all thought and reality, that is a great life work, which puts the preacher's soul much upon the Cross, but also raises it continually from the dead.

§

Behind all the differences between a positive Gospel and religious liberalism there keep reappearing the two elements, *personality with its immortality and sin with its witness to holiness.* The liberalism I speak of consistently tends to erase the personal element both from God and from the human future. Its note is some variety of Pantheism, with all the spell and appeal of that issue to those who have but an intellectual history. And it farther erases, like all Monistic systems, the decisive factor in history, the factor of sin and of God's holiness. The holiness of the Spinosist deity is not holy in the Christian sense, nor in any sense which leaves us with a real conscience. Even Hegel tends to erase that. For such a creed sin is not outside the vast process of reconciliation whereby the supreme idea finds in the ideas below something intrinsically serviceable to its final purpose when the hour comes for them to be absorbed and preserved (*aufgehoben*). There is something in sin which can be preserved and utilized for the divine purpose. That is to say, there is something in it (as sin, and not merely as free volition) which is due to the divine purpose, and may be incorporated in the great reconcilement. One day we may see (if at that far day we continue to exist capable of seeing anything) how our sin was a negative contribution to the divine event, and had its place in the divine scheme of things. And we may even be ashamed of the pother we made about it.

All this is absolutely incompatible with the sin that brought death to God in the Son of God. Sin as we see it by God's holiness in Christ's Cross contains nothing that can be absorbed by that holiness and given an eternal value. It is outside the range of reconcileable things. It can only be destroyed as in principle Christ did destroy it. Doubtless it must be made to minister to God's greater glory; but never by any kind of exploitation; and only by entire destruction.

In all the efforts to subdue Christian theology to be a province of the empire of pure thought there is discernible an inability which seems constitutional to gauge the fact of sin at its moral value. There is some lack of a moral retina. There is an absence of a personal moral history. There is a poverty of moral realism and of soul history as dis-

tinct from the mind's. Yet I venture to think that
there is more of a key to the divine method in the
tragedies of remorse and the shame of guilt than
in the fascinating processes of speculative thought.
The greatest of modern popular orators, a master
of laughter, tears, and all assemblies, often visited a
friend of mine. One day as they stood on a height
which commanded a noble view my friend missed
him, and on search found him some yards away, prone
on the heath, sobbing, with his head buried in his
hands. When he had recovered somewhat, and assured
his companion it was not illness, he said that from
time to time some sight of greatness suddenly
smote into him the shame of what he had been in
the years of his dissipation and sin. And the horror
of it never lost its freshness, nor did the freshness fade
from the wonder of his forgiveness. Moments like
these, and men like these, have a key to the spiritual
system of the world which the thinkers must fail to
turn till they insert in its ring much more than their
thought. And to have no such experience, or at
least the power to understand it, is to be a minor
in the moral life.

§

8. To gather the matter up. *The liberal theology finds Christ's centre of gravity in what He
has in common with us ; a positive theology in
that wherein He differs.* The one urges us to a
faith like Christ's, the other to a faith in Christ.
The one bids us imitate the religion of Jesus ;

the other cannot attempt to imitate a Redeemer, or criticize the judge of conscience; and it takes Jesus for our religion. The one preaches as the principle of Christianity the principle of indefectible human sonship, the principle of man's incorrigible spirituality, with Christ only as its classic case and supreme prophet; the other identifies the principle with Christ, and finds it secured only in the total act of His eternal person. Liberalism dwells on Christ's preaching, positivity on a Christ preached. The one finds the most impressive thing in Christ to be His perfect human nature; the other is much more impressed by His treatment of human nature than by His incarnation of it. The one dwells on Christ as the expression of humanity, the other dwells on His business with humanity. For the one He consummates it, for the other He redeems it. Liberalism offers Christ to a seeking world as its answer, or to a suffering world as its healer; positivity offers Him to a guilty world also as its Atoning Saviour. The one treats the sinlessness of Christ as the expression of the essential, though soiled, sinlessness of man; the other treats it as the sanctity possible only to the Holy One of God. The one regards it as a relative sinlessness; the other as an absolute holiness. The one takes stand on love; the other declares that the divine thing in love, as it is in Christ, is holy grace. For the one the divine reality is a calm and mystic presence and he joys that God is near in love; for the other it is a perpetual deed, and the nearness is a terror except as grace for love scorned.   A liberal theology discerns God's real presence in the mere *action*, process, or movement of the world ; a positive finds it in the *act* of the world, the supreme act of history which consummates the world.   The one is engrossed with the way God's *presence* pervades His world, the other with the way He realizes by redemptive act His *purpose* in the world.   The one finds Christ to crown the *immanence* of the divine presence in the world ;   the other finds Him to be the *incarnation* of the divine will with the world.   The one has the cosmological interest of evolution, the other the teleological interest of Redemption.   For liberalism the world is God's arena, His sphere of energy, where His substance, forces, and ideas play ;   for positivity it is becoming His Kingdom, where His purpose rules.   For the one the world is His organ, for the other it is His creature ;   and while He is immanent in His creature, He is incarnate only in His uncreated Son.   If the world is the creature of His holy love, the Son is more ;   He is its eternal counterpart.   For the one the world was created *for* Christ, or at least for Christ's ideal ;   for the other it was created *in* Christ.

§

Religion as it grows powerful grows positive.   But the constant drift of liberalism is away from positivity, and it devotes itself to the scientific study of religions.   Yet even that study might teach us that *the constant tendency of religion, as it rises in the scale, is to be more positive,* more historic, more defined, and more objective. There is no such thing anywhere as religion *per se,* religion apart from a specific form of religion—unless perhaps we find it in the decadents from the higher types, where you have a vague religiosity with the effort to detach itself from every form—Church, doctrine, or any other clear committal. But in the historic religions, as you rise in the scale of quality you grow in positivity. They become more historical, and more dogmatic, more explicit in regard to the gravest issues. They do not erase the frontiers, though they promote the coming and going of a freer trade. A positive religion is a concrete one. It is so intellectually ; and still more so morally. Experience, I keep saying, makes an appeal to our will and choice. It puts us upon our moral mettle. It takes a line. It stakes life and eternity on selection, decision, committal. It calls us to moral verve and vigilance. There are mature lives to-day which are darker than they would have been had they not at the early stage fallen victims to a vague and pathetic fallacy of fatherhood, in which the holy had no meaning and judgment no place. But how poor, how remote it all is. As we live we are being tried for our life. And that is the issue you face as preachers. One of these tendencies will make you preachers of a Gospel, the other will make you advocates of a culture. One will make you strangers and sojourners in the world, the other citizens of the world. maybe men of the world, One will make you apostles of Christ, and one will make you champions of humanity. One will make you severe with yourself, one will make you tender with yourself. One will commend you to the naughty people, and one will commend you to the nice.

Now of these two tendencies one means the destruction of preaching. If it cease to be God's word, descending on men and intervening in history, then it will cease as an institution in due time. It may become lecturing, or it may become oratory, but as preaching it must die out with a positive Gospel. People cannot be expected to treat a message of insight from man to man as they do a message of revelation from God to man. An age cannot be expected to treat a message from another age as they treat a message from Eternal God to every age. Men with the passion of the present cannot be expected to listen even to a message from humanity as they would to one from God. And if humanity redeem itself you will not be able to prevent each member of it from feeling that he is his own redeemer. If we owe everything to man's innate spirituality, asserting itself in various forms of life or worship, we have, in this spirituality, something all too vague for a Gospel, too familiar for a message, and too little positive to give a real preacher his text, or his authority, or even his audience. For if it is all a matter of innate human spirituality it is too innate to each hearer to dispose him to hear it meekly. How should he hear meekly a word which is not engrafted but evolved out of the common spiritual stock. Each man's own spirituality is in its nature as good as anything another man might bring him.

Is it not all really a serious issue, and a grave choice? The less seriously you feel the issue the more serious it is for you. Not to feel the immense gulf it cleaves is not to choose with open eyes. Whichever side you go to, go with an adequate sense of what is involved. Do not treat the matter as if to men of sense and soul there were but one rational possibility. One respects far more a man who really grasps the situation and deliberately goes to the wrong side—far more than one who goes there for want of knowing his subject, or who good-naturedly minimizes the difference and says we are all one at bottom. If we are so, it is either in a positive Christ, or in a pantheistic, monistic unity which is spiritually unmeaning and morally noxious. What we do not respect is the assumption of the liberal and superior note by men who have not wrestled with the subject, or measured the ground, but are the victims of epicurean reading, easy books, or popular expositors. This matter is really, for the preacher, an issue of the soul, a decision of the life, which turns study from a pursuit to a conflict, and makes the attainment of conviction a wrestling with God for your salvation. For the preacher, truly, the salvation of the soul is also the salvation of the mind. Your mind also must come to the obedience and service of faith. There is such a thing as the *sacrificium intellectus*. But it is not to an institution it is to the conscience. It is the recognition of that primacy of the moral which views sin as the crux of the ethical, i.e. the human, situation, and redemption as its only solution. Your charter as preachers is not contained in what the world says to your earnest thought but in what the Word says to your sinful conscience. And the question is not " What do you think of Christ ? " but, " How do you treat Him ? " It is not what is He *to* you. It is more even than what is He *for* you. And still more it is what is He *in* you. And are you in Him ? That last is in some ways the most crucial question of all. For by having Christ in you, you may mean no more than inheriting the results of His vast historic movement, and absorbing into your character the moral fruits of His legacy to men. So you might have Christ working on in you in a posthumous way. But when you ask yourself, " Am I in Him ? " you can say, Yea, to that only if He still live, and live as Himself our spiritual world, made unto us justification, sanctification, and redemption.

PREACHING POSITIVE AND
MODERN

VII

Preaching Positive and Modern

§

THEOLOGY, if it is to be of real use to the preacher, must be modernized. It is fruitless to offer to the public the precise modes of thought which were so fresh and powerful with the Reformers, or the schemes so ably propounded by the dogmatists of the seventeenth century, and so severely raked by the Socinians. The nineteenth century was not a theological century, but it has not passed without leaving a great and good effect upon theology. It was a century of scholarship, of criticism, and of heresy. But do we not recognize now that competent heresy is a negative blessing to the Church and its truth ? Only it must be competent. It is the dabblers on both sides that do the mischief. We must carry on the work of last century in modernizing theology.

But what does the modernizing of theology mean ? Does it mean that its control passes into the hands of modern theories of the soul and the world ? Does it mean that the Christian idea of a holy God shall

be at the mercy of what is a mere philosophical
ultimate ? Does it mean that theology must be
licensed by the cosmologies or psychologies of the
hour ? Does it mean that we start with a certain
scheme of creation and cut off all that projects
over its edge ? For instance, nothing more worthily
marks the modern Church than the idea of evolution,
especially in connexion with its own history. But
is our belief to be stretched on the pallet of evolution,
for instance, and everything to be trimmed down
which is beyond that scheme ? The Higher Criticism is a gift to us of the spirit which gave us the
Bible. But is the Bible to be put on the rack of
mere literary criticism, or historic, or even ethical,
and nothing accepted from it but what it emits
under such question ? Are the scholars, the savants,
the philosophers to be the Board of Triers for the
Gospel ? Is modern just eqivalent to *à la mode* ?

The result of that I have already discussed as
mere theological liberalism, which, in the effort to
discard dogma, only substitutes philosophic dogma
for theological. The error is in its start and standard. It begins from the wrong end. It begins
with a scheme of creation, a scheme of the world
or man, with which, in truth, religion is but indirectly
concerned. And it does not begin with the new
creation, with the evangelical experience, the
moral redemption, Eternal Life in Jesus Christ.
It begins with the world and not with the Word,
with thought and not faith, with love and not
grace, with kindness and not holiness. It is cosmo-

logical, or it is psychological, being preoccupied with the structure and action of nature or of mind ; whereas religion (and the Christian faith certainly) is teleological, being preoccupied with God's purpose and goal for things, and for history, and for the soul. The one makes a specification of life and knowledge, and requires any religion which tenders to comply. It thinks of man's rational structure more than his moral need, of his power to understand more than his weakness to trust and obey. The other lays hold of God's object with life, finding in Christ both the goal and its guarantee. The one gives no finality, because the schemes of life and drafts of the world are changing with progress ; the other has finality or nothing, because it begins with God's chief end for history in its salvation in Jesus Christ. In Christ it finds in advance the eternal and final purpose of God. We see not yet all things—but we see Jesus. It is teleological and redemptive. In a word, if theology is to be modernized it must be by its own Gospel.

The two methods differ in their start, then. The one begins with man, the other with God, the one with science or sentiment, the other with the Gospel, the one with the healthy heart and its satisfaction, the other with the ruined conscience and its redemption. The one begins with the world, (as I say) the other with the Word. But, in practice, we find this— that to begin with the world is to become dubious about the Word ; whereas to begin with the Word is to become sure about the world. A philosophy can bring us to no security of a revelation; but a revelation develops a philosophy, or a view of the world; it is adjustable to many schemes of the world; and it is hospitable to many of the modern principles of interpreting the world. It is not the victim of modern theories like monism, but it has welcome for many modern principles like evolution. In the face of modern *theories* or dogmas the Word of revelation is autonomous. It has its own dogmas by an equal right. But in face of modern *principles* it discerns in them, and often through their means, the hidden treasures of its own wealth. But whether on suggestion from without, or on impulse from within, it develops its latent wealth by its own native genius and freedom. It reforms and rediscovers itself, as it did in the Reformation. The creeds are discoveries of the Church to itself by the heresies, which are therefore negative blessings. And these two things, the Church's recognition of modern principles and its rediscovery of its own, combine to modernize the theology it presents to intelligence. It is friendly and reasonable to theories like evolution, but it is commanded by the fact of redemption and its experience. It claims that its experience of God reconciling in Christ is as real and valid as any experience of the world. Its faith is an organ of real knowledge.[1] What science does for our knowledge of things and forces, faith does for our knowledge of persons, our knowledge, above all, of our personal God and His saving will.

[1] See, among many others, *Paulsen's Ethik*, passim.

§

I. And if I may first ask what are the positive
doctrines which, amid all that is modernized in it,
make Christianity still a Gospel of the Grace of
God, the answer would in my judgment be this.[1]
They are the Eternal Sonship, the Mediatorship,
and the Resurrection of Jesus Christ.

1. *It is a Gospel of Jesus the Eternal Son of God.*
It sets Christ's person in the centre of theology
no less than of religion. If the nineteenth century
had done no more than restore the person of Christ
to the centre of theology, it would have done a
very great theological work. The historic Jesus is
personally identical with the Christian principle or
with the Eternal Christ. He stood thus in a unique
relation to Eternal God. It was a relation unique
not only as being unattained so far by other men.
For that is not denied by the liberalism of the
hour as a mere historic verdict. But He was unique
in a dogmatic sense, in a way unattainable not
only by any man but by collective humanity.
This unique relation to God constituted His person,
and it was not simply an exercise of His person. It
was not attained by Him, but He was constituted in
it. He began by being the Son of God in eternal fact,
though He ended by being the Son in historic power.
The idea of a metaphysical sonship is not absurd,
though our data make its express form tentative only.

[1] See **Theodore Kaftan,** *Die neue Theologie des alten
Glaubens.*

The metaphysical unity with God is postulated
by the evangelical unity, however far it may be
from being defined. It is a unity which is far more
than harmony of will. It involves parity of being,
which places the historic Jesus with the Creator, rather
than the creature, and beside the Creator, rather than
under Him. He was of Godhead. If we take in their
full earnest the words that God was in Christ reconciling we have in this Christ the real presence and
action of a forgiving God. The act of Christ was
still more God's act, and not a mere reflection of
it. His love was God's love, and not a mere response to it We have Christ doing what God
alone could do—forgiving sin committed against
God alone. None but the injured could either
forgive or save. If God was not saving in Christ,
if Christ was not God saving, He was saving from
God. And we can do but lean justice to Christ's
own description of His consciousness at the close
of Matthew xi., if we do not set Him apart in
kind as well as function from the rest of the race,
and find just there the secret of His unique
identification with the race. No one who was
simply one of the race could contain and shelter
the race as Christ felt He could when He said, " Come
unto Me all ye that labour." To come *unto* this
Christ is to come *into* Him. No one who was
simply of the race could identify himself so completely with the whole race as redemption demands.
And it was as God that He was worshipped by the
first Church. Be the story of His birth fact or

symbol, at least it proves that. In Jesus, then, we do not hear of God, we meet Him. He does not simply reveal God; He is God in revelation, the gracious God revealed.

§

2. *It is a Gospel of Jesus the Mediator.* He mediates the holy grace of God, not as the preacher does, but in a way that the preacher has to preach. He is the mediator and not the medium. He is the Redeemer, and not the champion, of mankind. He is the Revealer, and not the rival, of God. In His Cross He confessed and satisfied the holiness of God in a way so intimate, so absolute, that it was also the radical exposure of sin in all its sinfulness, and thus it became its destruction. If the sinless could not confess sin, He exposed it. He could, and did, confess the holiness which throws sin into complete exposure and ruin. The divine morality, established in the holiness of the Atoning Cross, is the true source of our modern ethicizing of theology and our future ethicizing of society. Christ's work was not to proclaim forgiveness in the loftiest, kindest, amplest way. Others did that. Israel did that— not indeed as a people, but in its elect and inner self as a Messiah people. But Christ brought forgiveness as the Son of God alone could, as God forgiving, as forgiveness incarnate, as one actually redeeming and not offering redemption, as the divine destroyer of guilt, as the Eternal Salvation in God made historic and visible. Christianity is a media-

torial religion always.   Always, through all Eternity,
Jesus Christ is our Mediator with the Father.   The
mediation of Christ belongs to the perennial nature
of communion with God, and not merely to a
historic point of our religion.   We are sons always only in Him who was Son in none.   We are
the sons of God's Grace, He alone is the Son of His
love.   God's relation to him is not the matter of
grace it must be for every one of us forgiven
sinners.   His place with God is by nature and
absolute right.   He was and ever *is* the Son that
I must *become* through him.   And His absolute
Sonship became effective and historic in the consummation of the Cross.

When we say that the Cross is a Gospel of holy
love, gracious to human sin, we mean that the first
concern of Christ was with God and not with man.
It was with God's holiness, and its accentuation
of man's sin.   He poured out His soul unto death,
not to impress man but to confess God.   Therefore
He impresses man infinitely, inexhaustibly.   There
is nothing that makes sin so terrible as its full exhibition before God by God's own holiness, by His own
holy one ; in whom the holiness goes out as love,
suffers the judgment, and redeems as grace.   Love
is only divine because it is holy love.   And only as
holy does it elicit the faith that has all love latent
in it.   It is in this holiness of God that all our faith
and all our theology begin.   It is this that must per-
petually exalt them, and correct them, and moralize
them, and infuse them with passion, compassion,

imagination and majesty. All the reconstruction
of belief must begin with the holiness of God. All
the recovery of faith from mere religion must be
brought about by His holiness. And when we come
to speak of God's love, and ask how it should differ
from the benignities of ideal gods, or nature gods,
how it should celestialize human love, the answer
is the same. It is as holy love. It is as the love
is in the Cross. The purity of the speculative idea
falls short, in practical religion, of the holiness in
the Cross. It is ethereal rather than divine, and
sublimated more than sublime. Herein is love,
not that we loved who easily forgo propitiation,
but that He loved, who so loved as to make His
own unsparing propitiation under the conditions of
judgment. Herein is love, not as we love, but as He
loves who loves His holy name before all His children,
His holy name before all His prodigals, and therefore
spared not even His only Son. Herein is our salvation
as sure and perennial as the holiness for which we
are saved. And love is thus sure, because it is the holy
foundation of the real, the moral world.

§

3. *Christianity is a Gospel of Christ's resurrection.*
The same Jesus who died also rose, and lives as the
King of heavenly Glory and Lord of human destiny.
The fact that He rose, and that *He* rose, is the main
matter; it is not the manner of it, or its circumstances. The point is that the same continuous personality that mastered life during life in death also

triumphed over death, appeared to sundry in that victory, and lives in its full power and glory for us evermore. The Son of God, in heavenly power and glory now, was and is our dear, real, earthly Jesus. The physical conditions are subordinate. The empty tomb I would leave a question as open as the Virgin Birth.[1] I believe the tomb was emptied—else the body would have been produced to refute the apostles. But, even if it had not been, the crucified body was not the redeeming person. And God could prepare, and Christ could take, for His purposes a body as it pleased Him.

The mistake we make here, especially in preaching, is in treating the Resurrection of Christ as evidence to the world, as a proof, instead of an exercise, of His divine power. The evidential value of miracles is quite gone. As has been said, " instead of the miracles helping faith it takes all our faith to help us to believe the miracles." It is a misuse of miracle to make it evidentiary. None of Christ's miracles

[1] Nothing would more help us to find where we are, and to deal faithfully with our crypto-unitarianism, than to realize that our real difference with the Socinians is not as to the Virgin Birth (which is irrelevant to the Incarnation) but as to the Atonement. The locus of the issue is not the cradle but the cross. It is where it was with the first Socinianism—a question as to the standing need and conditions of forgiveness, whether forgiveness is the one gift, the one all-inclusive gift of God in Christ (Rom. viii. 32). The Unitarian issue is the Evangelical. It is a question as to the Gospel in its true and Pauline sense. In a very true sense the issue of the hour is less about Jesus than about Paul.

were so used by Him (in the Synoptics at least).
Indeed, He did His best to hush them up. He
always refused them as a sign. They were pure,
almost irrepressible, acts of real pity and help.
They were not advertisements ; they were not
credentials. They were not given to unfaith,
but to faith. They were no mere exhibitions
of power. Christ was not thaumaturgic. He
was no impressionist. He would never coerce
faith. The reaction against miracle is largely a
protest against our un-Christlike abuse of it.
We have given it a wrong place, a place which Christ
would not allow it to have, even for His contemporaries. And we do not erase miracles, therefore,
when we restore them to their true and blessed
place for faith.

The resurrection of Christ, is thus not evidential, but it is real. It is not the surest thing
in scientific history, but it is an essential fact to
Christian faith. It gave faith back its Lord. It
roused faith to know itself and its Master. The
apostles did not critically examine the evidence
for the resurrection ; they hailed the risen Lord.
It was not a resurrection that impressed them, but
a returned Saviour. The matter of moment is the
reality of the risen Lord, the identity of the Christ
now in heaven with the Jesus of the finished victory
in the Cross. The great thing is the power given
to believers to say and feel with real meaning
that they are in Christ and Christ in them. It
is to realize that the victorious Jesus was seen of

many, and was in converse with them; that as Christ, He still rules the Kingdom He set up; and that (if He endure at all) He is not sitting apart, solemnly superannuate like a retired and cloistered emperor, and watching, with only a founder's interest, the progress of the realm which once He set going but which now runs of itself. Nay, but He watches the Kingdom as the King who ever rules. And the Kingdom will never be but what He is continually making it.

§

II. But now what has a modernized theology to offer in the way of recognizing modern principles as well as in the way of preaching its own?[1]

1. Ever since the Reformation Protestantism has grown in the recognition of one modern principle which it did so much to create—*the freedom of the individual from external authority.* Whether that authority be Bible, Church, or Dogma, merely as such, faith renounces them all. The Bible is no code of either precept or belief. It is not a doctrinal protocol. The Word of God is in the Bible, as the soul is in the body. The one authority is the grace of the Bible speaking to the soul of man. That is to say, the one authority is the Gospel not only in the soul and speaking to the soul, but making the soul. It is a spiritual, practical, creative authority. It is not prescriptive. To be sure, it is an authority which acts under psychological conditions,

_____
[1] I still make free use of Kaftan's essay.

which conditions alone psychology is competent
to explore. But with the sanctions of that authority no science is competent to deal, either in
challenge or support. The idea of authority is
not destroyed because it ceases to be external.
Because it ceases to be external it does not cease
to be objective, to be presented to consciousness
and not produced from it. The moral law which
hounds the sinner is nothing external, but it is fear-
fully, inevitably, objective. And the Gospel that
saves is no less objective and authoritative than
the law that damns. Its voice may be inward and
private. But these inner voices are what make
the real authority ; when the soul is spoken to by
another who is its own other. There is no voice
so poignant in condemnation as the voice that is
dear. Remorse is more than half the grief of
many a decent widower. There is no judgment
so serious as that of our kin, the judgment of
love. The most terrible accusers of the culprit's
crime are the children it brands and who never
upbraid. The law of Society bears so closely upon
us because we ourselves are not insulated wills but
products of the same society that made the law.
And there is no authority so ubiquitous, and therefore so objective, as the Word of God that emerges
in the colloquy or conflict of the soul God made.

It is quite true that a huge problem is set to the
Gospel in the present moral anarchy of western
civilization. We have not yet found for society the
Word which the individual freely finds, the Word

to replace for the public the external authority of
the medieval Church. But so long as the individual
is made to find that Word for himself in the historic
Gospel, there need be no fear that Society will
not find it in due course for purposes of public
control.

§

2. A second great modern idea is here suggested
which profoundly affects the type of our Christian
faith—the social idea. We always have been greatly
affected by the social idea in the shape of the Church.
Our Christian theology has been developed as the
intelligent expression on the face of a living Church.
It has been in vital connexion with the consciousness
of a living society. No church, no theology. But
it is also becoming amenable to the form and pressure of a society wider though not greater—civil
society ; and especially in respect of its weak.
The Brotherhood in the deep Christian sense becomes much affected by the Brotherhood in the
broad humane sense. In the past the *strength*
of Society has much moulded Christian thought
and institutions. The Holy Empire, the dynasties, the philosophies have all been shaping powers.
The ablest jurisprudence at one time much coloured
the theology of atonement, for instance. But now
the *weakness* and need of Society exert more
and more the modifying pressure. The appeal
from the helpless, the passion of pity, affects the
whole frame of Christian method, institution,

ethic, and even thought, in a growing way. It bears home to us the fact that every single soul is saved in an act which was the organic salvation, the salvation into a kingdom, of the whole race. We are not really saved if we are saved into neglect of a social salvation. The Gospel preached to the soul must be a Gospel which leaves the saved soul much more concerned than he used to be about the saving of civilization, the salvation of the just as well as of the lost, and the restoration of the poor as well as of the wicked. There are very great social changes involved in the modernization of our theology which is now going on. Christian truth must be socialized by the same power as socializes Christian wealth. And it ought in fairness to be added that medieval theology was much more social than Protestantism has been except on its Calvinistic side. It was far more social than our debased and individualized Calvinism. It is easy to see why Catholicism, Anglican or Roman, whose golden age was the medieval, should be more socialist than current Protestantism.

§

3. There is another point where the ethicizing of Christianity has been greatly affected by modern thought—*the rescue of personality from individualism the socializing of its idea.* The influence is social, but it comes from the psychological side. It proceeds first from that growth of the principle of personality which has been mainly promoted by

Christianity. Christ is certainly no less concerned than Nietsche that the personality should receive the fullest development of which it is capable, and be more and more of a power. The difference between them lies in the moral method by which the personality is put into possession of itself and its resources—in the one case by asserting self in the other by losing it ; in the one case by self-pleasing, in the other by self-renunciation. Christianity is interested in the first degree in the modern emphasis on personality, because it is its chief creator. But the influence I allude to is more than that. It lies, secondly, in the conviction that the *strength* of personality, after an early stage, is damaged by the mere *force* of individualism, and is a social product. Personality does not come into the world with us ready made, but it has a history and a growth. Education is not merely its training, it is its creation. In all of us the personality is incomplete ; and it misleads us in the most grave way when we use it as an analogy for the ever complete and holy personality of God. We are but persons in the making. Personality is created by social influences, and finds itself only in these. We complete our personality only as we fall into place and service in the vital movement of the society in which we live. Isolation means arrested development. The aggressive egotist is working his own moral destruction by stunting and shrinking his true personality. Social life, duty, and sympathy, are the only conditions

under which a true personality can be shaped.
And if it be asked how a society so crude, imperfect,
unmoral, and even immoral as that in which we
live is to mould a personality truly moral, it is here
that Christ comes to the rescue with the gift to
faith both of an active Spirit and of a society
complete in Himself, which in Him is none of these
evil things, the society of the Kingdom of God, which
plays a part so great in the modern construction
of the Gospel. We are saved only in a salvation
which set up a kingdom, and did not merely set it
on foot. We have the Kingdom not with Christ
but in Christ. Do not leave Christ out of the
Kingdom, as if He were detachable from it like any
common king. The individual is saved only in this
social salvation. And the more you insist that a
soul can only be saved, and a personality secured,
by Christ's finished work, the more you must contend that the Kingdom of God is not merely coming
but is come, and is active in the Spirit among us
now. There is the closest connexion, if not identity,
when you go deep enough, between the theology
of salvation and the moral principles of social
regeneration. The principle of our salvation is
the principle of human ethic, not only of private,
as has long been seen, but of public ethic, as we
now come to see. A great economist has lately
traced in an original and masterly way the vital
connexion between the ethic of Calvinism and
modern economics. To dismiss the moral necessity
for God of Christ's Cross is, in the long run, to banish

moral principles from public affairs; since the greatest public affair in history would then have in it no causation in the eternal and immutable morality of the universe.

§

4. With the modern stress laid by Christianity upon a kingdom, *we must recognize the distinction* so marked in recent thought ever since Kant *between theoretical and practical knowledge, and we must fall in with the modern stress on the latter.* Ethic is a far mightier matter than science, and Christian experience a far more precious thing than Christian correctitude. We move to a Gospel of act and experience, which in the long run is independent of either philosophy or criticism. The real Gospel of the Cross is beyond either. In the strict sense of the word theology, that too is immune. For it rests on the contact of indubitable history (viz. Christ's Person and Cross) with present experience. What is vulnerable is a theosophy, a secondary theology which has grown up round experimental theology, and is largely drawn from cosmic or juristic speculation. These speculations are, of course, bound to arise. For the more free we are in the practical experience of our positive Gospel, the more freely we discuss and appropriate from the theoretic world. The more sure we are in our positive Gospel, the less we are tempted to try to control and manipulate philosophy so as to take the danger out of it. But it is by no philosophy or

theosophy that we stand or fall. A man speculates with a free judgment if he is not speculating with the capital which means his livelihood. And so we have a new liberty for thought in the primacy of the moral, and the certainty of our moral redemption in experience.

And we are not only *free* to go on from that standpoint to be occupied with the interpretation of the world. We *must* so go on. The faith that makes us free is the faith of a universal, nay a cosmic, redemption. The truths and questions of science are not freaks or hobbies, arbitrary or gratuitous. They are necessary and inevitable. They rise from life, from actual contact with the world. They present real life to us in certain aspects. They represent not only the objective world, but the objective world as it emerges in human experience, in human consciousness and will. The philosophy which cannot license us yet does enrich us. It does not give us our grasp, but it enlarges it. It does not give us a footing, but it does give a horizon.

I venture to say, therefore, that that separation of the theoretical and the practical (with the stress on the latter) which has been so influential ever since Kant, and rises again with Neo-Kantianism, Pragmatism, and Activism like Eucken's, is a principle of great value both for the certainty and the freedom of our Christian faith in contact with the world. The more we are secured in our practical experience of the Gospel, the more we are free to listen to all representations from philosophy or science in shaping to a doctrine our capacious life with Christ in God.

All this means that our theology must be ethicized. It must be framed with more regard to the practical than to the speculative ideals of life and faith. To modernize theology it must be ethicized, but more from the revelation of God's holiness in the Cross than from the progress of natural or social ethic, however refined.

§

5. *Christianity in being ethicized, is popularized.* The classical and pagan view of the world was theoretic. It would solve the great riddle intellectually. But this was possible for the few alone. It was the work of experts. But when the problem is that of the conscience, it concerns us all. It is accessible to all, nay, it presses on all. The great issue is not being thought out, it is being lived out, loved out, worked out, and fought out. The power for life concerns all, the scheme of life but a few. The whole reality of life is on its moral side, and that is the side which the Gospel appeals to, and so it appeals to all. The last stand of the Gospel is in the whole reality of practical life, individual and social, in homes, marts, senates, and Churches. It is not in the schools. It is only paganism (whether Haeckel's or Hegel's) that rests in the self-sufficiency of thought or the idea. The Gospel is the moral, the universal, the final interpretation of life.

Christ came not with a reading of life but with its redemption, not with the answer to a riddle but with
the solution of a practical problem. He did not
come with a body of new truth, but with a
power of new reality, not with the profoundest
knowledge but with Eternal Life.

§

6. I need hardly include among the marks of a
modern Christianity *the extent to which its whole
outlook has been modified by the doctrine of evolution, and especially historic evolution.* This might
almost go without saying. Even the Roman Church
has recognized it, and the line of its apologetic has
been profoundly changed by its doctrine of development as formulated by Möhler and Newman. First
the blade, then the ear, then the full corn in the ear.
Protestantism has recognized the principle more
fully still. Dr. Adams Brown, in the most able
outline of Theology which we now possess in English,
has said that the three types of Christianity usually
given—the Greek, Roman, and Protestant—should
be extended by dividing the latter into two—the
Reformation type and the modern type ; because
the difference between these two is as great as that
between the Greek and the Roman type. And he
notes as the destinctive feature of modern Protestantism the effect of this doctrine of evolution.
(*Outlines of Theology, p. 62 n.*). There are other
features, as I venture to point out ; and I should
myself lay more stress on the new ethical note.

But the evolutionary idea is especially attractive to a scientific age. We have certainly no quarrel with that idea till it is lifted from being a method and elevated into a dogma—indeed *the* dogma; till it is treated as a *vera causa*, and made to explain not simply the mode of change but the principle of change, the germinating principle of the seed as well as the phases of its process. It is a philosophy which explains much, and makes us patient of much, and hopeful of more. But it cannot give us hope in the Christian and certain sense. Because it cannot give us the goal of its own movements any more than their real cause. And a religion has to do rather with the source and the goal than with the path, with the meaning rather than the method. We must welcome the new force given by this theory to many a word of Christ, and many a movement of the Spirit. It is really not evolution we have to watch, but the Monism which is so often supposed to be inseparable from it by those who have more science than philosophy, more imagination than either, little ethical insight, and theology least of all.

The whole attitude of the Church to its truth has been altered by the destruction though evolution of the idea of a final system of belief, or a monopolist form of polity. Its intellectual hospitality has been indefinitely extended. And it is free, with a large liberty, from a burden too great for even faith to bear. It can regard the new philosophies as helpers so long as they do not claim to be suzerains, so long as they do not aspire to prescribe belief but only to enrich it, to correct its statement, and to enhance its scope. They help to place us in a new relation of mastery and ease to the Bible and the stage which the Bible registers. And they give us a new grasp of the long action of the Spirit and its way with the Church and the world. The more subtle and plastic the Spirit, the mightier and more irresistible is its action. And the less monumental our Christ is, in a stiff Byzantine figure, the more pervasive He is as a constant and subduing power. When evolution escapes from the bondage of the physical sciences, and its mesalliance with monistic dogma, it is a distinguished badge and blessing of a modern Church. Only let it be taken as a supplement to creation, and not as a substitute for redemption, and it gives a wonderful flexibility and grace to much theological thought that once was formal and hard.

§

7. Nothing is more characteristic of the modern mind than its passion for reality. It is a passion that takes all sorts of extravagant, and some noxious, forms. But it is a worthy instinct. And it is a demand that elicits the moral realism, the unsparing spiritual thoroughness, of the Gospel. Hence the Gospel not only tolerates, it demands, science and criticism. If it can succumb to these it should. The criticism may be the moral caustic applied to Christian society by an Ibsen, or it may be the Higher Criticism of the Bible or the creeds

by the schools. Our treasure in Bible or Church is in an earthen vessel which is fairly exposed to the critic. And especially historic criticism touches us, as we have the water only in the historic vessel. But every historic phenomenon, in so far as it is historic, must admit criticism, and stand the test of that reality. Be it book or creed, or even Christ Himself so far as He is a historic personality—we cannot seclude them from competent criticism. But then the historic Jesus is no mere historic figure. Even in so far as He is historic, as the object of our faith He is, though not immune from critical action, yet secure. For the living person of Christ stands, and its consummation on the Cross, and its continued life in our experience. And that is where our real faith is fixed—on the finished redeeming work of the Saviour on the Cross, sealed indeed in the resurrection but finished on the Cross, published in the resurrection but achieved on the Cross. That is faith's reality, the reality that faith knows. No criticism can shake that if it be thoroughly settled into our experience. From that vantage ground we recognize the rights of criticism because we are in a position to deny its rule. That Jesus we cannot criticize either historically or morally. For we cannot criticize our Judge and our Redeemer. We can criticize His knowledge about the Old Testament and the like, but we cannot criticize his ownership of our souls. He is for us the last reality, which enables us to criticize all else. His saints shall judge the world.

§

III. Thus it is not with a critical issue we have really to do, it is with a dogmatic. And this I ask your leave to explain.

The question of recent criticism and its effect on your Gospel will often arise in your mind, or it will be put to you by others. And unless you found on the true rock it may cost you much trouble and pain.

You will be wise if you keep it out of your preaching. That is to say, do not preach much about it. Preach as men who know about it. Preach habitually neither its methods nor its results, but preach a Gospel which has taken due account of both. The Christ we have to declare is neither a residuum which the critics are pleased to leave us, nor an asbestos quite unaffected by the fire. What criticism acts on is the Bible, the record. And, closely as Christ is bound up with the Bible, He is more closely bound up with the Gospel than with the Bible. When it becomes a religious question, that is, a question of the Gospel, criticism takes quite a secondary place, and, in cases, may even be irrelevant. The matter then ceasing to turn on facts, but turning on a living person, passes into the hands of the believer, and through him to the theologian. It is a dogmatic question.

§

Take the case of the Bible itself for instance. The momentous question does not concern its mode of origin, its *provenance*, its constituent parts, authors, dates. It does not concern the equal value for historic science of every portion, or for theological truth of every thought it contains. It is a question of a special and real revelation from God to the conscience. Have we here, on the whole, the effective history of redemption ? It is not the history of Israel, or the biography of Christ, that the Bible exists to give. Its history is the history of grace, the exposition of a long action and a final act of grace. And, as I said at the outset, it is history not of a scientific but of a preached kind. It is a kind of history, and an amount of history, prescribed by the practical purpose of conveying the grace of God. It is sacramental history. It is broken bread—such portions of history as form sacramental elements, adequate for the spiritual purpose in hand. It does not exist primarily to instruct us about God, but to convey God to us. The New Testament is not a mere monument of the first century. Nor, on the other hand, is it a mere book of devotion. Revelation is not there to convey theology, nor to elevate piety, but to convey God Himself. It is His self-revelation, which means His self-communication. It is not concerned with thought, nor with mere hints or indications of His action, " making Him broken gleams in a stifled splendour and gloom." These you find in other religions. In a looser sense they too convey revelations of God, self-intimations of God, indications of His presence, His thought, His movement, in some sort. They suggest principles which Christ realized in a person. But we want more than signs of God's presence and movement. We want action positive and final. What we want in revelation is God's total final will, His purpose, His heart, His central and final self, the whole counsel of God in a compendious sense. We want answer to the question, not, Is He here ? Is He accessible ? But, What is He going to do with us ? What is He doing with us and for us ? What must I do to be saved ? And that is the question put and answered, once for all, in the Bible. The best that the religion of nature does for us is to wake us to a helpless sense of the contradiction and crisis in which we are, and make us feel that what we want is not knowledge but salvation. So that while in other religions the element uppermost is man seeking God, in Israel and in Christ the uppermost thing is God seeking man and finding him for good and all. But in all other religions God and man are seeking each other in the dark ; in Christianity they find each other.

We need fear no criticism which leaves us with that. That is the marrow of all the impossible old theories of inspiration. Their object was, often in very unfortunate ways, to secure the uniqueness, the immediacy, the reality, and the finality of God's self-revelation in the Bible. Let us do them that justice, even against themselves. Let us try, in so far as they survive, to get their advocates to see that if they treat the Bible with respect, we, who sympathize with the critical method, do so out of a respect greater still. We let the Bible speak for itself. The great question, then, as to the Bible is not about the historic impregnability of certain detailed facts under the full fire of criticism. It is a question whether the record as a whole is effective and sacramental, whether we have the history of a special movement and action of God for our redemption, or whether we have but a wonderful exhalation of the religious instinct and faculty of man. It is really a dogmatic question. Ὁ Θεὸς θεολογίζει.

§

So much for the Bible. Now it is so in a like manner with Jesus Christ. The great question is dogmatic. It is, who is He? What did He do? What does He do? What is His present relation to us and to the future? Was He really the Son of God, or was He but the choice epitome of man? Have we in Him the final approach and self-bestowal of God, the sempiternal presence and final action of the divine reality; or have we a distillation, so to say, of all that is best in religious humanity? Was He an achievement of human nature to make us proud, or was He an achievement of God's nature on our race, called out by the race's deed and shame? His work was an act of sacrifice, of faith, of pity and of love—was it the act of God? Was it God in action? Was He, is He, the true Son of God, for ever Mediator and for ever Lord; or was He just the greatest of all the prophets, apostles, and martyrs of the spiritual life? Do we possess in Him God, or a messenger from God? You can see what a difference must be made in our preaching, according as we answer these alternatives.

Criticism may settle that Jesus loved, taught, blessed, and died. It may decide that to His contemporaries He did pass for one who performed miracles, and accepted that reputation ; that He held Himself, rightly or wrongly, to be directly and uniquely from and with God, in the sense of Matthew xi. 25 ff. ; and that the first church was only made possible, historically, by its belief that He really rose from the dead. But these are not the prime questions. If they were, our faith would be at the mercy of the critics. The great question is, Did He do the things the apostles believed ? Was He really what He held Himself to be ? These claims and beliefs were actual. They existed as claims and beliefs. The claims were made, the beliefs were held. Were they real and valid ? Could He, can He, make them good ? Have we in the Jesus who so lived, and so thought both of Himself and God—have we the living God ? And do we have Him to-day as living, immortal, royal, redeeming Lord God ? Was He, is He, of Deity ? May we worship Him ? The New Testament Church did. They could not help it. The impression left on them was such that worship was a psychological necessity quite inevitable, quite intelligible, quite explicable, as the psychology of religion goes. But while thus inevitable was it really illicit ? Was it an extravagance which our better knowledge of reality must correct and reduce ? Must we beware of that tendency to worship Him, and arrest it ? Must we hear His own voice arresting us, ever fainter and farther as time goes on, " Why do you call Me so good ? Little children, keep yourselves from idols."

Now, the answer to these questions is not critical but dogmatic. No criticism can certify us of these things, and therefore no criticism can take certainty from us. The man, the Church, that is in living intercourse with the risen Christ is in possession of a fact of experience as real as any mere historic fact, or any experience of reality, that the critic has to found on and make a standard. And with that experience, a man is bound to approach the critical evidence of Christ's resurrection in a different frame of mind from the merely scientific man who has no such experience. This makes a great difference for criticism between the Old Testament and the New Testament. In the Old Testament we have no historic character with whom we are in daily personal relation still, and who is the greatest contemporary of every age. The fact that the risen Christ appeared only to believers is of immense significance ; as I have said, it impairs the value of the resurrection as proof to the sceptical world, and defines its chief value as being for the Church, for the revival of faith, and not its creation. The external evidence for it, I have owned, is not scientifically complete, nor, suppose it were, is the bearing of the fact upon the rational world, but upon the believing Church. It did not found redemption. That was done and finished on the Cross. But it founded the Church as a historic company, by the resurrection of its faith from the dead. It did not found redemption, but it put God's seal on the completeness of redemption, and it launched the Church. " If our knowledge of Christ closed with the grave, I fear no faith could have arisen in Christ's victory over death. It could not have been a postulate from the outcome of His early action. And if it had it would have been too weak to resist doubt." [1]

The living Christ who died has destroyed my guilt, and brought me God. That is not the action of the resurrection but of the Cross. I believe that the divine power in Him which wells up in my faith, rather than the irrepressible vitality of His divine " nature," is the power by which Christ rose. But it is still more the power by which He gained His finished victory on the Cross. Without the primary theology of the Cross the resurrection of Christ would have no more value than a reanimation. The most present and real fact of our Christian faith is the fact accessible to faith alone. It is the fact that Christ has brought us God and destroyed our guilt. You do not yet know the inner Christ who are but His lovers or friends. You need to have been His patients and to owe Him your life. That is Christianity. A Church without that experience at its centre is not Christianity. What makes a Church Christian is not the historic fact of His death, but the theological spiritual, experimental fact that His death meant

[1] Metzger quoted by Reischle Z. f. Th. & K. vii. 205.

that, and did that, and ever does it. Where there is no such experience it is hard, if not impossible, to convince anybody that His death was more than the close of His life, or the sealing of His witness with His martyr blood. But as a present fact that evangelical action of Christ's death is far more real, and therefore more effective, with us than the death of any Jewish martyr at Roman hands 2,000 years ago. Therefore dogmatic conviction of this kind may have a great effect on criticism, but criticism has only a minor effect upon it. We may be led to recast some of our ideas as to the historical conditions amid which the great life and death transpired. We may modify much in our views as to Christ's omniscience, and similar things affected by His emptying of Himself. He accepted some of the limitations of human ignorance. He consented not to know, with a nescience divinely wise. The story is all recorded in a book, and therefore literary criticism has its rights. Christ worked through history, and in the concretest relation to the history of His race and age ; and, in so far as you have history, historic criticism has its rights. Christ lived a real, and therefore a growing, human life, as a historic personality. Therefore, being in psychological conditions, He is amenable so far to psychological criticism. But allowing for all such things, the question remains dogmatic, Was He, is He, what Christian faith essentially believes ? Did these convictions, of His and of the Church, correspond to reality ? Was He, is He, in God what He thought

He was, and what He was held to be ? When the
first Church worshipped Him with God's name, and
set Him on God's throne, were they a new race of
idolaters ? Was his influence so poor in quality
that it could not protect them from that ? He
thought Himself redeemer ; did He really redeem ?
Did God redeem in Him ? Was God the real
actor in His saving action ? These are the questions ; and in all such questions, criticism is *ultra
vires*. These things are settled in another and
higher court, and criticism must work under that
settlement. The soundest criticism is the criticism
by a believing Church, daily living on the Grace
of the Cross and the venture of faith.

It is quite true that these truths become dogmas
which, in their statement, are fair matter for criticism.
The theology of the Church is not a closed product of
the Holy Spirit, any more than the Bible is a closed
product of verbal inspiration. A process of criticism,
adjustment, and correction has always been going
on. Theology, on the whole, has been constantly
modernized. But it all proceeds on the basis of a
reality above logic and beyond criticism, the reality of
experienced redemption in the Cross, of faith's knowledge, and the Church's communion with Christ. It
is thus something within dogma itself that is the great
corrective of dogma. Christian truth in a Church
carries in itself the conditions, and the resources, of its
own self-preservation through self-correction. The
Church's dogmatic faith is the great corrective of the
Church's dogmatic thought. The religious life in a

risen and royal Redeemer is always ahead of the religious thought about the nature and method of Redemption. The old faith is always making theology new. The true critic of Christian history is its primary theology. You expected me perhaps to say the true critic of a Christian theology is its history. But that is now a commonplace. I meant something less obvious. It is a theological Christ we have centrally to do with—an atoning Christ. And it is only a theological Christ that we need take immense pains to preserve for the future. It is that piece of experienced theology, an atoning, reconciling, redeeming Christ, that has made all the rest of theology. And it must therefore be its living test. With historical criticism, simply as a branch of exact science, pursued by the scholars, and taught in the schools, you have as preachers only a minor concern. You may take it up as you might any other science, only as your nearest pursuit. But you do not wait on it for your message. You must deliver that message while the critics are still at war. Christ is there and urgent, whatever is happening to the story of Christ. A knowledge of criticism may help you to disengage the kernel from the husk, to save the time so often lost in the defence of outposts, to discard obsolete weapons and superfluous baggage, and to concentrate on the things that really matter for eternal life and godliness —like the Reconciliation of the Cross. All true science teaches us also its own limits, and so destroys its own tyranny. But the real criticism with which

we have to do, from which all our religion starts
when we take the whole Christian field into account,
is not our criticism of Christ, but Christ's criticism
of us, His saving judgment of us. The higher
criticism casts us on the highest. There is a secondary theology of corollaries from faith, and there is a
primary of faith's essence. To handle this great
and primary theology the first condition is the new
man. Our most judicious thing is to treat Christ
as our judge, to know Him as we are first known
of Him, and to search Him as those who are
searched to the marrow by His subtle Spirit.

§

Might I venture here to speak of myself, and of
more than thirty years given to progressive thought
in connexion, for the most part, with a pulpit and
the care of souls. Will you forgive me? I am
addressing young men who have the ministry before
them, as most of mine is behind, strewn indeed
with mistakes, yet led up of the Spirit.

There was a time when I was interested in the
first degree with purely scientific criticism. Bred
among academic scholarship of the classics and
philosophy, I carried these habits to the Bible, and
I found in the subject a new fascination, in proportion as the stakes were so much higher. But,
fortunately for me, I was not condemned to the
mere scholar's cloistered life. I could not treat
the matter as an academic quest. I was kept
close to practical conditions. I was in a relation

of life, duty, and responsibility for others. I
could not contemplate conclusions without asking
how they would affect these people, and my word
to them, in doubt, death, grief, or repentance. I
could not call on them to accept my verdict on
points that came so near their souls. That is not
our conception of the ministry. And they were
people in the press and care of life. They could
not give their minds to such critical questions.
If they had had the time, they had not the training.
I saw amateurs making the attempt either in the
pew or in the pulpit. And the result was a warning.
Yet there were Christian matters which men must
decide for themselves, trained or not. Therefore,
these matters could not be the things which were
at issue in historic criticism taken alone. Moreover, I looked beyond my immediate charge, and
viewed the state of mind and faith in the Church
at large—especially in those sections of it nearest
myself. And I became convinced that they were
in no spiritual condition to have forced on them
those questions on which scholars so delighted and
differed. They were not entrenched in that reality
of experience and that certainty of salvation which is
the position of safety and command in all critical
matters. It also pleased God by the revelation
of His holiness and grace, which the great theologians
taught me to find in the Bible, to bring home to
me my sin in a way that submerged all the school
questions in weight, urgency, and poignancy. I
was turned from a Christian to a believer, from a

lover of love to an object of grace. And so, whereas I first thought that what the Churches needed was enlightened instruction and liberal theology, I came to be sure that what they needed was evangelization, in something more than the conventional sense of that word. "What we need is not the dechurching of Christianity, but the Christianizing of the Church." For the sake of critical freedom, in the long run that is so. Religion without an experimental foundation in grace, readily feels panic in the presence of criticism, and is apt to do wild and unjust things in its terror. The Churches are not, in the main, in the spiritual condition of certainty which enables them to be composed and fair to critical methods. They either expect too much from them, and then round upon them in disappointed anger when it is not forthcoming. Or they expect so little from them that they despise them as only ignorance can. They run either to rationalism or to obscurantism. There was something to be done, I felt, before they could freely handle the work of the scholars on the central positions.

And that something was to revive the faith of the Churches in what made them Churches ; to turn them from the ill-found sentiment which had sapped faith ; to re-open their eyes to the meaning of their own salvation ; to rectify their Christian charity by more concern for Christian truth ; to banish the amiable religiosity which had taken possession of them in the name of Christian love ; and to restore some sense not only of love's severity,

but of the unsparing moral mordancy in the Cross
and its judgment, which means salvation to the
uttermost ; to recreate an experience of redemption,
both profound and poignant, which should enable
them to deal reasonably, without extravagance
and without panic, with the scholars' results as
these came in. What was needed before we discussed the evidence for the resurrection, was a revival
of the sense of God's judgment-grace in the Cross,
a renewal of the sense of holiness, and so of
sin, as the Cross set forth the one, and exposed
the other in its light. We needed to restore their
Christian footing to many in the Churches who
were far within the zone which criticism occupies.
In a word, it seemed to me that what the critical
movement called for was not a mere palliation of
orthodoxy, in the shape of liberal views, but a new
positivity of Gospel. It was not a new compre-
hensiveness, but a new concentration, a new evangelization, that was demanded by the situation.

But the defective theological education of the
ministry seemed to put a great obstacle in the way
of such a revival as I have described. For, incredible as it may seem to many, and even alarming,
theology was, (for reasons on which it would be
ungracious for me to enter,) not only distrusted,
but hated by many of the stewards of the Θεοῦ λόγος.
And I have longed and prayed to see the man
arise to alter all this, with an equal knowledge of
his sin, his Saviour, and his subject, to do the
work that had to be done in rearing men with a

real, thorough, humble and joyous belief in their own message, and to do it on a scale to compel the attention, and even the concern, of our Churches.

Meantime my own course seemed prescribed. It was, in the space of life, strength, and work which was yet mine, to labour as one who waited for that messianic hope, and to try to persuade those who would hear to join me in preparation for so great a gift of God. I withdrew my prime attention from much of the scholar's work and gave it to those theological interests, imbibed first from Maurice, and then more mightily through Ritschl, which come nearer to life than science, sentiment, or ethic ever can do. I immersed myself in the Logic of Hegel,[1] and corrected it by the theology of Paul, and its continuity in the Reformation, because I was all the time being corrected and humiliated by the Holy Spirit. To me John Newton's hymn which I spoke of is almost holy writ. My faith in critical methods is unchanged. My acceptance of many of the new results is as it was. This applies to the criticism of traditional dogma no less than of scripture. But the need of the hour, among the only circles I can reach, is not that. The time for it will come, but not yet. It is a slow matter. For what is needed is no mere change of view, but a change and a deepening in the type of personal religion, amounting in cases to a new conversion. There is that amiss with the Churches which free criticism can

[1] I desire to own here how very much I owe to Dr. Fairbairn.

never cure, and no breadth or freshness of view
amend. There is a lack of depth and height, an
attenuation of experience, a slackness of grasp, a
displacement of the centre, a false realism, a dislocation of perspective, amid which the things
that make Christianity permanently Christian are
in danger of fading from power, if not from view.
In a word, I was driven to a change of front though
not of footing—to the preacher's and the pastor's
treatment of the situation, which is also the
New Testament view, and which is very different
from the scholar's. The savant may or must frame
results and utter them regardless of their public
effect, but the preacher may not. The order of
truth he deals with has its own methods, his office
has its own paedagogic, and his duty its own conscience. In most cases the best contribution the
preacher can make at present to the new theology
is to deepen and clear the old faith, and to
rescue it from a kind of religion which is only
religion and hardly Christian faith. What has
often passed as the new theology is no more, sometimes, than a theology of fatigue, or a theology of
the press, or a theology of views, or a theology
of revolt. Or it is an accommodation theology, a
theology accommodated only to the actual interests
of the cultured hour.[1] The effort made is to

[1] While I was writing this I read the address of
an estimable preacher of up-to-date theology who was
demanding that the theologians should come down and
accept a theology imposed by three things—physical

substitute for the old faith something more human in its origin, more humane in its temper, and more halting in its creed, something more genial and more rational and more shallow. It is that rather than the effort to deepen the old theology by a sympathetic re-interpretation, which pierces farther into its content of revelation, and speaks the old faith in a new tongue. The tongue is new enough, but it is not certain that it speaks the old thing, or develops its position from a profounder acquaintance with the holiness of the love of God within the Cross. It analyses the Bible, but it does not reconstruct from the Bible, but from what is known as the Christian principle, which is mainly human nature re-edited and bowdlerised.

I am sure no new theology can really be theology, whatever its novelty, unless it express and develop the old faith which made those theologies that are now old the mightiest things of the age when they were new. Well do I know how little a theo-

science, historical study (especially as to the origin of the Bible), and comparative religion. Well, these results are pretty familiar to most of us by now, and very sterile. But you will hardly believe that there was not a word about the study of the Gospel, our application to the contents of Christ's revelation of God, the implicates of his idea of God, or the principles of his work. No, that would have put the preacher beside the theologians. He would have had to ask questions about what was meant by God's most holy love in Christ, questions which no science of nature, history or religion can answer. Our spiritual shyness of God's holiness has more than some thing to do with the ordinary reaction against theology.

logy in itself can do, and how the mighty doer is
the living faith.   But I know well also that that faith
is not the real thing unless it compels and loves an
adequate theology; and if it cannot produce it it
dies.   I know well also how seldom it is really
objections to an outworn system that keep men
from Christ, and retard the Gospel.   I am sure
that, if we had a theology brought entirely up to
date in regard to current thought, we should not
then have the great condition for the Kingdom
of God.   It is the wills of men, and not their views,
that are the great obstacle to the Gospel, and the
things most intractable.   The power to deal with
those wills is the power of the Gospel as the eternal
act of the will and heart of God.   And the power
of the Gospel as a preached thing is shaped in a
message which has had from the first a theological
language of its own creation as its most adequate
vehicle.   To discard that language entirely is to
maim the utterance of the Gospel.   To substitute
a vocabulary of mere humane sympathies or
notions for the great phrases and thoughts which
are theology compressed into diamonds is like the
attempt to improve a great historic language, which
is a nation's record, treasure and trust, by reducing
it to Saxon monosyllables, and these to phonetics.
I cannot conceive a Christianity to hold the future
without words like grace, sin, judgment, repentance,
incarnation, atonement, redemption, justification, sacrifice, faith and eternal life.   No words of less volume
than these can do justice to the meaning of God,

however easy their access to the minds of modern men.
It needs such words to act on the scale of God and
of the race. And the preacher who sets to discard
them or, what is more common, to eviscerate
them, is imperilling the great Church for a passing
effect with the small. For a living and modern
theology our chief need is a living and positive
faith, moving in those great categories, and full
of confident power to absorb and organize the
sound thought of the time. To rouse and feed
this faith is the great work of the preacher. And
thus the service the preacher does to theology is
at least no less than the service theology does to
him. A mere theology may strain and stiffen
the preacher. But the preacher who is a true
steward of the Christian Word makes a living
theology inevitable, which, because it lives, demands
new form and fitness for each succeeding time.

In closing his recent admirable *History of New
England Theology*, Dr. Frank Hugh Foster says:
" The questions of the present hour are more
fundamental than those with which New England
Theology, or it immediate successors, have had to
concern themselves. A ringing call is sounding
through the air to face the true issue—the reality
of God's supernatural interference in the history
of man *versus* the universal reign of unmodified
law [or ideas and processes]. The question is not
whether the old evangelical scheme needs some
adjustments to adapt it to our present knowledge,
but whether its most fundamental conception,

the very idea of the Gospel is true. Before this all the halfway compromises of the present day must be given up. Men must take sides. They must be for the Gospel or against it."

And for or against a historic Gospel, is what Dr. Foster means

THE PREACHER AND MODERN ETHIC

VIII

The Preacher and Modern Ethic

FROM the varied features of modern life that I have
indicated I should like to select for further treatment the ethical interest and its development.
There is no note in the modern mind more welcome or hopeful to us than this ethical note, the
moralizing of society in its ideas, its conduct, its
systems, and its institutions. In the case of institutions you may be more struck with the *humanizing*
of them, as for instance, of war. But the *moralizing*
movement is much deeper, and much more
permanent, and it carries the other, the humanizing
element, with it.

It is most to our purpose to note the ethicizing
of theology, among other legacies of the past. I
must have already said that a modern theology is
not simply theology *à la mode*. The main part of
the modernizing of theology is the moralizing of
it,—this much more than its rationalizing. But
indeed this tendency is nothing new. It is but
continuing a long process in the Christian Church.
It was Christ's own action on Judaism. It was Paul's
task with his Pharisaism. And a great step in this
movement was taken in the Middle Ages, when

the work of Christ ceased to be regarded as a traffic with Satan for His captives, and became for Anselm a satisfaction made by Christ to the wounded honour of God. It was another step when the principles of a great social discipline like jurisprudence were applied to explain the situation. It was a real advance when the Reformation introduced the idea of public justice, instead of wounded honour, as the object of satisfaction. The much decried forensic idea was ethically far ahead of the previous idea which recognized in Satan rights of property in souls, ahead also of the feudal idea of the honour of God. And still we move up the moral scale as we substitute for retributive justice with its individualism, universal righteousness and eternal holiness with the social note. So also when we discard the idea of equivalent penalty in favour of Christ's obedient sanctity as the satisfying thing before God. The whole great movement of thought on that question has been on an ascending moral scale. The more we modernize it the more we moralize it. And the modifications called for to-day are in the same direction. Our revisions but continue the long process of moral refinement in the Christian mind. And it appears *en route* that we cannot ethicize Christianity without pursuing a doctrine of Atonement ever more positive. The more ethical we become the more exigent is holiness ; and therefore the more necessary is Atonement as the action of love and grace at the instance of holiness and in its interests.

Let us only flee the amateur notion that in the Cross there is no ultimate ethical issue involved, that it is a simple religious appeal to the heart. The pulpit is doomed to futility if it appeal to the heart in any sense that discredits the final appeal to the conscience. I mean it is doomed if it keep declaring that, with such a Father as Christ's, forgiveness is a matter of course ; the only difficulty being to insert it into men's hearty belief. There is no doubt that is a very popular notion. ' How natural for God to forgive. It is just like Him.' Whereas the real truth is that it is only like the God familiar to us from the Cross, and not from our natural expectation. Real forgiveness is not natural. Nor is it natural and easy to consent to be forgiven. The more quick our moral sensibility is the more slow we are to accept our forgiveness. And that not through pride always, but often through the exact opposite—through shame, and the inability to forgive one's self. Is it Newman who says that the good man never forgives himself ? I wish a great many more said it. We should then have a better hold of the forgiveness of God. We should realize how far from a matter of course forgiveness was for a holy, and justly angry, God, for all His love. A free forgiveness flows from moral strength, but an easy forgiveness only means moral weakness. How natural for God to forgive ! Nay, if there be one thing in the world for ever supernatural it is real forgiveness—especially on the scale of redemption. It is natural only to the Supernatural. The

natural man does not forgive. He resents and
revenges. His wrath smoulders till it flash. And
the man who forgives easily, jauntily, and thought-
lessly, when it is a real offence, is neither natural
nor supernatural but subnatural. He is not only
less than God he is less than man.

§

Is not God's forgiveness the great moral paradox,
the great incredibility of the moral life, needing
all the miracle of Christ's person and action to make
us realize it when we grasp the terms ?   A recent
authority on preaching warns us that the effective
preacher must not be afraid of paradox. For the
politician, or the journalist, on the other hand,
nothing is more fatal.   But that is the region of the
ordinary able man, for whom all things must be plain
—with a tendency to be dull.   In that world an epigram is a frivolity, an antithesis mere ingenuity,
and a paradox is mere perversity.

Are there not two distinct classes of mind ?   The
one finds in what is given him just what is given,
and he is impatient of anything beyond.   His world
is as obvious as the primrose quotation from
Wordsworth would here be.   The other   tends
always to divine in the given the not yet given.
The second truth, the rest of the truth, the hidden
truth, the dark twin, is the weighty, fascinating
pole of it.   The idea latent, the subtle illusion, the
mockery of the face-value, the slow result, the subver-
sive effect, the irony of providence, the absurdities

of God stronger than all the wisdom of men, the mighty futility of the Cross—these are the things that appeal to such a mind, rather than the obvious which smites you in the face. To have the palpable thrown in its face is what the public loves, and it turns the other cheek. And many are the professors of the obvious, and traffickers in the simple, and great is their reward in the heaven of their *clientèle*. But, for all that, when the soul, even of the public, is moved to its depths, it is beyond the reach of help or comfort from the obvious. The review satisfies not, the politician aids not, and the simple pulpit has no stay. Then do we lift our eyes to the hills, even to the twin peaks of Parnassus ; and we flee for strength to the truths of paradox, and to the men who see all things double one against another. Then we find more sense in those who speak of " dying to live " than in those who say " all that a man hath will he give for his life." There is more in those who bid us lose our soul if we would find it than in those who would find our soul for us at a price current. There is a poverty that makes many rich. And Christian wealth consists in our ceasing to possess. And you will remember a whole series of these pregnant epigrams as the only expression of the Apostles' experience in 2 Cor. iv. 8–11.

Life from its beginning is a vast vital contradiction. It proceeds by the tension and balance of forces that destroy and forces that build. We are born with the death sentence in us. We die every hour we live. We live, spiritually, moreover, in a standing contradiction of liberty and dependence, freedom and grace, object and subject. Personality itself is—I will not say an illogical—but an alogical unity ; else it could not be a power. All scientific experience is paradoxically against the personality whose unity and continuity alone make any experience possible. *Credo quia absurdum* is much less absurd than it looks. A dogma which contains a contradiction like that of the God-man may, for that very reason, be the only adequate expression for the experience of the soul at its last and greatest height.

However it may be with the writer, the preacher must not be afraid of paradox. It is his dread of paradox, his addiction to the obvious, that so often makes him a bore. His simplicity succeeds only in being bald and passionless. Of course, a string of paradoxes may easily bore us, but not more than a string of commonplaces. And a string of paradoxes, ingeniously invented, is one thing. It is smart, metallic, offensive. But the great recurrent paradox of the spiritual life, revealed or discovered, is another thing. The haunting moral paradox of the Cross is another thing. And if we shun that, and water that down, and extenuate that, we have no Gospel to preach, or we preach what we have without passion. Who has tasted the spiritual life that knows nothing of the deep, eternal, commanding nonsense of "rejoicing in tribulation" or being "more than conquerors" as the "slaves of Christ." Nonsense is just the word a cultivated Roman would have used for such speech. The offence of the Cross, the scandal of it, the blazing indiscretion and audacious paradox of it, has not ceased. Nor has its appeal ceased to that region of us to which we come when our plain palpable world startles and deceives us by smiting us to the dust and rolling over us—as if a man should lean upon a wall and a snake bit him, or went for a walk and a lion met him. We do not touch the deep illogical things of God till we find paradox their only expression. Life under God is one grand paradox of dependence and liberty. These two logical incompatibles are only solved in the living active unity of the moral person, especially towards God. So with life and death. The tremendous passion for life is God's paradoxical way of expressing the intense significance of death as life's consummation and solution. What we call the passion of Christ is the divine reflection of the passion of human life. His awful death is but the obverse and not the doom of His solemn and abounding life. And it not only embodies life's intensity but interprets it. It is the whole passion and power of life *sub specie eternitatis*. The passion of life with which we shrink from death is the negative, but eloquent, expression of the intensity of life's Immortality. That massive and peaceful lake has slumbering in it all the volume and power of the roaring river of earthly life that fills it. Thoughts like these serve to compose and dignify us, where the plain is but the trivial, and the clear is but the thin.

Now holy forgiveness is the greatest moral paradox,

the most exalting, pacifying paradox, the greatest
practical paradox, in the world.   Do not think that
the word of your Gospel is not a moral paradox—
law and love, the just and the justifier of the unjust,
the holy and the sanctifier of the unholy, holy severity
and loving mercy, yea, the Holy made sin.   Of
their union the Cross is not only the evidential fact
but the effecting fact.   It not only reveals it, it
brings it about.   That God might be just and
also the justifier of the sinner meant all the moral
mystery of the Cross, and all its offence to the
natural moral man.   The natural moral man either
does not forgive—and there are none more unfor-
giving than some sticklers for morality ; or else he
forgives as he shaves—" I suppose I ought to ; "
or as he dines—" because I like to."   He believes
in a God who either does not forgive, or who forgives of course—*c'est son métier*.   But the true
supernatural forgiveness is a revolution and not
an evolution—yea, it means a solemn and ordered
crisis within God Himself.   But crisis is Greek for
judgment.   The forgiveness of the world can only
be accomplished by the judgment of the world
That is the indispensable paradox whereby Christianity makes morality spiritual.   And not to realize
that means a step back and not forward in the great
modernizing drift which moralizes spiritual things.

§

It is a poor error to think that the ethicizing of
religion is its prompt application to present problems,

or the reduction of religion to ethics, and faith to cold morality. Rather, by concentrating religion in a crisis between holiness and sin it gives to it a moral nature and a moral core, a moral focus and a moral soul. Sin, it has been said, is the one fact in which religion and morality are inseparably bound. It is still more true of Christ's conquest of sin. In particular, the ethicizing of the Cross means this. It does not mean simply treating the Cross as the apotheosis of that self-sacrifice which is the crown of humane ethic, or the epitome of that altruism which cements society. It does not mean that the Cross is viewed as the grand object lesson in ethics to men, and the great lever in the hand of a changeless God to lift them back to the rails they had left. It does not mean that the Cross must be construed wholly by the moral category of fatherhood instead of the juristic category of judgment. Those who so speak forget that there are other and larger moral categories than the domestic relations, and a world far vaster than the home. Christ's domestic life was a tragedy. His family thought him mad. He has nothing to say of family feeling or fireside joy. " Who doeth the will of God is to me kith and kin." And Paul was of like mind. Those who would translate God's ways wholly in homely categories forget that when we are dealing with God we are dealing on the scale of all human society, dealing with the social and not merely the affectional conscience, indeed with the eternal moral order of existence. They forget that juristic principles form one aspect of

that social ethic which is such an enthusiasm of the
modern world. They forget that to moralize the
Cross means to explain it not simply by the enlargement of the best private ethic but by the introduction of the largest public ethic of the time. This
was so when the jurists played such a part as theologians, at the close of the middle age. And to-day
the demand for social righteousness rather than charity ("Curse your charity! give us work!") when
it is applied to the Cross as the centre of the Kingdom
of God, means the demand for its explanation in
terms of the holiness of God rather than His pitying
love or altruism alone. But to this I must recur later.

§

To ethicize religion, I say then, does not mean to
reduce it to pedestrian morality but to recognize
in its heart the action of the greatest influence in
the higher movement of civilization—I mean *the
primacy of the moral.* To the preacher this is an
observation of the first importance, for it means
the primacy and finality of the holy in his construction of the Gospel. Faith is not ethic, but it
is nothing if it be not ethical. We could not have
faith even in infinite love were it not *holy* love.
That is what makes the eternal steadfastness on
which faith rests. Faith acts on the heart but its
seat is in the conscience, and its reflection is found
in the pure bench of a great realm no less than in
its kindly homes. The rational, therefore, must here
take a second place, and with it goes the hegemony
of the doctrinaire. With it goes the rule of

intellectualism, whether as orthodoxy or heresy, and the reign of the sentimental, which rationalism always brings as a sweet sauce to moisten its sapless drought.

In almost every department we are forced to recognize this ethicizing movement. I need not waste time in pointing out to you that it is identical with the purification of society, its reform, its rescue from politics and commerce, from the tyranny of monarchy, aristocracy, democracy, and plutocracy. I need not remind you how much more it means than philanthropy, how it means the salvation of philanthropy itself, and its provision with staying power. For we preachers have this great advantage in these days. The primacy of the moral, the leadership of the will among the faculties, is really the same as our cardinal principle of justification by faith alone. For faith is the greatest moral act a man can perform, as the grace it answers is the supreme moral possibility for God, the supreme triumph of His holiness. Faith is the moral act which covers, pervades, and assigns the whole man as a living person. Therefore this modern claim for the primacy of the moral is one which we preachers should welcome, for we have in our charge the supreme means of giving it effect. Much of this, however, may be among things obvious.

But it may be less obvious, and it may not be beyond our purpose, if I make special allusion to the spread of this movement in philosophy, and especially in psychology; to the defeat of rationalism, even of the nobler kind, with the retreat of Hegel;

and to the triumph of voluntarism in a revised Kant, through men like Schopenhauer, Paulsen, Wundt, Eucken, and James. Even positivism worked in this direction of subduing intellectualism to the will of love. The reason is but the tool of the will. The will is real life. Reality is experience, and experience is the contact of personalities. It is a plexus of wills. Life is not a shadow, or a thing, but an energy, a will to live, as God Himself is not an infinite spiritual presence in repose, but an infinite spiritual power in essential action. Even for Aristotle God was an $\dot{\epsilon}\nu\dot{\epsilon}\rho\gamma\epsilon\iota\alpha$. The moral will is the will to live fully, the passionate self-asseveration of life, slowly shaped by relations social and divine, by humanity and God. Life rises from the unit, through the social stage, to eternal life. Action is good which promotes the life of the race in all its resources ; and the life of the race is good when it fulfils and enriches the life of God in all its fulness. That is to say, man is good not in happiness but in perfection ; that is in holiness. The good is what enhances true life, the bad is what cramps and kills it. Life, spirit, is the first thing and the last. Energy, vitality, fulness of experience takes the place of mechanism, constructions, and schemes. Action takes the place of vision ; the redemption of the world takes the place of its interpretation. Science therefore, retires to its due place. Our first need is to know the destiny of the world and not its scheme. It is not ability that has the secret of life but energy moral power. Reality is life, and not mere truth, it is life as will, as power, as spirit. It is spiritual ethical, personal life, a world of moral values, becoming absolute and eternal in God's holiness. We need urgently that we get over the aesthetic idea of holiness, the idea of white and even burning purity as of Eternal light, and attain the active idea of Eternal *Life* and absolute moral and personal energy. God the holy is not like a snowy peak on the roof of the world wreathed with the incense of our contemplation ; but rather is he a sun of power in our heaven and the source of all vital force. This will-life, personal, but more, is the prime and creative factor in the soul. Men must achieve themselves, and acquire their souls, rather than think correctly. The theologian, for instance, should first be not a philosopher but a saved man, with eternal life working in him. Christian theology is the theology not of illumination but of conversion. The supreme Christian gift is not eternal truth but eternal life, more life, fuller life, godlier life, holier life, a life inspired spiritually from the past but not ruled romantically by the past, ruled rather by perfection. Life, which began in spontaneity and not in thought, is raised by a faith passing logic to share in a spontaneity infinite and eternal in the Spirit. To the eye of spiritual reality we are outgrowing the age of science. We are outgrowing intellectual constructions of the world, whether they be those of modern physics, or of the ecclesiastical systems which represent the best science of centuries ago. Our chief business is not to pourtray the world we are in but to realize and effect it. We have to divine rather than define. We have to divine its meaning rather than make pictures and concepts of its state. We are in an actual situation and not in a painted scene. Our first concern is not a sketch, narrow or broad, but a purpose. It is not, How is our world built ? but, What does it intend ? We interpret not from a knowledge of the past but from a revelation of the perfect. There is no such thing as totally disinterested knowledge. It is all in the interest of life, all dominated by the will to live. There is no such thing as pure science, absolutely poised and impartial. There are no pure intelligences. They would be monsters. Intellect is a function of personality. Beliefs depend on the will to believe. The ideals we live by are not a product of the intellect, but of the will, of our life energy, of life's ideal, of life energizing at its future best. They are, so to say, the retroaction of our life's urgent future and fulness ; or the beneficent pressure of posterity, which plays a part so much greater than heredity. An ideal is a value, not a mere vision ; and a value is a judgment of the will. If you have no will you have no ideals ; and no description of ideals by any preacher will move you. Knowledge always follows life-interest in the long run. We prosecute the knowledge of what we are interested in, of what appeals to life, feeling, force, concern. We hate and dread the ennui which is the absence of these things. Religion is so far superstition in that both represent the deep instinct of escape from the rational. We interpret men and movements diversely

according to our supreme interest in life. No doubt
sects and parties thus arise. But they are better than
a unanimity of frozen thought like the Greek Church,
or of imperious thought like the Roman. No scheme
of the world can give us more than an orthodoxy
or a heresy. It cannot give us the main thing,
which is the meaning, the drift, the issue, the goal,
the settlement of the world. That meaning resides
in its action, its movement, its history, its destiny,
its purpose. It resides, in a word, in its God, its
immanent, transcendent, relative, absolute, and final
God. It is only that sectarianism of thought which
is called specialism that denies a theology. A theology is borne in upon us the more urgently the
larger our purview of the world is.

This moral movement, therefore, so conspicuous
in society and philosophy, affects theology no less.
The burthen of a real theology is not a cosmology
but a teleology. It reveals and assures the moral
purpose of the world. It presents us with our
future in advance. It builds on the supremacy
and finality of intelligent action toward a moral
purpose, toward a consummation of life, not of
science, whether sacred or secular. A real theology
is that which is framed under the primacy, not of
the rational or scientific, but of the moral, that is, of
the holy. Everything here turns on the hegemony
of personality, on its central organ as conscience,
on its central energy as will, on its central malady
as sin, on its central destiny as redemption. The
great object of things is not the self-expression of

the Eternal in time but His self-effectuation as holy in a kingdom. The work of Christ was not simply the revelation of a new world but its achievement. The world is not God's expression, but His action, His conflict, His conquest. What theology has in charge is the message of a final and holy consummation, awaiting history, yet anticipated in history, in the consummate, victorious Christ. It is the prepayment of our divine destiny. We see not yet all things put under either God or man but we see Jesus, faith's source and consummator alike.[1]

§

I said the interpretation of history comes not from a scientific or inductive knowledge of the past but from the idea of life's perfection, i.e. the revelation, which is also the effectuation, of life's destined holiness. I am particular to say its destined holiness, and not its innate or essential, because it is not intrinsic to man but is the gift and revelation of God. Where then is that creative revelation ? For the Christian it is given in history, but it is not an induction from history, nor an intuition of consciousness. It is given first in the inner history of a people with a moral destiny, a select people, Israel, issuing secondly in the life and action of an elect person, Christ. That gift is the great charter of the preacher. He has to do with a situation which is moral above all things, with men and interests that have their

---

[1] See for the continuation of this line of thought the Appendix to this lecture.

raison d'être there, whose bearing and action are on the will. He is also the steward of a historic act in Christ, whose perennial power over life is in striking contrast with our success as yet in giving any rational account of it. The Apostles were not made preachers by a theology but by a personal act and the experience of it, by a new life and not a new creed, a new power and not a new institution. There was, indeed, a new society but it was made by the new power. What roused the Apostles was Christ as the crown of a long revelation coming through historic action. And when they gave such supreme value to Christ's death, it was not simply the Judaic notion of symbolic sacrifice that moved them. Symbols make poets but not missionaries. The missionary needs a much more real and ethical inspiration. Symbols but reflect, they do not effect. And the effectual thing was the ethical action at the core of Israel's destiny, the long action of election, righteousness, judgment, love; which had its consummation in Christ, and gave Christ His unique appeal as Captain of the elect to Israel's choicest sons. In the ethicizing of theology by the idea of the holy we but return to the fountain head.

§

The trust of Israel and its gift to the world was not mere monotheism. It was the ethical monotheism which could not rest till it rose to grasp the one God only as the holy God. The God of Israel

was not a monopolist.   He was not sole as ousting and
consuming other deities by sheer push and power ;
but as the unity of righteousness and peace, of
judgment and mercy, of unapproachable sanctity
and of approaching grace.   The very history of the
word holiness in the Old Testament displays the
gradual transcendence of the idea of separation by
that of sanctity.   It traverses a path in which the
quantitative idea of *tabu* changes to the qualitative
idea of active and absolute purity. The religious grows
ethical, that it may become not only more religious
but the one religion for the conscience and for the
world.   The one God can only be the holy God.

When Israel sank to Judaism the ethical element
retired before official rule and imperial ambition
—as to-day Curialism and Ultramontanism have
submerged the ethical spirituality which made
men like St. Bernard in the great medieval Church.
When Christ came the ethical Israel was in the
trough of a wave. Judaism had come to what some
of our active and forward Churches have reached.
It had lost the sense of sanctity in the pursuit of a
righteousness based, now on equity, now on charity,
but always disjoined from grace. For Judaism it was
the formal righteousness of an ecclesiastical society,
for us it is the distributive justice of an economic
society.   But, for both, righteousness and kindness
submerge holiness and grace. We are far more
kind to our neighbours than we feel God gracious
to us. For many in our Churches a meal to poor
children or cripples is associated with more stir

of interest and sense of benefit than the Communion. There is more heart-certainty and satisfaction about it. If that spread it means that *philanthropia* is taking his place of *philadelphia*, the natural brotherhood of the supernatural, pity of faith, and man of Christ. The one is taking the place of the other, instead of growing out of it. The true Christian love of man is that which blossoms on a far deeper and more lively faith in Christ. Let us not linger to lament this state of things but let us interrogate it and understand it. It means inordinate affection which is idolatry. It means the loss of the insight of holiness. We may be getting ready, when the critical time comes, for a blunder as stupendous as that which Judaism made. For does it matter at last what amount of well-doing mark a Church; will that keep it a Church? If it has lost the sense of holiness and what is due to it, if it has lost that worship and culture of holiness which centres about a real Atonement, is it not deserted by the Holy Spirit? And unless He return it may be any kind of admirable society for the promotion of goodness and mercy, but it ceases to be a Church. It may contribute much to civilization, culture, and charity, as Judaism does to this day, but it ceases to be the unearthly organ of the holy Kingdom of God.

When this dullness of spiritual ethic rejected Christ, Judaism kept the monotheism but lost the holiness whose consummation Christ was. And hence Judaism ever since, while it has produced plenty

of geniuses in many kinds, and plenty of mystics,
has not produced moral leaders for the world.   If
it has produced saints they are not such as have
by their sanctity impressed the world.   It is too
tribal for the last universality, too narrow, however
fine, in its practical ethic.   The finer and wider
ethic of Judaism is no more to-day than Hillel was
in Pharisaism, or Stoicism in Greece and Rome.   It
cannot save the situation.   Only when ethic rises
to holiness can it become really universal ; and
only when holiness gets effect in an Atonement real
and not symbolic.   The Atonement to God's holiness
is the focus of Christian (that is, of all) ethic, the one
meeting-point of religion and morals, of grace and
conscience, and therefore it is the real secret of
Christ's universalism.   It was the atoning Cross that
made Christ absolutely · human.

Is it not so ?   Is not the great universality that
of the conscience ; and the final universality—is it
not God's conscience, that is, God's holiness, of
which the Cross is the supreme energy ?   It was in
Christ and, within Christ, in His Cross (as Paul was
crushed to discover) that the ethical soul of the
Hebrew God broke into white flame.   The true
Israelites always found in Israel's God no mere
autocrat, whose doings were limited only by logical
possibility, but a moral Jehovah, whose power
was governed by the absolute holiness of His own
nature, and even limited into history in order to
achieve the purpose of that holiness.   He led His
people in the paths of righteousness for His own

name's sake. A God of mercy, truly, but also a
God of right ; a God, therefore, whose passion of
mercy could act only by way of historic redemption
into righteousness. He was a God of grace, but
of grace that could never sacrifice His moral nature,
or simply waive His moral order. He must honour
it. And He could not simply honour it in secret,
bear the cost and say nothing about it. That
would not be to the ethical point. For it would
not be honouring holiness where it was defied, or
establishing it in the presence of its enemies. The
judge of all the earth must do public right. And,
besides, He was a God of revelation, of self-bestowal. He must be shown as honouring His own
holiness in the motive and act of the revelation
itself. He must not be revealed simply as one who
incidentally held His holiness in respect. But the
act of revelation must be the act of respect, the
self-respect of the holy. He must be revealed in
the act of honouring it, honouring it by the very
act that gave and saved. He must pity in a way
to set up for ever the public right and glory of His
holiness. That is to say, He was a God whose great
act of grace was also, because he was holy, a great
act of judgment. For to Israel the Messianic time
was always a great day of judgment—terrible, but
still more glorious than terrible, a time of hope
more than fear. Such, then, was the Hebrew idea
of God. Such was God's revelation of Himself to
Israel. It was a revelation, and a God, supremely
ethical, as being supremely holy — so supremely

holy that, from the Cross onwards, holiness ceased
to be an attribute of God, and became, in the
Holy Spirit, a constituent father and active subject in the Godhead itself.

This is the God that was in Christ reconciling,
redeeming the world. The more we grasp this
function of the Cross the more we ethicize it. And
it is the only radical way of ethicizing it. To
moralize Christianity anew we must replace the
idea of judgment among all the gains we have won
for the other and sympathetic side of faith. The
consummation of this historic union of grace and
judgment was in the death of Christ. And as the
grace of God was on Christ, and not only through
Christ on us, so also the judgment of God was on
Christ and not only through Christ on us. That
is the serious solemn point, disputed by many,
and to be pressed only with a grave sense that it
alone meets the moral demand of holiness and completes it. Christ not only exercises the judgment
of God on us; He absorbs it, so that we are judged
not only by Him but in Him. And so in Him we
are judged unto salvation. " The chastisement
of our peace was on Him."

In the Cross, then, we have the ethical consummation, perfect and prolific, of the old paradox of grace
and judgment. During His life Christ was at one time
pitiful, at another severe. He was merciful to one
class, and stern to another. But in the Cross this
separation of grace and judgment disappears, as the
distinction of all times and classes disappears in the

one issue of the universal conscience. And the goodness and the severity of God are perfectly one, as God is one in His passion of movement toward the sinner and reaction from his sin, of grace to the one and wrath to the other.

It is not wonderful that the Disciples with their national past should find in Christ's death something else than the priestly idea of sacrifice symbolized in their ritual. They found in Him a living epistle *to* the Hebrews, and not merely *from* the Hebrews. He was as much a manifesto to Israel from God as from Israel to the world. They found in Christ the priest no less than the sacrifice. They found also this prophetic note of blended grace and judgment, which made them preachers of a Gospel in His death rather than narrators of His memorable life. Even in Paul there was more Hebraism than Judaism, far more prophet than priest. The great prophetic note finds itself at last in the apostolic. Prophetism by its very failure was itself a prophecy. Its holy ideal strained on and up into the Holy One, His doom, and His work, wherein history changed key into eternity. The Apostles found in the Cross that involution of mercy and sanctity, of grace and righteousness, that revelation of sin as well as love, which met at once the greatest intuitions of their religious history, and the deepest needs of their shamed conscience. The Cross, which was the chief shame of their soul, personal or national, became their sure moral triumph. In it the national past found itself in historic effect, and their personal

past found itself in a regenerate life. Some of them
had denied it, one had betrayed, and one had perse-
cuted it ; but they all came to find in it a moral
power from which they never went back. It was
final for them and their hereditary ideals, because
it was the last judgment and the last mercy in a
nation whose history and whose song had all along
been of mercy and judgment. The justified had
the last judgment behind them. The holy morality,
eternal in the heavens, became actual on earth. It
was the Holy made Sin, the absolute moral miracle—
or else the merest ingenuity of nonsense.

§

A gospel which is not final is a mere programme
of reform, and there is no finality in any Gospel which
ignores the moral element of judgment in God's revelation of love. And therefore there is in such a Gospel
no indefectible power. Yet that element is widely
ignored in the popular Gospel of sympathy which has
replaced the once popular Gospel of orthodoxy.
The primacy usurped by the intellect has been taken
by the humane affections instead of the evangelical conscience. Judgment has ceased to be
preached as an essential factor in a revelation of
holy love. Where it is preached it is often in crude
forms, without insight, and with non-moral associ-
ations which rob it of its practical power. It is
preached as "the last day" or the "great assize" or
the "quenchless fire." But it is useless to put judgment at the close of history if it have not a decisive

place at the centre of history. Indeed it is impossible. The judgment day of the great future assize draws its true solemnity of meaning from the judgment day in Pilate's hall. To repudiate as mere theology this element of judgment in the Cross, to eliminate the awe of it from our practical habit of piety, is to subside in due course into a non-ethical religion, which finally becomes but a sweetened paganism. For it is in the moral element in the Cross that the real *differentia* of Christianity comes to light. It is the Cross, and it is this in the Cross, that makes Christ more than man. The Incarnation as an article of our faith rests on our experience of the Atonement alone, on our ethical experience there, on the treatment of our sin there, on what God found precious and divine there. Christ must be chiefly for us what He is chiefly to God. We press to a historic view of Christ and we do well; but we must do better, and press still more to the theological view of Him, which sets out what He is to God. We must learn to regard Him as God does. And that is as the consort of His throne, in whose Cross and its judgment the Eternal holiness found itself for the universe again. To minimize the judgment really effected on evil in the Cross once for all is to subside into a humane paganism, in which, after due and usual course, the paganism will submerge the humanity. Our gentler, sweeter, more sympathetic piety will show itself, as it often does show itself, unable to bear up our public life against the moral declensions, seductions, vulgarities, and crimes of a too rich, prosperous and miserable world. Some sweet and facile evangelicals have had a bad business name. You might thus find a charming and pious home, where yet the business activity of its head could best be described as preying on the public. People object to the pagan suggestions of a word like expiation. But it is the want of the thing, truly and ethically understood, that is the real pagan danger, the absence of any satisfaction in holiness to the grieved holiness of God. It is a satisfaction which man, as he came to his senses, would insist on making, even if God did not insist on providing it. For this lack the conscience of the Church comes short at its creative centre— just as it came short when to expiation was given but the pagan and unmoral sense of mollification. The conscience of the Church loses its moral source and bracing school. And Christianity falls victim to fanciful subjectivity, bustling energies, religious romancers, or the fireside pieties.

These things are attractive enough to a humanist age and to half-culture. And they take often far nobler and graver forms than would be suggested by the words I have just used to describe their effect in many. But they are ineffectual for the great public purposes of the Kingdom. They are in-effectual against the pagan ethic of the natural man, or a society full of moral failures and moral vulgarities. If the death of Christ be preached only for the *pathos* of its effect on us and not for the *ethos* of its effect on God, we lack that prime

hallowing of His name which exercises on us the profoundest moral effect of all, and which bases our ethic
on holiness immutable and eternal. For, as I have
already said, the spectacle of Christ dealing with
God for us and our sin moves us more deeply than
the spectacle of Christ dealing with us for God.
As our priest and victim he is far more subduing
than as a prophet of the Lord. Yet each without
the other is false. It is a redemption by revealed
grace through effective judgment that is the moral
principle of social regeneration. Whether the public
take or refuse the dogmas of theologians as such is a
light matter. But it is a great matter if the dogmas
of the theologians cover living powers and moral energies, by which society stands or falls. And that is
the aspect of theology by which theology and society
will stand or fall—the aspect of it which equips the
preacher to be not only a voice but an authority to
his time. Public freedom at last depends on spiritual
freedom, and spiritual freedom is not in human
nature but in its redemption. And the first principle
of the Christian redemption is the holy recognition of God's wounded holiness, its holy satisfaction
in Christ's holy obedience amid the last conditions
of human wickedness. The moral perfection of
our race is to offer that obedience in sequel and in
detail. Man's chief end is not to make the most of
himself, but to glorify a holy God by the holiness
which alone can satisfy holiness. And that is what
sinful man can do only in the power of the atoning
holiness of Christ.

§

I know there are those whom we have great reason to honour, who press duly into the heart of the Atonement with the lamp of modern ethic, but who light their lamp at the social and moral relation of fatherhood. That, they say, is the one key put into our hands, by the very constitution of society, for the moral world. The true authentic word of the conscience is the word of father and son. The pillar and ground of social ethic is the family. It was this Word that Christ took up and clothed with eternal validity. It was the Father He preached, and for the Father He died. It was in the name of a disowned Father that He dealt with the conscience. It was to a holy Father that He offered His own conscience. And He retrieved our case by His perfect sympathetic unity with His Father on the one hand, and with His brethren on the other. Accordingly, this theory is offered as a real and near point of attachment for the preacher who has to address people that care more for their families than anything else—Bible, Church or Gospel.

But do they who speak thus go to the bottom of their own plea that it was to a Holy Father that Christ offered His own conscience ? Do they grasp the fact that it was not in the Fatherhood but in the holiness of it that Christ's originality lay ? Do they realize the immense difference it makes when we extend the fatherhood which we learn in the small kind area of family sympathy, to a universal

fatherhood—a fatherhood which is the guardian
of the whole moral order, amidst warring interests,
and of the absolute holiness of the Eternal against
those who hate the holy for its holiness ? Are the
paternal affections the only, or the chief interest of
history ? Is the Father of our Lord Jesus Christ
the crucified simply a magnified and supernatural
sire ? Had Jesus much of the family feeling ? Was
His family experience quite happy ? Was Joseph
a type that he had simply to enlarge to find God ?
Where do we find the authority for erecting the
house-father, at his spiritual best, into God ?
The reply is of course that the authority is
Christ. Well, we all admit that Christ is our
authority. The question only begins after that.
What aspect or action of Christ is selected as the
vehicle of the supreme revelation ? Where in
Christ is the oracle of the Father's will ? Where
is the Father's authentic Word ? Where is *the*
revelation of the Father ? Surely in the act into
which was put the whole life and pesonality of
the Son. Surely in the redeeming act, if the main
work of a Father or a Son, in a case like ours,
be redemption. Surely in the Cross. Everything
turns on the interpretation of the Cross. And
what is to interpret it ? Must it not interpret itself, and all else, if it be the focus of revelation ?
Must not the redemption it brings to pass create in
us the power to interpret it ? Must it not be
interpreted by its effect rather than by its antecedents ? Antecedents may account for it, explain

it, but not interpret it. All great interpretation
is teleological. The supreme spiritual events have
their meaning either in themselves, or in their
outcome, rather than in their *provenance.* That
is the Christian way of treating evolution. The
interpretation of the series is at its summit. It is
man that interprets the world, and not the world
man. And, by the same principle, as it is Christ
that interprets Israel, so it is the Cross that interprets Christ. It is not the teaching of Jesus that
interprets the Cross ; it is the Cross that interprets
the teaching of Jesus. It may have been so even
to Himself. On that I cannot enter here. I will
only express my conviction that, unless Christ was
principally a teacher aiming at a right interpretation
of God, rather than a Redeemer effecting the
righteous action of God in the reconstruction of
man, it is to the Cross we must look for the true
interpretation of Fatherhood in Him. The Cross
interprets the Father, not the Father the Cross. And
that interpretation was seized and given by John,
when the Cross had had more of its perfect work—in
John with his manifold insistence upon the *Holy*
Father. The nature of the Cross is more revealed
in the adjective than in the noun. It is the adjective there that represents the Cross's own interpretation of itself. We thus understand the insight
of Luther when he found the true commentary
on Christ in the Epistles rather than the Gospels.

I am afraid the thinkers whom I regret here to
oppose use an analogy as a revelation. They over-

look the fact that the seat of revelation must be sought in the centre of redemption ; that it lies not in our experience, paternal or filial, but in our faith of salvation ; and that all Christ ever said about God has its true gloss only in what He did about God, and still in our conscience does. And through the effect of the Cross upon the whole conscience, and especially upon the sinful saved conscience, we are driven to think of its prime action as being objective upon God, or upon the evil power, or both. It is there that we have the chief source even of its effect on us. The chief value of the Cross is its value for God, rather than for man.

If that be so we must not allow ourselves to be led by either our affections, or even the seeming words of Christ, to interpret the Fatherhood of God as the apotheosis of the natural heart and of the sympathetic, endlessly patient and hospitable sire. If the Cross and not paternity is the supreme locus of the conscience of the race, if, that is, it be a historic locus and not a sociological, then our effort to ethicize faith must begin with the ethic of the Cross. We must not start to ethicize the Cross at a standard of fatherhood brought from elsewhere, whether that elsewhere be in social psychology, in the voice of our affections, or even in the words of Christ Himself. My case would be that the highest ethic is the ethic of holiness ; and that we cannot bring that ethic to the Cross to explain it, but we must draw it from the supreme assertion of holiness, from the Cross and

its revelation in the conscience it redeems. I
hope it may not be thought an unfair thing to
say that, as the great jubilants of the Cross have
been the great sinners it saved, so its great interpreters are men who, *ceteris paribus*, have that
scorching of hell upon them, even in heaven, which
so many who are interested in theology seem to
lack. And because of the lack, when they seek
to ethicize they but humanize. They have more
humane sympathy than evangelical experience.
But the Cross comes with its own ethic in broken
and contrite men. All that is provided by the new
ethical or paternal interest in modern society is a
congenial *nidus* for Christian ethic ; it does not
provide the illuminative principle. The Cross is
really luminous only where it is active. It is its
own energy that makes its own light. And its
truest interpreters, *ceteris paribus*, are the sinners it
has plucked from the gates of death and the
mouth of hell. The greatest apostolate is made out
of deserters or persecutors, of prodigals more than
model sons.

§

The Church has very properly returned to a scriptural interest in *the Kingdom of God*. Her theologians, like Ritschl, have led the way, and her
preachers press the new ideal. But it does not seem
to meet from the mass of Christians a response
which corresponds to the enthusiasm for it of the
pulpit. It falls on many as a somewhat archaic
conception, too small and primitive for the compass

of a modern and complex society. And why ? For one reason because its advocates so often forget that it was only the Cross that founded it, it was universalized by the Cross, the apostolic Cross first gave it range and currency. When Christ had overcome the sharpness of death He opened the Kingdom of Heaven to all believers. People plant themselves too exclusively on Christ's teaching of the Kingdom—often expressed in forms more germane to the first century than the twentieth, and to the East rather than to the West. The Saviour is really a more modern idea in these democratic days than the King ; and the Cross has an ethical significance more immortal than the kingdom. In construing the social relations by Christianity, therefore, our first duty is not to analyse the metaphor of the Kingdom. Christ has given us the thing. Christ Himself translated the metaphor into reality for us by His death. He was condemned because of His claim to be a king, and "He did not die for a metaphor." It was there that He really founded the revelation, not in His parables, prophecies, or precepts. These were addressed to Jews. And some of them are heavily coated with the apocalyptic colour of the time. Our first charge in the ethic and service of the Kingdom is to accept and apply love as we find it in Christ crucified, as saving holy grace. All the Kingdom is latent in that Cross. All its ethic has its creative centre there. Christian ethic consists in living out the life of the Cross freely in the Spirit, rather than in obeying all the precepts of the Sermon on the Mount as precepts, which but leads to the attractive crudities of Tolstoi. The true nature and universality of the Kingdom broke out in the Cross. It was Christ's first and final appeal to the world as distinct from Israel. There, for instance, the true charter of missions lies, not in certain injunctions, or " marching orders," which are at the mercy of criticism. Accordingly the doctrine of Christianity as an ellipse, with its two centres of the Kingdom and the Cross, will not hold good. If we speak of two centres they must represent the two great categories for interpreting the Cross—Reconciliation and Redemption, which pass but do not fade into each other. We have but the one centre of the Cross for the Kingdom, for the new humanity, and for its ethic. Even in the Lord's Prayer we have the Cross before the Kingdom. The hallowing of God's name is a prior interest to the coming of the Kingdom. It is the action in the heavens which is the constant prelude of the doing of God's will on earth. The Eternal Spirit of Christ's self-oblation to God is the inspiration of the new world. There we find the resources of the Kingdom in one fontal act where that eternal sacrifice looks forth. And it is there that we find it in the ethical form native to the inner Israel, and equally relevant to every age. There we have the focus of that moral eternity of action, that spiritual universe of energy, which is the contemporary of every age, and therefore is always modern. Christian ethic in Christian

society is the mutual relation of sons, not under a loving father, but under a certain kind of
loving father—under the Father revealed by a
Cross whose first concern was holiness and the
dues of holiness. See what manner of love
the Father hath bestowed on us. God so loved
that He gave His Son to be a propitiation and to
hallow His name. It was not enough that evil
should be mastered ; holiness had to be set up and
secured in history. And the continuous agent
of that holiness is the conscience in us which was
first created on the Cross by the offering of holiness
to the Holy One. The prime vocation of the society
of the Cross is holiness unto the Lord. And as
human society grows more Christian this must
become its waxing note. It sounds the dominant
over all—even over love. It is the power, the
life, which all love serves. If we are to fill life
full, and spread the reign of love, let us preach
the holy God, and the Cross where He is at His
fullest and Holiest of all. Our Gospel is not simply
God is love, but God's love is holy, for the Holy
One is love.

What is this final appeal even of love to holiness
but asserting for God what everything that is best
in modern life tends to assert for man—the primacy
of the moral, the supremacy of life and will to
thought or truth. What is it but the ethicizing of
religion. For God the moral and the supreme is His
holy will of love. You cannot ethicize either religion or life without adjusting it to the holiness of

God. And that practical adjustment, objective
and subjective, was Christ's work in the atoning
Cross. Pardon is the perpetual demand of our
actual moral situation. And pardon is only pardon,
not when it wipes the slate, but as it is the supreme expression and establishment of moral reality.
Its conditions are those required by moral reality
on an eternal scale—that is, by the holy.

§

What an advantage, then, the preacher of holiness
as it is in the Cross has in addressing the society
of these days, set upon moral righteousness as it
never was before. For both the Cross and the
public the moral is the first thing. I do not mean
that the preacher should preach the moral philosophy of the Cross, or confine himself to Christian
ethics, but he has to preach a Gospel which has
supreme in its heart this moral note of holy grace
and judgment love; and he preaches it to a public
in which the moral passion is rising steadily. The
modern appeal to the will is the native note of
the Christian apostle, the appeal to the moral will,
to the conscience.

There is nothing you will oftener hear from pulpits
that strive to be abreast of things than this : " Christianity is not a creed ; it is a life." What is meant
by it ? Not surely that Christianity is but a
certain course or manner of living. That drops
all to mere moralism. Not that it is a way of feeling,
a certain sympathetic strain. That makes it a senti-

mentalism. Not that it is simply the copying of a heroic example. That makes it a depressing legalism, or a no less depressing idealism. If it mean anything it surely means that Christianity is a solution of the problem of life, which is a moral problem. And Christianity means still more, giving us the moral solution of life as a present. Here is another paradox—the gift of a moral achievement, moral victory, as a present. You can compare it with that parallel audacity " The Father hath *given* the Son to have life *in Himself*. Such is the secret of Christianity and such its gift—the gift of a life that masters the supreme moral condition of holiness— eternal life, as it was achieved in the Cross, in the holy satisfaction of the Cross. Such is the paradox of the cross, its alogical nature, its defiance of a perfectly consistent theology, its ethical offence to monism, its inner contradiction as the only adequate harmony of religious experience, its dualism as the only condition of the moral and holy life.

§

This Gospel appeals not only to the strength of modern society—its interest in righteousness, and in a social righteousness—but also to its weakness. Because the weakness of the hour (for all our ethical progress) is a moral weakness. In every other respect society is stronger than it ever was before. Never was man's mastery of the world so complete. Never had he such resources in dealing with it, and compelling it to his purpose.

Yes, but it is the matter of his purpose that is the
weak place. What is his purpose when he has
one ? What is to repair his lack of one ?   Our
trouble is the paganism of the age, with its moral
hollowness and its shell of self-confidence. On
the one side you have the weakness of over-energy—
men engrossed with practical activity, like old
Rome, till they have neither leisure nor power to
note the crumbling of their moral interior. That you
may have in a young country. And, on the other
hand, you have what you find in the old and deca-
dent lands—the weakness of no-energy, the hebetude
of the outworn, the failure of will, the lack of moral
interest. You have the conscience narcotised by
civilization, by science, by culture, by religion,
by morality itself. All these things conspire to
stifle in the conscience the deepest issues which
drive us to the Cross. Even religion in this respect
can be very mischievous to Christianity, on the
principle that the good is the enemy of the best.
And at the extreme end you have the moral para-
lytics, who find life no longer worth living except
in moments of some kind of intoxication ; you
have the moral degenerates or *cretins*, the victims
of the age's overfed individualism and its moral
fatigue, who live in a perpetual depression because
they have no motives ; and you have the moral
melancholics and irresolutes, who, by the very
wealth of their ideas, have so many motives that
they are unable to choose any one of them. I
am thinking on the one hand of the famous Melan-

cholia of Dürer, limp and listless in the midst of all the resources of science and art. I think on the other hand of a victim of " psychological rumination " so noble yet so over-interested as Amiel. And between these two extremes you have a varied gamut of people whose trouble is moral marasmus, and who so often leap at the manifold quackeries of volitional religion, or self-salvation, or will-idolatry. They all betray a narcotised conscience, a light sense and a light healing of our mortal wounds. Nothing reveals the incompetency of much popular religion more than its inability to gauge the poignancy of the moral situation on the one hand, or the true depth of the moral resources of Christianity on the other.

§

In those circumstances let the preacher who is sure be of new cheer. It is the prophet's opportunity. The conscience of society is awake but it is not illuminated ; and where illuminated it has not power. It is awake enough to cry for a redemption, but not enough to take the Christian redemption home, far less to bring it to pass around. It is power for the conscience the preacher brings. His great object is not to produce either loving affections or correct views of Christian truth, whether broad or narrow, neither sympathies, liberalisms, nor orthodoxies, but the moral power of the Christian Gospel. The correct science of our faith is all very well, but, whether old or new, it is not faith. And the ethics of love, gather-

ing about the dear person of Christ, is very well,
but it is only a partial solution of the problem
offered us by the world. That is a moral, a
practical problem, a problem not of the sympathies,
but of the will and conscience. The ethic of love
has more effect on those who are in the Church
than on the world. It moves chiefly the already
well disposed. It is a Gospel for the sensitive. And
it lacks the note of authority which is the modern
world's chief need, and which is heard in its power,
not in the heart but the conscience. Authority's
seat and source is not God's love, but God's holiness.
Have I not said that the love in God must itself
rest on the holiness of God, that we can trust love
with real faith only if it show itself absolutely
holy. That is to say, the Church's Word, the
preacher's Word, must issue from a Gospel not
of love alone but of holy love. It sounds from a
Cross which does not merely show love but honours
holiness. It flows from a grace which does not
merely display compassion, but effects judgment,
achieves redemption, does the one deed demanded
in the real moral situation by the holy authority of
God. The Word of grace is a deed of God. And
the answer of faith must be a deed no less. Faith is
not a sympathy but an act. It is the moral victory
that overcomes the active world by an act greater
still, inspired from a world more active still The
faith that the preacher would stir is the greatest
of moral deeds. It searches the deep and devious
recesses of the conscience upon the scale of the

whole world—yea of the holy world unseen. And it breeds that new mystic life which is the only condition of a new heaven and a new earth wherein dwells holiness. " This is *the* work of God that they should believe in Him whom He hath sent to be a propitiation for us."

May I resume ? The history of the world morally viewed is a tragedy. All the great tragedy of the world turns upon its guilt. Aeschylus, Shakespeare, Goethe, Ibsen, all tell it you. The solution of the world, therefore, is what destroys its guilt. And nothing can destroy guilt but the very holiness that makes guilt guilt. And that destruction is the work of Christ upon His Cross, the Word of Life Eternal in your hands and in your souls. The relevancy of His Cross is not to a church, or a sect, or a creed, but to the total moral world in its actual radical case. The moral world, I say, is the real world, the ever modern world. And the supreme problem of the moral world is sin. Its one need is to be forgiven. And nothing but holiness can forgive. Love cannot. We are both forgiven and redeemed in Jesus Christ and in Him as crucified unto the world for the holiness of God and the sin of men.

APPENDIX (p. 308)

THERE is one qualification which has to be made, however, when we use the Pragmatism or Voluntarism of recent philosophy as a calculus for the specific action of Christianity. Action is indeed the material of truth (*Wesen=Actus*) —the organ, too, by which we reach it as well as spread it, and become true as well as see true.   But we have to do with something more than the action either of nature, of men, or of mankind.   To fall back thus on the will, energy, or resource of man is to make religion in the end impossible, except by a kind of moral positivism which leaves humanity to worship but itself and its deed.   What we have to realize is a spiritual world not simply in man but in which man is, a world that has to temper him and master him, that has to prevent him from taking his needs, passions and energies for charter or standard, a world that has to stand over him, test him, sift him, lift him, and end by setting him on a totally different base from the egotism in which he began.   That is, we have to do, above all, not simply with an ideal world of process, but with a spiritual world of value.

And this spiritual world is not quiescent but active. It does not simply envelop us, it acts on us, and we react on it ; and in that reaction we find ourselves, and we grow into spiritual persons with which we never set out. It does not swathe us and erase us, it besets us, it applies itself to us.   It does not simply stand at the door, or pass and suck us into its wake ; it knocks, enters, finds, and saves us—all in the way of creating our moral personality and giving us to ourselves by rescuing us from ourselves.   It is an active not a static world.   It moves, it works, it creates.

Its movement is not process, as so many to-day are seduced to construe it, in the wake of the great cosmic processionalist and marshal, Hegel, with his staff of subordinate evolutionists.   This of Hegel's, indeed, is a conception which lifts us over much of the triviality and slavery of life ; but only to substitute for petty bondage a vast tyranny, and to replace a prison by a despotism, with a first show of freedom but a final atmosphere of death.   And especially it leaves us with a loss of moral liberty, and ethical dignity, and spiritual initiative and personal consummation.   The actual course of history is not a process. And it is not through yielding to a process that history is created by its great actors.   There are stagnations, too, degenerations, enmities which forbid us to call life a process,

at the same time as they prevent us from treating its
movement as our being rolled over and ground up in a
greater process. Mere process ends in mechanism, coarse
or fine, and extinguishes a soul. Behind everything that
seems process on any large scale our active moral soul
insists on placing an act, and an act from a new world—
something ethical and personal in its kind.

If this spiritual world, so active, be one ; if we are
to escape pluralism, as well as monism ; if we are not
to escape being rolled over by a vast process only to be
crushed by the active but awful collision of more spiritual
worlds than one ; then its action must be one infinite and
unitary *concursus*, one compendious personal act, the *actus
purus* of an infinite personality who is not only ethical but
self-sufficient in his ethic. But what is an infinite moral
self-sufficiency, an active, changeless, self-completeness,
but *holiness*. The total action of the spiritual world both
in us and around is holiness. We find ourselves before and
within a holy God, a spiritually moral personality, self-
determined and self-complete.

But no less, if this spiritual world and power be universal,
it must assert itself supremely in the region of *history*. If
its inmost nature be action we cannot think of it as secluded
from that one region where action has real meaning and
effect for man. It must assert, express, reveal and effect
itself in history for the holy and mastering power it is.

Yet such a power cannot adequately reveal itself *dis-
persed through* history, or merely parallel with it, nor even
in "mutual involution." For such a diffused revelation
would not represent, and might even belie, a spiritual
power whose nature was not only action but action of
the sole kind which possesses moral unity, namely, the
action of a moral person. If it reveal itself—I do not
merely mean assert itself—in history it must surely do
so in an act corresponding to its own total ethical nature in
the spiritual world, in an act which gathers and commands cosmic history, as its nature is to focus and utter
all spiritual being. A world of spiritual action with moral
coherency can only be revealed in history by a supreme

spiritual act, the supreme act of a person who both gathers up and controls human existence, and delivers it from that submersion in self and the world which in the long run is fatal to man's action as man.   If spiritual existence be an infinite and eternal act, such must also be its revelation.

And this is the act of Christ in the *Cross*, the act of the Gospel.   It is the act of God's grace, met by the act of our faith—an act into which a whole divine life was put, and one that issues in a whole life on our part.   This act is the gift of God ; whose freedom we attain by no mere development of our own liberty, but by a free act which renounces our liberty for His, breaks with what is behind and beneath us, breaks with the old self, and, by accepting a new creation, exchanges an assertive individualism for a redeemed personality.   The energy of such a spiritual world as we postulate in God can only act on us in the way of redemption and not more evolution from the world of our first stage.   We cease to be self-made men, and we are men who let God make us, and make us by His grace and not His evolution.   We achieve by this grace a personality we had not at the first.   As we reach our freedom we acquire and attain ourselves ; and we reach our freedom by surrendering it to God's.   The best use we can make of our freedom is to forgo it, and to sign it away to one whose work and joy it is to create in us a freedom we can never acquire.   We are but persons in the making, and we are not made till grace make us and faith is made. Our supreme ethical act is the faith that gives us at once our Saviour and ourselves.   We exhaust our own exertions, and we deliver ourselves to a faithful Creator.   And our perfecting God is a God of grace, not only because He finishes us, but finishes us as alone we can be perfected— by redemption, by a change of base, centre, and affection. He is a gracious God and not simply a benevolent God, because He lets us exhaust, and even wreck, our private powers, instead of only guiding their education, so that with His free and creative act He may make of us what all our native force could never do.

THE MORAL POIGNANCY OF THE CROSS

IX

The Moral Poignancy of the Cross

THE leading doctrine of much modern theology is the Fatherhood of God in a sense I have already indicated. It offers us a God genial, benignant, patient, and too great in His love to make so much as Paulinism does of the sin of a mere child like man. Now, how does such a conception really affect modern preaching? It is another form of the question if we ask how it affects the Church whose voice preaching is. No such vast doctrine can be tested by either the feeling or the character of an individual, even if he be a most successful preacher. There are plenty of individuals, and indeed one whole sex, to whom a religion of naïve fatherly love is perfectly satisfactory—so much so that they can not only think of nothing beyond, but they grow impatient when anything more is pressed, as if it were a sophistication, an impertinence, or a foray of dogma. But the real question is not about individuals, but it is this—Is that the faith once committed to the Church? Is it the faith that has formed the real *continuum* of the Church, its distinctive note and staying power in history?

And what would the moral and religious result be if the whole Church accepted that position, and lived on that level and climate of faith ? What would be the result then to the preacher's message, and to his ultimate moral effect on life or society ?

It is easy, of course, to say that above all things we need a simple religion, and that this gospel of fatherly love is of the simplest ; that it speaks the language of the heart, and the piety of our mothers' knee ; and that it is the order of faith that befits an age of democracy, when Christianity is straining every nerve to get at the untaught mass.

§

Now, on this there are several remarks. First, Is the test of a Gospel the welcome it receives, the rapidity of its success ? Is the distinctive note of the Church's Gospel that which immediately appeals to the democracy or the minor ? Is Christianity to stand or fall by its direct effect on the workman or the youth ? Is it great, universal, and final as a religion because it is within the effortless comprehension of the ignorant or the weak ? It shall, indeed, be for these. The wayfaring man, though a fool, need not err therein. But is he the criterion of the religion ? Is everything to be sacrificed from Bible, Church, or Creed which does not attract or hold the masses of the natural man ? Is it the case that what we now find most valuable in Christianity has arrested and commanded the prompt welcome of men in its course through

history ? These are questions which it is not superfluous to discuss in the connexion.

§

Second, the situation of the soul is not a simple
one. The moral difficulty of society is not that we are
strayed children, great babes in a wood. It is that we
are sinful men in a sinful race. We are mutinous. It
is not a pathetic situation that the preacher con-
fronts so much as a tragic. The first question for
a Redeemer is still the old one, *quanti ponderis sit
peccatum*. The forgiveness of sin is the foundation
and genesis of Christianity ; it is not an incident in it,
nor in the Christian life. Not to know sin is not to
know Christ. That is true for the race if not for
every soul in it. No one can describe the situation
as simple who has earned the right to an opinion by
gauging that fundamental question, or by knowledge
of the moral world round him. Let us not go to
war without counting the cost. A remedy for such
a situation which is merely simple is a pill for an
earthquake, or a poultice for a cancer. The disease
is mortal. And, moreover, what is in question is a
diseased world. It is a society that is sick to death,
and not a stray soul. We have to deal with a radical
evil in human nature, and spiritual wickedness
in deep places. We have not only to restore the
prodigal but to reorganize the household of the elder
brother. In life's daily affairs it may be wisdom
not to take things tragically. But they have to be
taken tragically somewhere if we are to have moral

realism at all.   And the men of power and thoroughness do so take it, whether Kant or Ibsen.   The
world as a world has to be tragically taken, and
converted to a *divina commedia*.   If it is our wisdom
not to be tragic it is only the wisdom of faith, which
does not ignore the tragedy, but is able to cast it
on One who did take things tragically, and who
underwent and overcame at the moral centre of men
and things.

§

And, thirdly, we may ask how far this view does
justice to the revelation which is the κήρυγμα of
the Church, and the preacher's capital in the Bible.
The Church has not only to read the present situation ; she has to read her own Gospel before that ;
which is what multitudes of people, and even
preachers, are not doing.   How far does this view
do justice to the revelation " God is love," in the
face of such a world of muddle, misery and anomaly,
of guilt, grief, and devilry.   The preacher's business
is to make that principle of love real and effective
in a world of extreme wickedness, a world with
Goneril in it, and Regan, and Iago, and Mephis-
topheles, with the Inquisition in it, and the Russian
bureaucracy.   It is not Hamlet that is the real
trouble, though he most arrests the attention of to-
day.   And the preacher's first inquiry is, How is
that revelation ' God is love ' made effective by God ?
How does God Himself face the world's worst in
the Gospel which is put into the preacher's hands ?

It is not the unwieldy mass of a gross average world
that makes the problem of the Cross, but the world's
wickedness, condensed, organized pointed, deliberate,
and Satanic, not missing or losing God but challenging Him. It is not a misunderstanding but war *à la
outrance*. It is sin's death or God's. For we must
keep urging that what is given the preacher is not
a truth but a Gospel; nor is it an offer of God at
the mercy of human experience, but an objective
finished deed. What is this deed? How does God
reveal Himself as love? I should like to devote this
lecture to an answer to that question more explicit
than my previous references, because all these
references have been accumulating such a necessity
for me; and because it is the question which goes to
the root of the preacher's power; meaning thereby
chiefly the Church's message as the preacher to the
world. For it is easy (I said) to be misled by the
effect of idiosyncrasy in individual preachers, or by
their effect on individual cases. An invalid might
be greatly consoled by a kindly preacher whose net
public effect was to undermine the Christian Gospel.

§

We are all agreed that the Gospel is the revelation
of God's love to the sinful world. My points are,
first, that no revelation of divine love to such a
world is possible unless the revelation is an act of
redemption. Men had to be delivered into the very
power to see a revelation; so that mere manifestation
is but one factor in revelation. And my second point

is that the redemption of man is inseparable from
the satisfaction of God in an Atonement.

§

1. On the first head, I would begin by recalling
the educational principle, that as no lesson is really
taught till it is learned, so revelation is not
revelation till it get home, till it return to God in
faith. And we have to be saved into faith before
we are saved by it. The power of sin is such that
we cannot believe to saving purpose except we are
redeemed into that power. We cannot believe even
when we wish to. The voice of our distress is,

> "*Hilf, Vater mein,*
> *Dem Knechte dein,*
> *Ich glaub' und kann nicht glauben.*"

Faith itself, we say, is the work of the Spirit.
And the Spirit itself proceeds from the Cross, and
is the Spirit of our redemption. And just as a
great and original artist like Turner, or a similar
poet like Browning, had first to create the very
taste that understands them, so it is with the tremendous and creative revelation of God in Christ.
It had to recreate man, and redeem him into the
very power of realizing it. The difficulty in believing in an Atonement is in great measure due to
the fact that the belief needs self-surrender. The
real necessity of an Atonement only comes home
where it has done its work—only to the conscience
redeemed. You cannot prove it to the world, or
force it on the natural man. If a man say 'I do

not see the need of it ' you can go little farther with
him, beyond a caution that he shall not make his
myopia the standard of vision.

We may, and we must, modernize our theories of
Atonement, but for preaching, in such a world as
this, the Church must have the thing, the deed.
It cannot act effectively in a world where evil is
so able, so practical, so passionate, so sordid, and
so established, with a mere exhibition of fatherhood; nor can it treat the history of sonship as
man's natural evolution under Christ's benignant
sunshine up to a spiritual plane.

How then are we to do justice to God's holy love ?
Well, how did He ? He might conceivably have
done it through a sage that taught this love. But
that is too futile, and He did not act so. He might
have done it through a prophet, inspired by his own
experience of such righteous love, and aglow with
its passion. But prophetism, with all its moral
fervour, was a failure for the saving either of Israel
or the world. Yea, as a prophet only, Jesus Himself was a failure both with the people and His disciples. Or He might have done it by a sinless but
statuesque personality, who embodied His love,
and visualized it to us as its living image and our
perfect example or type. But even that is more of
a spectacle than a salvation ; it is something more
aesthetic for our spiritual contemplation than dynamic for our moral redemption. So to view Christ is no
doubt a great matter. But it is the nature of a *tableau
vivant*. It leaves Him still a somewhat inert per-

sonality, a spiritual figure finished all but the arms.
He cannot take hold of the world and wrestle with
it. He is not among the mighty doers of the race.
He remains but a gracious influence. We meet in
Him with that nearness of the divine presence
which marks an early stage of religion, but not
with His searching divine act which makes God the
last moral reality. The last moral reality is a person
not in repose but in action with the world. The
real God is present in the soul, active in history,
and master of the world. Now the pure and sinless
personality of Christ leaves us indeed with a divine
presence in whom our selfhood may be lost, but
not with the divine act of new creation in which
we are given our true moral place in a saved world.
It leaves us with a religion of worship but not with
a religion of power, with a message which exhibits
rather than achieves, and says rather than does.

And, therefore, God's way of carrying home His love
to the world was by a person who was realized in one
act corresponding to the unity of the person and the
scale of the world ; a person whose consummation of
Himself was in the great man's way of crucial action ; an
action giving effect to His whole universal personality
and therefore having effect on the whole of man's relation to God. God in Christ's Cross not only manifests
His love but gives effect to it in human history. He
enters that stream, and rides on its rage, and rules its
flood, and bends its course. He reseats His love in command upon the active centre of human reality. He does
the thing which is crucial for human destiny. Christ

effected God's purpose with the race, He did not
merely contribute the chief condition to that end.
The Cross *effects* the reconciliation of man and
God ; it does not simply announce it, or simply
prepare it. It does not simply provide either a
preliminary which God needs in a propitiation, or
the stimulus man needs in a spiritual hero, or a
moving martyr. The propitiation is the redemption.
The only satisfaction to a holy God is the absolute
establishment of holiness, as Christ did it in all but
the empirical way. The Cross is the redemption in
principle and effect. It does not avert the great
last judgment, it is the action of that judgment.
Do not persist in thinking of the last judgment as
mainly dreadful and damnatory. In the Bible and
especially in the Old Testament, I have already
said, the day of the Lord is an awful joy, as the
final vindication of goodness, the final establishment of righteousness. Judgment is the grand
justification, not prepared by the Cross, but
effected and completed on the Cross and the justification there. The justified have the last judgment
behind them. There the eschatological becomes
ethical, the remote near, the last first. The justification in the Cross does not produce the
salvation ; it is the salvation. In Christ we
have no mere preface or auxiliary to the
supreme crisis of humanity. We have that crisis.
The day of the Lord is here. We are in its midst.
Only as the race is living out Christ's death, for
weal or woe, can we truly say *Die Weltgeschichte*

ist das Weltgericht. The work was finished there as
well as begun. But it was finished more than begun.
It began its career as a finished work. But to this
point I must return later.

§

Christ does not come to us merely announcing
His view of God.   Nor does He come afire with the
ardour of holiness.   Nor does He come to present
to the world a perfect but lapidary sanctity.   What
He carries home to us is not the existence of God
but the grace of God.   He comes to be the standing,
saving action of a holy God in and on the world.
He is in it as one who is in perpetual conquest over
it.   He is in it sacramentally, not as immanent
but as incarnate, not as its substance but as its
purpose, not as filling it but as effectuating it, not
pervading it but subduing and reclaiming it, not
as its ground but as its King.

In Christ God does not simply announce Himself,
and He cannot be preached by a mere announcement.
He gives no mere revelation about Himself.   The
revelation *about* God is the bane common both to
orthodoxy and to rationalism.   Both are the victims
of that intellectualism.   What we need, what
God has given, what preaching has to convey,
is Himself.   It is Sacramental work.   His revelation is His actual coming and doing.   He is there
in Christ, not *through* Christ.   Revelation is self-
communication ; and it is self-communication which
is not the mere offer of Himself but the actual

bestowal of Himself, His effectual occupation of
Man-soul and not His mere claim of it, not the soul's
opportunity but the soul's seizure by an act of conquest. God is the matter of His own revelation ;
and, therefore, He only succeeds if he win, not the
soul's assent, but the soul itself. If it was Himself
He gave, it is man's self He must have. And He
is not really revealed to man, for all His outgoing,
till He receive that answer, till He redeem, and return upon Himself with man's soul for a prey. Revelation must take effect in restored communion. God
is not really opened to me till He opens me to Him.

All this is only possible if revelation and preaching
be much more than declaration. Revelation must be
an act. Reality is action. *Im Anfang war die That.*
Christ spoke far less of love than he practised it. He
did not publish a new idea of the Father—rather He
was the first true Son. Christ as God's revelation is
God's act ; and our conveyance of Christ in preaching
is Christ's act. Otherwise, God's love would be a mere
lenient word, or a mere affection on His part, lacking
in moral energy and in power to give effect to itself.
God then would not fully identify Himself with the
human case. He feels for men, and speaks to them
but He does nothing. He sends, but He does not
come. This sending, no doubt, is a great thing, but
it is not a Gospel that inspires preaching in the high
and powerful sense, in a sense commensurate
either with tragic humanity or a triumphant Church.
And the philanthropy based on this, prolific as it
may be for a time, has not a future, for lack of staying

power. The divinest love which could not put its whole self into a saving act might but wring its hands on the shore, or wade a little in, as many do, who mean the very best, but who can only tickle the evil of a world with which they cannot grapple. When we preachers ask about the revelation of God's love what we ask for is its deed.

Remember above all things that the love we have to do with is holy love. And holiness is the eternal moral power which must do, and do, till it see itself everywhere. That is its only satisfaction and atonement, not the pound of flesh but entire absolute response in its own active kind. And that is what we have in Christ as our head.

§

The modernizing of theology (I have urged) means above all things its ethicizing. And its ethicizing can only mean its control at all points by the supreme ethical power. But that must mean not its reformation from without but its self reformation from within. For the supreme ethical idea is one which the Gospel itself provides, which the Gospel alone provides, and, still more, puts in action and makes effective. It is not an idea imported from culture as a corrective to faith. It is given in faith as the idea and the power which necessitated the Cross of Christ and made it mighty, the idea and power of God's holiness, its word and deed.

And what does that holiness mean and demand if we become more explicit ?

Turn to man himself. Begin with him as a moral personality. Man finds the moral order of the world uttered for him in his conscience. In that conscience he even finds the voice of God. He carries back the moral order, whether in himself or without, to God. God as holy is its absolute ground.

For that conscience is not a voice from a corner of man's being. It is the verdict of his whole moral self. It is himself, as a complete moral personality, pronouncing on himself as something else, either short of that, or hostile to it. It is the expression of his own moral autonomy. In so far as it is a law to him it is the law of his full free moral self.

But it has power over him not only as being his, but as taking the same supreme place for every moral being. It has this supreme place therefore for humanity. The sanctity of man is the sanctity of man's full, free, and collective moral self.

But that very complete fulness must go back on a divine ground of it all, the ground of our very autonomy. We are again confronted with the paradox of dependence and freedom " He hath *given* the Son to have life *in Himself.*" " Work, for it is God working." We go back to secure our autonomy on an autonomy which has its ground in itself, that is to say, to God. Without this divine autonomy, underlying and guaranteeing all ours, we have no principle that gives the moral law a supreme sanction, and raises it above all our wilful doubt or passion.

Now this principle is the holiness of God. Or

rather it is God the holy. It is God as self-complete and absolute moral personality, the universal and eternal holy God whose sufficiency is of Himself, the self-contained, and self-determined moral reality of the universe, for which all things work together in a supreme *concursus*, which must endure if all else fail, and must be secured at any cost beside. Better it were that man should wreck than that God's holiness be defiled and defied. " The dignity of man himself is better secured if it break in the maintenance of God's holiness than if that holiness suffer defeat for man's mere existence." It is a holiness whose claim must be not only made, but made good, and given unmistakable effect. (I beg you to bear with my phraseology often. For we are here almost beyond the limits of human speech and caught up to the verge of realities which it is not given to man to utter.)

It is not enough, therefore, to emphasize the person of Christ, to set it again in the centre as modern theology was bound to do, and has done ever since Schleiermacher, in order to repair much historic neglect. We may dwell on the person of Christ and mean no more than a perfectly saintly soul reposing in God. But this is a conception too sabbatic for a universe which is an act, and whose energy runs up into human history. Christ's person has its reality in its active relation to other persons— God or men. We must find the key to it in something Christ did with His entirety, and did in relation to that holiness of God which means so much more than all Humanity is worth.

The true key to Christ's person is in His work. It lies not in a miraculous manner of birth, nor in a metaphysical manner of two co-existent natures, but in a moral way of atoning experience. It lies in His personal action, and in our experience of saving benefits from Him. It lies not in His constitution but in His blessings. His love to us is not the image, the reflexion, or even the result of God's love, it is a part of it, the very present action of it. We feel this particularly when we are forgiven. It is only the holy love we have so wronged that has the right to forgive. And the forgiveness we take from Christ is taken directly from the hand and heart of God, immediately though not unmediated. Christ is God forgiving. He does not help us to God, He brings God. In Him God comes. He is not the agent of God but the Son of God ; He is God the Son. As we must preach Christ and not merely about Christ, so Christ does not merely bring access to God, He brings God. God is Love only if Jesus is God. Otherwise Jesus would become our real God.

God's love then is love in holy action, in forgiveness, in redemption. It is the love for sinners of a God above all things *holy*, whose holiness makes sin damnable as sin and love active as grace. It can only act in a way that shall do justice to holiness, and restore it. Short of that, love does no more than pass a lenient sentence on sin. It meets the strain of the situation by reducing the severity of the demand. It empties of meaning the wrath of God. And it reduces the holy law of His nature to a bye-law He can suspend, or a habit He can break.

§

Any conception of God which exalts His Father-hood at the cost of His holiness, or to its neglect, unsettles the moral throne of the universe. Any reaction of ours from a too exacting God which leaves us with but a kindly God, a patient and a pitiful, is a reaction which sends us over the edge of the moral world. And it robs us of moral energy. The fatherly God of recent religious liberalism is indeed a conception for which we have to bless Him when we look back on much that went before. But the gain brings loss. It is a conception which by itself tends to do less than justice even to God's love. It tends to take the authority out of the Gospel, the sinew out of preaching, the insight out of faith, the stamina out of character, and discipline out of the home. Such a view of God is not in sufficient moral earnest—though nothing could exceed the moral eagerness of many who hold it. It does not descend into hell nor ascend into heaven. It does not pierce and destroy our self-satisfaction. It has not spiritual depth, real and sincere as the piety is of many of its advocates. It has not what I have already called adequate moral mordancy. The question at last is not of its particular advocates but of the result that would follow if this become the view of the whole church. " As is Thy majesty so is Thy mercy," says the sage. But what I

describe is a view of mercy which does justice
neither to the majesty of God, nor to the greatness of man. It has certainly no due sense of
the human tragedy, the moral tragedy of the
race. And, accordingly, it takes from preaching
the element so conspicuous by its absence to-day,
the element of imaginative greatness and moral
poignancy. It lacks the note of doom and
the searching realism of the greatest moral seers.
It is no more true to Shakespeare than to the Bible,
to Dante than to Paul. It robs faith of its energy,
its virility, its command, its compass, and its
solemnity. The temperature of religion falls. The
horizon of the soul contracts. Piety becomes
prosaic, action conventional, goodness domestic, and
mercy but kind. We have churches of the nicest,
kindest people, who have nothing apostolic or
missionary, who never knew the soul's despair or its
breathless gratitude. God becomes either a spectacular and inert God, or a God who acts amiably ;
with the strictness of affection at best, and not the
judgment of sanctity ; without the consuming fire,
and the great white throne. He is not dramatic in
the great sense of the word. He is not adequate
to history. He is not on the scale of the race. He
is the centre of a religious scene instead of the
protagonist in the moral drama of Man and Time.
The whole relation between God and man is reduced to attitude and not action—to a pose, at
last. It is more sympathetic than searching. The
Cross becomes a *parergon*. We tend then to a

Christianity without force, passion, or effect ; a suburban piety, homely and kindly but unfit to cope with the actual moral case of the world, its giant souls and hearty sinners. We cannot deal to any purpose with the great sins or the great fearless transgressors, the exceeding sinfulness and deep damnation of the race. Our word is as a very lovely song of one that has a pleasant voice and can play well on an instrument. And the people hear, but do not. They hear, but do not fear. They are enchanted, but unchanged. Moral taste takes the place of moral insight. Religious sensibility stands where evangelical faith should be. Education takes the place of conversion, a happy nature of the new nature. Love takes the place of faith, uneasiness of concern, regret of repentance, and criticism of judgment. Sin becomes a thing of short weight. It was largely our ignorance ; and when we thought of God's anger we were misreading Him by reading into Him our choleric selves. Our salvation becomes a somewhat common thing, and glorious heavens or fiery hells die into the light of drab and drowsy day. Much is done by enlightened views in the way of correcting our conception of God, to fit it into its place in the rest of knowledge, and to lift it to a higher stage in the long religious evolution. But it is all apologetic, all theosophic. It aims at adjusting the grace of God to the natural realm rather than interpreting it by our moral soul and our moral coil. It is not theology ; it is not religion, it is not vital godliness. It does not do much in the way of effectively restoring the actual living relation between God and the soul. I am compelled to recognize often that the most deeply and practically pious people in the Church are among those whose orthodox theology I do not share. I even distrust it for the Church's future. But they have the pearl of price.

§

To lay the stress of Christ's revelation elsewhere than on the atoning Cross is to make Him no more than a martyr, whose testimony was not given by His death, but only sealed by it. His message must then be sought in His words ; and His death only certifies the strength of conviction behind them. Or it may be sought in the spell of His character to which His death but gives the impressive close.

But His message was of Himself, even through His words and deeds. " Come unto Me," " Confess Me if in the judgment you would have Me confess you." The cup of cold water was blessed like the cup of the supper—for His sake. I need not add to these passages. If, then, He was a martyr, He was a martyr to Himself. But a man who is a martyr to Himself on this scale is either a megalomaniac egotist, or He is a redeeming God. But Christ's long moral majesty and influence with man forbid the former alternative, unless the whole race is a moral lunatic and history a freak. He was God, therefore, and His death was God in action. He was not simply the witness of God's grace, He was its fact, its in-

carnation. His death was not merely a seal to His
work ; it was His consummate work. It gathered
up His whole person. It was more than a confirm-
atory pledge, it was the effective sacrament of the
gracious God, with His real presence at its core.
Something was done there once for all, and the
subject doer of it was God. The real acting person
in the Cross was God. Christ's death was not the
sealing of a preacher's testimony ; it altered from
God's part the whole relation between God and man
for ever. It did not declare something, or prove
something, it achieved something decisive for
history, nay for eternity.

If it be otherwise, does it not but add another to
our moral problems, and the greatest of them all ?
If the holiest of men but suffered here the last
calamity, and if it was not the Holy God gaining the
last victory, then we have but another, and the
greatest, of the many problems that haunt us about
God's justice or love in history. The imaginative
greatness of the problem is no sufficient answer to
it. How could we read God's love in the sinless
Christ if His death was but another case of fate
submerging love. Even His resurrection would be
no proof of love's final victory had that victory not
been essentially won in His death. Resurrection might
then be no more than a personal reward for extreme
but futile fidelity. It would not seal love's final
victory for the race, it would not confirm redemption
on the world scale. The Cross would simply be the
last and worst case of the stoning of love's prophets.

And we should be presented with the alternatives,
either that the supreme power was ignorant of it,
or indifferent ; or, if not indifferent, he was an angry
spectator ; and, in His anger, either helpless, or accumulating a wrath which would break, one day, upon
us in avenging judgment and nothing more. This is
a dilemma which we escape only if we can regard
Christ, not as the witness, nor even as the mere æsthetic
incarnation of God's holy love, but as that love itself
in its crucial moral act of eternal judgment and grace.

§

If sin be man's fatal act the Cross is God's vital
act.   But it is action we have to do with.   It
is will meeting will, yet not in transaction but
interaction.   It is redemption mastering perdition.   What slew Christ was an act of man,
but it was for Him much more than an in-
fliction and a fate of which He was the passive
martyr.   It was much more than man's act and
Christ's fate.   It was an act on His side much more
even than on theirs ; and an act, not of resignation
but of conquest absolute over both His own fate
and ours.   He was more active in His death than
was the world, the fate, the sin, which inflicted it.
Rather, when we view things on the largest scale,
we must reverse the positions. It was not His
fate and the world's act, it was His act and the
world's fate.   The world's condemnation of Him
was His condemnation of the world—but a condemnation unto forgiveness and salvation. In the

Cross the world was doomed to—salvation. All
were shut up unto sin, that there might be mercy on
all. The world's one sin was made by grace the
world's one hope.

It was the world's one sin ; and it was so because
it was committed against the one central visitation
of man by God. The crucifying of Christ was the
greatest crime of history, not in itself, but because
it was inflicted on the Holiest. It is not the tra-
vesty of justice that is so unique, it is not the crime
against humanity. Against humanity alone other
crimes may have been as great or greater—political,
papal, dynastic, Napoleonic, Russian crimes. But
this was the crime against the unique action of the
Holy God, the sin against the Holy Ghost. And
therefore to Israel as a national unity it is un-
forgiven. It was man's sin indeed, but it was
through Israel. And for the salvation of the whole
the offending member was cut off. Israel died as
the body, that its spirit, as Christ, might conquer
mankind.

As, therefore, the one sin was consummate in the
act of man the one salvation can be nothing less than
the act of God. The death of Christ completes by
action God's love embodied in His person. It is the
one thing that gives His person its full scope and
effect. And it does so as a decisive creative act, an
act of God and not merely a martyr act. It copes
with man's act, it does not but endure it meekly.
It was not merely the evidence of a divine love,
sensitive yet unpierced at the centre by sin. It was

the deed of a love stung to the core, stung to act for
its life, to act once for all and make an end

§

II. But in His death Christ not only acted and
redeemed, He suffered and atoned.[1] He acted
as only a divine sufferer could. His act of sacrifice
became an endurance of judgment. Nothing else
than atonement could do full justice to Love.
Love might do much, but if it did not suffer, and
suffer not only pain but judgment, it could not
do its divine utmost. That is to say, it might
have contact with us, and blessed contact, but it
would be short of identification with us. It could
not enter into our self-condemnation. But surely
love divine could not stop short of such an identification with our suffering as made Christ's suffering
judicial. Must a divine love not go so far with us
and for us as to enter the wrath of holiness ? Even
that was not beyond Christ's love. He was made
sin. God did not punish Christ, but Christ entered
the dark shadow of God's penalty on sin. We
must press the results of God's holy love in completely identifying Himself with us. Holiness is
not holiness till it go out in love, seek the sinner
in grace, and react on his sin by judging it. But
love is not divine identification with us till it become
sacrifice. Nor is the identification with us complete

[1] I do not say much in these lectures about the reconciling
effect of His work upon men. That may not be understood
as it should, but it is better understood to-day than the
other aspects of his work.

till the sacrifice become judgment, till our Saviour
share our self condemnation, our fatal judgment of
ourselves in God's name.   The priest, in his
grace, becomes the victim, and completes his confession of God's holiness by meeting its action
as judgment.   To forgive sin he must bear sin.

As He took the suffering He took and bore the
sin that caused it—the sin and not its consequences
only.   If he could not confess, sin, He could and
did confess, in experience and act, the holiness of
God in its reaction on sin.   He confessed the
holiness, but the guilt He could not confess in the
same sense.   He could but realize it, bear it, as only
the holy could, and so expose it in all its sinfulness.
The revelation of love is a revelation no less of
sin, because the love is holy love.   That holy
confession in act of the injured holiness, amid the
conditions of sin and judgment, was the satisfaction
He made to God.   And the necessity for it lay in
God's holy name.   It was thus that He offered to
God, and acted on God.   He not only acted from
God on man, but from man on God.   I do not
mean that He changed God's *feeling* to the race.
That was grace always, the grace that sent Him.
But He did change the *relation* between God
and man.   The reconciliation of one always means
a great change for both parties.   He made communion possible again on both sides.   To do this
He had to bear the wrath, the judgment, the
privation of God.   He could not otherwise enact
and reveal love, and do the revelation justice.

The more love there is in a holy God, the more wrath. Sin, in the sinner He loves, against the law of His own nature, which He loves better still, could not leave Him either indifferent, or merely pitiful. For Love would then desert its own holiness. And being holy, God's concern with sin is more than pity, and more than pain. It is holiness in earnest reaction. It is wrath unto judgment. That wrath Christ felt, not indeed as personal resentment, but as the dark valley, as the horror of thick darkness. And He felt, moreover, that it was God's will for Him, not indeed inflicted, so far as His conscience was concerned, but still laid on Him by God through His sympathy with us. It was not merely a darkening of His vision of the Father ; it was desertion by the Father in sympathy with the complete fulfilment of their common task. As one might in certain circumstances say " I love you, but I must leave you," " I love you, but for the sake of all that is at issue I may not show it." And it was by recognizing, honouring, this very desertion as the wise, righteous, loving will of God, that Christ converted it for us all into a new and deeper communion. It was thus He approved His Godhead, and achieved the Redemption. The real Incarnation lay not in Christ's being made flesh for us, but in His being made sin. And the dereliction was the real descent into hell, the bottoming of salvation. Here beneath the depth of sin is the deeper depth of God. " If I make My bed in hell, Thou art there."

Love, then, must go to entire identification (short of absorption). And Christ, in identifying Himself divinely with sinful man, had to take the sin's consequence, and especially its judgment, else the identification would not be complete, and the love would come short. He must somehow identify Himself in a sympathetic way, even *with man's self-condemnation which is the reflection of his judgment by God.* I need hardly allude to the familiar illustrations in the shame which innocent people feel through the crime of a kinsman. If the chief function of Christ's love was to represent man in a solidary way, a priestly way, He must make offering to God ; He must offer to God's holiness by a holy obedience, and not merely to God's love by loving response. He could not experience sin, for then He would be short of holy identification with God ; yet He must experience and endure God's wrath against sin, else His love would be short of sympathetic identification with us. And unless he felt God's holy wrath and reaction against sin, He could not show forgiving love in full. No one can forgive in full who does not feel the fullness of the offence. To feel the fullness of the offence as the Holiest must, is also to feel the wrath the Holiest feels. But for one in perfect sympathy with man to feel what the Holiest feels is to feel the divine wrath, not as its holy subject only, but as its human object. Christ could not show the power of forgiving love in full unless He felt the weight of God's wrath in full, i.e. not God's temper but God's judgment; which for Him was God's withdrawal, the experience of God's total negation of the sin He was made. Grace could only be perfectly revealed in an act of judgment—though inflicted on Himself by the Judge. Atonement to God must be made, and it was only possible from God.

No one can feel more than I do that if all this be not absolute truth it is sheer nonsense. So it sifts men.

§

This aspect of the matter is not indeed vital to personal Christianity, but it is to the Church's total message and to the final prospects of Christianity. It presents the last issue in the moral war of God and man. It is essential to a full interpretation of God's love. God so loved the world, not quantitatively but qualitatively, not only so intensely, but in such a unique manner, that He gave His Son to be a propitiation. It is the provision of a propitiation that is the distinctive mark of God's love as transcending humane pity or affection in holy grace. Surely it must be so. The greater the love the closer it must come to life, and to the interior of life. It can the less ignore the realities of life. It does not leave us to ourselves, in a careless affection; it enters our ways, and sounds our depths, and measures all our tragic case. It has a comprehending, and not merely a kindly pity. It does not merely feel for our case, it assumes it wholly. Therefore, it must regard the last reality of sin, and deal with it accord-

ing to *all* the circumstances—especially those
visible to holiness alone, and to us in proportion
as we are redeemed into holiness.   So dealing
with sin it forgives it ; and forgives it effectually—
not by way of amnesty, not by mere pardon, not
by way of mere mercy upon our repentance, but
by the radical way of redemption ; not by indulgence, not by treating it as a matter of ignorance,
weakness, misfortune, but as the crime of our freedom, grave in proportion to our freedom, most
heinous in the face of the grace that gives our
freedom.   And as grace is far more than indulgence,
so sin is far more than indifference.   It is the
nature of indifference to go on to become hate, if it be
given time and occasion.   The mercy, therefore, comes
as no matter of paternal course, as no calm act of
a parent too great and wise to be wounded by a
child's ways.   God is fundamentally affected by sin.
He is stung and to the core.   It does not simply
try Him.   It challenges His whole place in the
moral world.   It puts Him on His trial as God.
It is, in its nature, an assault on His life.   Its
total object is to unseat Him.   It has no part
whatever in His purpose.   It hates and kills Him.
It is His total negation and death.   It is not His
other but An other.   It is the one thing in the
world that lies outside reconciliation, whether you
mean by that the process or the act.   It cannot be
taken up into the supreme unity.   It can only be
destroyed.   It drives Him not merely to action but
to a passion of action, to action for His life, to action

in suffering unto death. And what makes Him suffer most is not its results but its guilt. It has a guilt in proportion to the holy love it scorns. The greater the love the greater the guilt. And the closer the love the greater the reaction against the sin, the greater the wrath. Hence the problem of reconciliation—both of God and man—a problem so integral to Christianity, and so foreign to even the finest kinds of theism. It is not the reconciliation of man with his world, the establishment of his moral personality against nature. That were mere apologetic. But it is the reconciliation of man within himself and God. The channel of holy love must be the bearer, the victim of holy wrath. To bear holy love to us He must bear holy wrath for us. The forgiver of sin must realize inwardly the whole moral quality of the guilt—as Christ did in His dereliction in the Cross. Inwardly he must realize it, experimentally, not intellectually. No otherwise could a God, a love, be revealed, which would not let us go, yet was in absolute moral earnest about the holy.

It may freely be granted also that the reconciliation of God (by Himself in Christ) is not very explicit in the New Testament—for the same reasons which forbid the missionary preaching to his heathen on such a theme. The New Testament represents but the missionary stage of Christian thought and action. But the idea is not therefore untrue. If not explicit in the New Testament, it is integral to the Gospel. It is involved in the moral quality of holy forgiveness

and in its divine psychology. In this respect it is
like the full doctrine of the Trinity, and many
another. The holiness of God, moreover, does
not explicitly occupy the same supreme position
in the New Testament as it does in the Old. Yet it
is the very Godhead of God. It is the essence of
Christ's idea of God. And (I think I have said) it
really receives in the New Testament a position above
any it had in the Old Testament. For it forms
much more than an attribute of God. In the Holy
Spirit it becomes a constituent element in the
Godhead, on its way to become at last a coequal
person in the Trinity.

§

To handle this matter means at the last a treatise.
I have no such purpose. I wish but to point out that
the expiatory idea of Christianity which is concerned
with the notion of satisfaction, is quite necessary to
do justice to the conception of God as love, and to
the closeness of His identification with us. It is
not an outgrown notion, a relic of moral immaturity,
like the patristic idea of Christ cheating Satan
by His death, or even the Anselmic satisfaction
of God's honour. I have sought to construe the
satisfaction to a holy God as consisting only in a
counterpart and equal holiness rendered under the
conditions of sin and judgment. And especially I
have wished to indicate that an expiatory atonement gives expression, by its searching moral realism, and its grasp both of holiness and sin, to an

element in Christianity which has a crucial effect on the depth, wealth, and moral penetration of the preaching of the Gospel. The matter is, of course, a doctrine of the Church, and not a test of personal Christianity. It is not a *Quicunque vult.* I will only venture to say I never knew my sin so long as I but saw Christ suffering for me—never until I saw Him under its judgment and realized that the chastisement of my peace was upon Him.

There is something lacking to our preaching, by general consent. It lacks the note, the energy of spiritual profundity and poignancy as distinct from spiritual sympathy, and of moral majesty as distinct from ethical interest. And I am convinced that this is ultimately due to the loss of conviction as to a real, objective, and finished redemption, and to the disappearance from current faith of a real relation to the holiness and the wrath of God. The note of judgment has gone out of common piety. It is not here a question of either denouncing or unchurching those who cannot recognize an expiatory element in our Salvation. I would simply express the conviction that their interpretation of the Cross does less than justice to the Gospel, and cannot continue to carry the full κήρυγμα of the Church. It has not the promise of the moral future of the world. It is not sufficiently charged with repentance and remission. It does not break men to Christ, but only train them, or at most bend them. And it does not embody that break with the world which, after all, has been a leading note in all the great victories of the Cross.

Epilogue

§

Certain things, I trust, will have appeared among others, in the course of our journey.

1. Preaching to the Church must recognize more fully the element of judgment, and preaching to the world the element of love. Judgment must begin at the house of God. We must preach more severely to the Church, and more pitifully to the world. We must make the demand on the Church heavier than the demand on the world.

2. There is nothing the Church needs more profoundly, though there are many things it needs more loudly, than an ethical conversion in regard to its great doctrines. These early went astray in a metaphysical direction. Metaphysic we must have, but even to this day the whole ethic of the Churches suffers incalculably from the long prepossession by metaphysical instead of moral interests, by pursuing the notion of substance instead of subject, by intellect cultivated at the cost of conscience. This appears in the interminable, and often barren, strifes about the nature of Christ in the Church's early stage, and of the sacrament in the later. And in inverse proportion

to the engrossment of ability with these insoluble
problems (or rather with their pursuit on insoluble
lines) has been the moral insight and energy of
the Church, especially on the public scale. So
that its idea of justice has become a by-word.
Ecclesiastical justice is sport for the Philistines.
The justice of a church court or of ecclesiastical
politicians is a matter of mockery. In the great
churches—the Catholic, Orthodox, or Established—
men of personal honour and uprightness lose the
sense of social justice as soon as a question arises
which threatens the interest of their Church. They
are perfectly sincere, and equally incapable of
grasping the just thing. It is a hereditary or
'miasmatic' paralysis, and not a personal vice.
Something is very wrong in some vital place.
And the deep root of it all lies in the Church's
long moral neglect of the great justification by God.
The mighty moral meaning there, original to itself
and imperial for all else, has been submerged,
where it should have been elucidated, by the
maxims of human instincts, utilities, and codes.
The intellectualism of the Church, and the counter-
intellectualism of its critics, have sucked the sap
and vigour from its ethic. Its conscience has not
been educated at its Cross. Its eye, from peering
into inaccessible heavens, has seen the moral values
upon earth only through great flakes of darkness.
Holiness has become mere sanctity, and righteousness but justice which is less equity than legal-
ity.

So that the very institution which was founded upon God's supreme act of public justice—the Church—has become the dullest to public justice of any institution, and as selfish as any association for the defence of a trade, a monopoly, or an ascendancy. From the point of view of Christian ethic there is no word more base-born than that word ascendancy.

3. The more ethically we construe the Gospel the more are we driven upon the holiness of God. And the deeper we enter that sacred ground the more we are seized by the necessity (for the very maintenance of our spiritual life) of a real and objective atonement offered to a holy God by the equal and satisfying holiness of Christ under the conditions of sin and judgment.

4. We must be critically liberal without ceasing to be theological. We must be free in our treatment of history, whether as doctrine or as Bible. But we must be firm on our faith's base in history. However we treat the Bible we must be positive in our treatment of the Bible's Gospel. We must reduce demand as to the Bible, and press it as to the Gospel. That way lies the future. That method meets the actual present situation. A mere abstract liberalism without content or responsibility, liberty to go anywhere and believe anything, is pseudoliberalism. What makes us free at the last ? For what are we made free ? Not for certain views broad or narrow. But for the faith of a positive Gospel, understood as I have defined

it, modified, perhaps, but certainly unchanged. Liberty of view is now assured. What is not secure is liberty of soul. And the only thing that can secure it is the faith of a positive Gospel. Liberty of view is a matter of mere science. It is religious liberty that concerns the public most. And that is only the fruit of the Gospel.

Nothing in the world is so precious as faith, hope and love. But the preacher of the Gospel must be sure on what abysses these rest and abide.

INDEX OF AUTHORS AND PROPER NAMES

INDEX OF SCRIPTURE REFERENCES